# JIM BLINN'S CORNER
# NOTATION, NOTATION, NOTATION

# The Morgan Kaufmann Series in Computer Graphics and Geometric Modeling

# Jim Blinn's Corner
## Notation, Notation, Notation

Jim Blinn

Microsoft Research

**MORGAN KAUFMANN PUBLISHERS**

AN IMPRINT OF ELSEVIER SCIENCE

AMSTERDAM   BOSTON   LONDON   NEW YORK
OXFORD   PARIS   SAN DIEGO   SAN FRANCISCO
SINGAPORE   SYDNEY   TOKYO

Publishing Director *Diane Cerra*
Publishing Services Manager *Edward Wade*
Editorial Asistant *Mona Buehler*
Cover Design *Ross Carron Design*
Cover Photography *Christine Alicino*
Text Design *Studio Arno*
Composition and Technical Illustration *Technology 'N Typography*
Copyeditor *Robert Fiske*
Proofreader *Sharilyn Hovind*
Indexer *Ty Koontz*
Printer *The Maple-Vail Book Manufacturing Group*

Morgan Kaufmann Publishers
An imprint of Elsevier Science
340 Pine Street, Sixth Floor
San Francisco, CA 94104-3205
*www.mkp.com*

07 06 05 04 03 5 4 3 2 1

**Library of Congress Control Number: 2002104303**
ISBN: 1-55860-860-5

This book is printed on acid-free paper.

# Contents

# Preface

This book is the third collection of articles originally published in the *IEEE Computer Graphics and Applications* journal. All of these articles, of course, have something to do with computer graphics. The first four were originally written at Caltech and describe how I drew planets for the JPL flyby movies. The rest of them were written after I came to Microsoft Research and cover a pretty wide range of topics, from assembly language optimization for parallel processors (Chapter 7) through exotic usage of C++ template instantiation (Chapter 18) to theoretical mathematics (Chapter 20). There should be something in here for everyone.

The previous two collections reproduced the original columns with only a few updates and fixes. For this volume, however, I succumbed to the urge to do major surgery on many of the columns. I changed some of the mathematical notation to something I liked better. I added a lot more diagrams (as befits a graphics book). I added answers to questions that I hadn't found when the original columns were written. So even if you've read the original magazine articles, go ahead and read this book. It's a lot better. (I'm especially proud of the improvements to Chapters 5, 18, 20, and 21, if anybody wants to compare them with the originals.)

One of the things people say they like about these articles is their irreverent style. This makes them a lot more fun to read than to write. I usually suffer greatly in writing them, going through six or seven major drafts. Only after I get the exposition and mathematics right (usually involving chasing down rogue minus signs) do I make the "joke pass." For the joke pass over this book I had the following idea. Have you noticed that when a movie is re-released on DVD they usually enhance it with a collection of deleted scenes and hilarious outtakes? How about setting it up so that I could advertise this book as containing "deleted scenes" and "hilarious outtakes"? This joke would only work, however, if these actually contained meaningful content instead of just fluff. I have, therefore, included some deleted scenes, stuff that was somewhat interesting but not on the main topic or some half-formed ideas that I never pursued further. But what should I do about outtakes? My model would be the wonderful fake outtakes at the end of the recent Pixar movies. I have to admit, though, that I came up a bit dry. How about "And then we see that the determinant of the matrix is plus one, er no, minus one, er (dissolve into helpless laughter)." Or how about "As we see in Figure 2.5 . . . hey who drew the moustache on Figure 2.5?" Maybe this concept doesn't translate well to this medium. You can, though, be charitable and give me a chuckle as though I actually did it.

When looking over these columns and searching for some common theme to use as a book subtitle, I realized that one of the things that I did a lot in these columns was to experiment with mathematical notation. I have some general comments to make on this, but if you're like me you don't read the prefaces to books. So I put these comments into a new first chapter. Since one of the notational conventions I use is to start vector component indexing from 0, I have named this Chapter 0.

# Acknowledgments

I want to thank Bobby Bodenheimer, Rick Szeliski, and Jim Kajiya for helpful comments about matrices; Steve Gabriel and Gideon Yuval for giving me some new insights into floating point; and Matt Klaasen for turning me on to Hilbert's book, referenced in Chapter 19. Thanks to Kirk Olynyk and Paul Heckbert for providing the inspiration for Chapter 13; to Todd Veldhuizen and William Baxter for inspiring Chapter 18 and encouraging me to make it better; and to Jon Paul Schelter for finding typos.

A long time ago (before these columns got started), I attempted to write a computer graphics textbook, but I never got very far with it. Writing a column for *CG&A* seems to be the only way that I can get enough stuff finished to make a whole book. The series of short deadlines breaks the problem down into manageable chunks. Once again I would like to thank my editors at the IEEE, Robin Baldwin, Nancy Hays, Linda World, Alkenia Winston, and Anne Lear, for their infinite patience in coping with my lateness. If it were not for them, these columns would never have gotten to press.

Finally, I would like to thank Microsoft Research for giving me an environment where I could do all the thinking and tinkering that produced the articles in this book.

# Notation

APRIL 2002

A common thread running through the original articles that became this book is experimentation with mathematical notation. You might think mathematical notation would be the most consistent and systematic form of representation possible. You'd be wrong! Mathematics is a natural language, made up by humans, and contains just as many inconsistencies and arbitrary rules as any other natural language. In this chapter, I want to begin by making a few observations on this language, and to explain some of the conventions I use in this book.

## Mathematical Symbols

When someone says "Consider the $x$, $y$, $z$ values," you immediately think they are talking about 3D coordinates. When someone says "the quantity $\theta$," you usually guess that they are talking about an angle. When someone writes $\alpha \mathbf{P}_0 + (1 - \alpha) \mathbf{P}_1$, it is likely that they are interpolating two points. Whenever you write a mathematical expression, there is often a lot of subtle and unstated meaning packed into the symbols you use. Let's take a brief look at some of the choices we have in building up a mathematical symbol and the meanings these choices imply.

### The Base Symbol

The first choice we make is which letter to use for the base symbol. The alphabetic position of the letter is our first opportunity to pack extra information into the symbol. Coordinates of points usually come from the end of the alphabet $(x, y, z)$. We use the beginning of the alphabet for polynomial coefficients $(ax^2 + bx + c)$ or for the coordinates of lines and planes $(ax + by + cz + dw)$. Subscript indices come from the middle of the alphabet $(P_i, Q_{jkl})$. Texture coordinates are often from the end of the middle $(u, v)$, $(s, t)$.

Foreign language fonts give us a whole raft of new choices, each with their own conventional usage pattern. We use Greek letters for angles $(\theta, \phi)$, for blending ratios $(\alpha)$ and for some physical constants like display intensity functions $(V^\gamma)$ (see Chapter 9). And, of course, there are constants like $\pi$. We use epsilon $(\varepsilon)$ to represent a small quantity and delta $(\delta)$ to represent a change in a quantity. We also use epsilon and delta to represent certain constant matrices (see Chapter 20). Other language fonts such as Fractur, Hebrew, Cyrillic, and various script fonts and double line fonts are typically used to represent various types of sets.

Once you've chosen a letter, you still have some choices as to how it is drawn. It's typical to use italics for scalar quantities $(a, b, x, y)$ and boldface for vector and matrix quantities $(\mathbf{pT}.)$ And, as this last example shows, to use lowercase for vectors and uppercase for matrices. You can also use case to pack yet another bit of meaning into a symbol, something I call the "variation-on-a-theme principle." Suppose you have two quantities that are related in some way. To emphasize this similarity, it's useful to have their symbols be (nearly) the same but to have some other property (like case) that distinguishes them. For example, I use case to distinguish between homogeneous $(x, y, w)$ vs. nonhomogeneous $(X, Y)$ coordinates of the same point, or 2D vs. 3D versions of a polynomial (see Chapter 20) or covariant vs. contravariant components of a tensor (see Chapter 20 again).

## Accessories

Once we've gotten our base letter, it's time to trick it out with chrome sidewalls and fuzzy dice to add even more information. And often these attachments can have more than one meaning.

**Subscript** A subscript is most often used to index elements of a vector $\mathbf{p} = (p_0, p_1, p_2)$ or a matrix $M_{1,2}$. (In the notation of Chapter 20, these would be contravariant indices.) Sometimes, though, a subscript represents a partial derivative $F_x = \partial F / \partial x$. And sometimes a subscript is just a name extender to distinguish between different variations on a particular base variable, such as $(x_{min}, x_{max})$, or between elements of some unordered collection such as $\mathbf{p}_a, \mathbf{p}_b, \mathbf{p}_c$. I have also used subscripts to indicate which coordinate system a point is in or which systems a matrix transforms between: $\mathbf{p}_e = \mathbf{p}_d \mathbf{T}_{de}$.

**Superscript** A superscript usually means exponentiation $\left( ax^3 + bx^2 \right)$. Sometimes, however, we use a superscript as a placeholder for another type of index, a covariant index $\begin{bmatrix} p^0 & p^1 & p^2 \end{bmatrix}$. This distinguishes them from contravariant indices, which are written as subscripts. Often you can tell the meaning of a superscript by context: exponentiated variables are usually added to other exponentiated variables, while variables with contravariant indices are usually multiplied by variables with covariant indices $\left( p^i p^j Q_{ij} \right)$. Hopefully, authors will warn you if the usage is at all ambiguous.

Other types of adornments look a bit like superscripts but really aren't. They can indicate some sort of function operating on the base symbol: $\mathbf{M}^T$ is the transpose of the matrix $\mathbf{M}$; $\mathbf{Q}^*$ is the adjoint of the matrix $\mathbf{Q}$. (Older notations use $\mathbf{Q}^\dagger$ for adjoint and $z^*$ for complex conjugate.) Various numbers of primes $\left( F', F'', F''', F^{IV} \right)$ often mean various orders of derivatives of the base symbol. But . . . sometimes a prime is just a prime; it's just another type of name extender to indicate another variation of the base symbol. For example, a transformed version of $\mathbf{p}$ could be written $\mathbf{p}'$.

**Overhead** Other adornments can appear over the symbol. Again, these can indicate some function of the base symbol ($\bar{z}$ means the complex conjugate of $z$, $\hat{\mathbf{v}}$ means a normalized version of the vector $\mathbf{v}$, and various numbers of dots—$\dot{x}, \ddot{x}, \dddot{x}$—can again mean various numbers of derivatives of $x$). They can be a sort of type declaration (an arrow, $\vec{\mathbf{v}}$, means that $\mathbf{v}$ is a vector), or they can again be simple name extenders. I often use $\bar{x}, \tilde{x}, \hat{x}$ as variations on the theme of $x$.

**Underfoot** Similar sorts of attire can appear underneath the symbol. I don't happen to use this much myself.

## A Standard Notation

Wouldn't it be nice if we could establish completely consistent rules for the meanings of all these choices? Wouldn't it be nice. The problem is that it's almost impossible to have a completely consistent notation that applies to all of mathematics. There just aren't enough squiggles to represent everything uniquely. And it's actually not even desirable. In different contexts, different properties are important and need to be emphasized. You want to use the adornment that is the most visually obvious to indicate the property that is most important intellectually. About all you can do is to tell readers explicitly what the add-ons mean.

# Computer Languages

The introduction of computer programming languages adds an interesting set of constraints and freedoms to mathematical notation. Most importantly, it is still inconvenient for variable names to have all the attachments we have just described. We make up for it by using multiple-letter variable names.

## Variable Names

Just as in biology, the most popular operation in mathematics is multiplication. It's so popular that it has many notational variants. You can say $a \times b$, $a \cdot b$, $(a, b)$, or you can simply write the two symbols to be multiplied next to each other, $ab$. This minimalist notation raises the specter of ambiguity unless we insist that all mathematical symbols consist of only one letter (but possibly decorated extremely nicely). Computer programming languages, though, have more positional precision with their characters so they afford the possibility of multiple character variable names without problems. This does, however, raise a translation issue between the typical mathematical way of writing something and a programming language–friendly version. You will see in this book various examples of this where the translation should be fairly apparent. Mathematical notations that are just used as name extenders translate easily:

$$\tilde{X} = \texttt{Xtilde}$$
$$X_{min} = \texttt{Xmin}$$
$$\mathbf{P}_1 = \texttt{P1}$$

Subscripts used as indices translate into

$$\mathbf{P}_1 = \texttt{P[1]}$$

and annotations that imply functions are written

$$\mathbf{M}^T = \texttt{M.Transpose()}$$
$$\mathbf{A}^{-1} = \texttt{A.Inverse()}$$
$$\mathbf{Q}^* = \texttt{Q.Adjoint()}$$

## Indexing

Another bit of culture clash between conventional mathematics notation and computer programming is the starting index for vector/matrix elements. Mathematicians start counting with 1:

$$\mathbf{v} = \begin{bmatrix} v_1 & v_2 & v_3 \end{bmatrix}$$

Computer scientists start counting with 0:

```
Vector3 v; v[0]=1; v[1]=42.; v[2]=sqrt(5);
```

It is sometimes possible to diddle the compiler into starting the indexing at 1, but this is language dependant and often makes for obscure code. I did a quick survey of my colleagues around the lab and the consensus was that it would be less confusing to alter the math notation. So for the purposes of this book, all indexing, including that in mathematical equations, starts from index 0:

$$\mathbf{v} = \begin{bmatrix} v_0 & v_1 & v_2 \end{bmatrix}$$

I didn't do this in the original articles, but I believe that I've caught all such instances in revising the chapters for this book. If you see something that looks wrong, consider that it might be one that I've missed. And to start out on the right foot, we begin this book with Chapter 0.

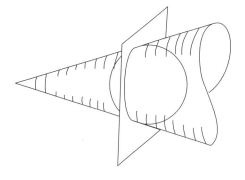

# CHAPTER ONE

# How to Draw a Sphere Part I, Basic Math

J A N U A R Y  1 9 9 5

Once upon a time (before the invention of ray tracing), I could claim the honor of having drawn more spheres than anybody in the world. This was because of all the moons and planets I drew for the *Voyager* flyby movies at JPL. I could have drawn spheres by hacking them up into scads of polygons, but that would have been the coward's way out. Instead, I wrote a special-purpose program that was highly optimized for drawing spheres. There are quite a variety of interesting tricks involved in this program, but when I started out to write about them I realized that a whole bunch of matrix mathematics is necessary to understand the algorithm. This chapter, then, consists largely of the matrix mathematics necessary to manipulate (and ultimately render) second-order surfaces. I'll get down to the rendering next time.

## Mathematical Context

I always have some trouble in writing these columns in deciding how much math to assume that you already know. Rather than repeat a bunch of stuff I've described before, I'll just refer you to Table 1.1 for the typographic conventions I will use here, and Table 1.2 for a quick review of homogeneous coordinates. In addition, some of my past articles are

**Table 1.1**  *Typographic conventions*

| Quantity | Typeface | Example |
|----------|----------|---------|
| Scalar | Italic | $x,y,z,s$ |
| Vector | Bold lc roman | **p,e** |
| Matrix | Bold uc roman | **T,Q** |

**Table 1.2**  *Homogeneous representations*

| Two dimensions | | Three dimensions | |
|----------------|--|------------------|--|
| **Geometry** | **Algebra** | **Geometry** | **Algebra** |
| Homogeneous point | $\begin{bmatrix} x & y & z \end{bmatrix} = \mathbf{p}$ | Homogeneous point | $\begin{bmatrix} x & y & z & w \end{bmatrix} = \mathbf{p}$ |
| Nonhomogeneous point | $\begin{bmatrix} X & Y \end{bmatrix} =$ $\begin{bmatrix} x/w & y/w \end{bmatrix}$ | Nonhomogeneous point | $\begin{bmatrix} X & Y & Z \end{bmatrix} =$ $\begin{bmatrix} x/w & y/w & z/w \end{bmatrix}$ |
| Point at infinity | $\begin{bmatrix} x & y & 0 \end{bmatrix}$ | Point at infinity | $\begin{bmatrix} x & y & z & 0 \end{bmatrix}$ |
| Point transformation | $\mathbf{pT} = \mathbf{p}'$ | Point transformation | $\mathbf{pT} = \mathbf{p}'$ |
| Homogeneous line | $\begin{bmatrix} a \\ b \\ c \end{bmatrix} = 1$ | Homogeneous plane | $\begin{bmatrix} a \\ b \\ c \\ d \end{bmatrix} = 1$ |
| Line at infinity | $\begin{bmatrix} 0 \\ 0 \\ c \end{bmatrix}$ | Plane at infinity | $\begin{bmatrix} 0 \\ 0 \\ 0 \\ d \end{bmatrix}$ |
| Line transformation | $\mathbf{T^*l} = \mathbf{l}'$ | Plane transformation | $\mathbf{T^*l} = \mathbf{l}'$ |

particularly relevant here.[1,2] (Don't you just love it when authors reference only their own papers? It makes them seem so smug.[3])

The description and manipulation of second-order curves and surfaces is a very nice example of the use of homogeneous coordinates and

1  Blinn, Jim, *Jim Blinn's Corner: Dirty Pixels*, Chapter 9, "Uppers and Downers, Part I," Morgan Kaufmann, 1998.

2  Blinn, Jim, *Jim Blinn's Corner: A Trip Down the Graphics Pipeline*, Chapter 18, "The Homogeneous Perspective Transform," Morgan Kaufmann, 1996.

3  Blinn, J. F., personal communication.

projective geometry. Since we will be dealing with spheres in perspective, the capability of homogeneous coordinate geometry to deal with points and planes at infinity will be especially useful.

# The Goal

I wanted an algorithm that drew a texture-mapped sphere arbitrarily scaled and translated and placed into perspective. It must work for *any* view of the sphere (this will turn out to be trickier than it seems). Oh, and I want it to be fast.

I'll first give a peek at the final operation of the algorithm to see what sorts of geometric problems we will need to solve. This will motivate the math in the remainder of this chapter.

I'll use a basic scan line algorithm consisting of two nested loops, one for *y* and one for *x*. We must be able to calculate the range of scan lines covered by the sphere to determine the range for the outer (*y*) loop. Likewise, for each scan line, we must calculate the *x* extent of pixels covered to find the range for the inner (*x*) loop.

The focus of attention in making a rendering algorithm fast is the inner loop. Inside this loop we will need, at each pixel, a normal vector to use for illumination calculations and texture coordinates to use for texture mapping. Going across a scan line we will find, first, that the *z* coordinate as a function of the horizontal position, *x*, has the form

$$z = \sqrt{z_2 x^2 + z_1 x + z_0}$$

and, second, that the normal vector and the position on the unit sphere (for texturing) are linear vector functions of *x* and *z:*

$$\mathbf{n} = \mathbf{n}_x x + \mathbf{n}_z z + \mathbf{n}_0$$
$$\mathbf{p} = \mathbf{p}_x x + \mathbf{p}_z z + \mathbf{p}_0$$

With the appropriate initialization, we can calculate many of these quantities incrementally. My final inner loop will look like the following (using the Vector/matrix classes defined in the Appendix):

```
float zs = sqrt(zSqrd); zSqrd += dzSqrd; dzSqrd += ddzSqrd;
Vector3 P = zs*Pz + PxXplusP0; PxXplusP0 += Px;
Vector3 N = zs*Nz + NxXplusN0; NxXplusN0 += Nx;
```

That's a square root, two scalar additions, two vector-scalar multiplications, and four vector additions.

Now my task is to show you why this works and how to actually calculate the $x$ and $y$ ranges and the $z_i$, $\mathbf{n}_i$, and $\mathbf{p}_i$ values. To do this, we must wallow a bit in matrix algebra.

# Second-Order Curves

I'm going to go through this rigamarole first in just two (homogeneous) dimensions to keep the diagrams and equations simpler. Most everything will easily generalize to what we really want—3D surfaces.

For a second-order curve, the equation has only second powers of the coordinates. The most general such equation is

$$0 = Ax^2 + 2Bxy + 2Cxw$$
$$+ Dy^2 + 2Eyw$$
$$+ Fw^2$$

We can rewrite this in matrix form as

$$\begin{bmatrix} x & y & w \end{bmatrix} \begin{bmatrix} A & B & C \\ B & D & E \\ C & E & F \end{bmatrix} \begin{bmatrix} x \\ y \\ w \end{bmatrix} = 0$$

I'll call the $3 \times 3$ symmetric matrix $\mathbf{Q}$, so another way to write the equation is

$$\mathbf{p}\mathbf{Q}\mathbf{p}^T = 0$$

This formulation satisfies the homogeneous condition that any non-zero scalar multiple of $\mathbf{Q}$ represents the same curve. For the most part, these curves will be conic sections. Examples of the possible curves and their defining matrices appear in Table 1.3.

Notice that some matrices will give degenerate conic sections; that is, the curves are really two intersecting first-order curves (i.e., lines). This will occur if you can factor the original second-order equation into two first-order equations with real coefficients. The matrix $\mathbf{Q}$ is singular in these cases. Another form of degeneracy happens when a matrix is satisfied for one point only. You can think of these as circles with a radius of zero. This will occur if the equation cannot be factored (without resorting to complex numbers). The matrix will be singular in this case also.

The preceding two cases of degeneracy happen when the rank of the matrix is 2. A further degeneracy occurs when the rank is reduced to 1. In

**Table 1.3**  *Types of second-order curves*

| Classification | Shape | Standard equation | Homogeneous equation | Matrix Q |
|---|---|---|---|---|
| Nondegenerate | Unit circle | $X^2 + Y^2 = 1$ | $x^2 + y^2 - w^2 = 0$ | $\begin{bmatrix} 1 & 0 & 0 \\ 0 & 1 & 0 \\ 0 & 0 & -1 \end{bmatrix}$ |
| | Parabola | $Y = X^2$ | $x^2 - yw = 0$ | $\begin{bmatrix} 1 & 0 & 0 \\ 0 & 0 & -1/2 \\ 0 & -1/2 & 0 \end{bmatrix}$ |
| | Hyperbola | $Y = 1/X$ | $xy - w^2 = 0$ | $\begin{bmatrix} 0 & 1/2 & 0 \\ 1/2 & 0 & 0 \\ 0 & 0 & -1 \end{bmatrix}$ |
| Degenerate: two intersecting lines | $X$ and $Y$ axes | $X = 0$ or $Y = 0$ | $xy = 0$ | $\begin{bmatrix} 0 & 1/2 & 0 \\ 1/2 & 0 & 0 \\ 0 & 0 & 0 \end{bmatrix}$ |
| | Diagonal lines | $Y = X$ or $Y = -X$ | $x^2 - y^2 = 0$ | $\begin{bmatrix} 1 & 0 & 0 \\ 0 & -1 & 0 \\ 0 & 0 & 0 \end{bmatrix}$ |
| Degenerate: single point | Origin | $X = 0$ and $Y = 0$ | $x^2 + y^2 = 0$ | $\begin{bmatrix} 1 & 0 & 0 \\ 0 & 1 & 0 \\ 0 & 0 & 0 \end{bmatrix}$ |
| Doubly degenerate: two coincident lines | $X$ axis twice | $X = 0$ twice | $x^2 = 0$ | $\begin{bmatrix} 1 & 0 & 0 \\ 0 & 0 & 0 \\ 0 & 0 & 0 \end{bmatrix}$ |
| Nondegenerate but boring | Null curve | $X^2 + Y^2 = -1$ | $x^2 + y^2 + w^2 = 0$ | $\begin{bmatrix} 1 & 0 & 0 \\ 0 & 1 & 0 \\ 0 & 0 & 1 \end{bmatrix}$ |

this case, the equation can be factored and the two factors are equal. The resulting curve is two coincident lines.

The final case can occur when no points satisfy the equation.

## Transformation

Given a quadric curve matrix $\mathbf{Q}$ and a homogeneous transformation matrix $\mathbf{T}$, we want to be able to derive a new matrix $\mathbf{Q}'$ that represents the transformed curve. That is, given

$$\mathbf{pQp}^T = 0 \text{ and } \mathbf{p}' = \mathbf{pT}$$

we want to find $\mathbf{Q}'$ such that, for points on the curve,

$$\mathbf{p}'\mathbf{Q}'\left(\mathbf{p}'\right)^T = 0$$

To solve this, first flip the equation for transforming points around:

$$\mathbf{p}'\mathbf{T}^* = \mathbf{p}$$

Then substitute this expression for $\mathbf{p}$ into the original quadric curve definition:

$$\mathbf{p}'\mathbf{T}^* \, \mathbf{Q}\left(\mathbf{p}'\mathbf{T}^*\right)^T = 0$$

Then expand the parenthesized expression and regroup:

$$\mathbf{p}'\left[\mathbf{T}^* \mathbf{QT}^{*T}\right]\left(\mathbf{p}'\right)^T = 0$$

By comparing the expression in square brackets with our desired expression for $\mathbf{Q}'$, we arrive at the answer:

$$\mathbf{Q}' = \mathbf{T}^* \mathbf{QT}^{*T} = 0$$

In other words, to transform a quadric curve, multiply on the left by the adjoint (i.e., generalized inverse) of the point transformation and on the right by the transpose of the adjoint. Quantities that transform in this manner are called *tensors*.

## Categorization by Eigenvalues

This transformation technique lets us simplify the categorization of quadric curves a bit. We apply a theorem from matrix algebra that says that, if a matrix is symmetric, it is possible to transform it into a diagonal matrix. The values on the diagonals are called *eigenvalues*. Furthermore, by using

**Table 1.4**  *Types of second-order curves via eigenvalue sign*

| Eigenvalue signs | Curve type |
|---|---|
| | **Nondegenerate** |
| $(+,+,+)$ or $(-,-,-)$ | Null curve |
| $(+,+,-)$ or $(-,-,+)$ | Conic section |
| | **Degenerate** |
| $(+,+,0)$ or $(-,-,0)$ | Single point (circle with radius = 0) |
| $(+,-,0)$ or $(-,+,0)$ | Intersecting lines |
| | **Doubly degenerate** |
| $(+,0,0)$ or $(-,0,0)$ | Coincident lines |

the appropriate scale factors, we can scale any nonzero diagonal elements to be $+1$ or $-1$. The only thing we can't do (with a nonsingular transformation) is change the sign of an eigenvalue or the number of eigenvalues that equal zero. Furthermore, since multiplying the whole matrix $\mathbf{Q}$ by $-1$ will produce the same curve, flipping the signs of *all* eigenvalues will yield the same curve type. Thus, all the curve types are covered by the possible patterns of +, -, and 0 for the three eigenvalues. See Table 1.4.

Note that this categorization does not distinguish between shapes that are different only due to homogeneous transformations (perhaps including perspective). Since any (nonsingular) transformation won't change the signs of the eigenvalues, any transformation of a curve of a particular type is the same curve as far as homogeneous projective geometry is concerned. Thus an ellipse, parabola, and hyperbola are all in the same category. You can think of a parabola as an ellipse that is tangent to the line at infinity. You can think of a hyperbola as an ellipse that pokes through the line at infinity and wraps around back to normal local space.

## Inside vs. Outside

The quadric form we have been using allows us to compute a number for any point, even those not on the curve:

$$\mathbf{p}\mathbf{Q}\mathbf{p}^T = f$$

If $\mathbf{p}$ lies on the curve, the value of $f$ will, of course, be zero. If $\mathbf{p}$ is not on the curve, the sign of $f$ can tell us if the point is inside or outside the curve. Which sign means inside, and which means outside? Look at the value we get by multiplying the arbitrary point $\begin{bmatrix} x & y & w \end{bmatrix}$ by the matrix for the unit circle at the origin:

$$f = \begin{bmatrix} x & y & w \end{bmatrix} \begin{bmatrix} 1 & 0 & 0 \\ 0 & 1 & 0 \\ 0 & 0 & -1 \end{bmatrix} \begin{bmatrix} x \\ y \\ w \end{bmatrix}$$

$$= x^2 + y^2 - w^2$$

$$\hat{=} X^2 + Y^2 - 1$$

If $f$ is positive, the point is outside the circle; if negative, it is inside. We must be a bit careful, however. Remember that in homogeneous coordinates $\begin{bmatrix} -x & -y & -w \end{bmatrix}$ has the same geometric meaning as $\begin{bmatrix} x & y & w \end{bmatrix}$, and $-\mathbf{Q}$ has the same geometric meaning as $\mathbf{Q}$. Using the point $\begin{bmatrix} -x & -y & -w \end{bmatrix}$ in the preceding equation still gives us the same sign, but using the matrix

$$\begin{bmatrix} -1 & 0 & 0 \\ 0 & -1 & 0 \\ 0 & 0 & 1 \end{bmatrix}$$

flips the sign. Since the inside/outside test must be kept unambiguous, we shall only use the version with two $+1$s and one $-1$. Note that a geometric transformation will not change the sign of $\mathbf{Q}$ even if a negative scale factor is involved. This is because the transformation is being multiplied twice, and the negatives cancel.

## Line Tangency

An important feature of homogeneous geometry is the two-for-the-price-of-one theorem, otherwise known as the *duality principle*. This states that if you take some true statement about points, lines, and matrices, you get another true statement by interchanging the words *point* and *line*, and replace the matrices with their adjoints. For example, the statement

point $\mathbf{p}$ is on curve $\mathbf{Q}$ if $\mathbf{pQp}^T = 0$

becomes

line $\mathbf{l}$ is on curve $\mathbf{Q}$ if $\mathbf{l}^T\mathbf{Q}*\mathbf{l} = 0$

In other words, you can test if a line is on (tangent to) a curve by multiplying it by the adjoint of the curve matrix.

We can generalize this discussion about inside/outside for points by looking at the case of the unit circle at the origin and the horizontal line $Y = y_H$. We represent the line by the column vector

$$1 = \begin{bmatrix} 0 \\ 1 \\ -y_H \end{bmatrix}$$

The adjoint of the unit circle matrix is

$$\begin{bmatrix} 1 & 0 & 0 \\ 0 & 1 & 0 \\ 0 & 0 & -1 \end{bmatrix}^* = \begin{bmatrix} -1 & 0 & 0 \\ 0 & -1 & 0 \\ 0 & 0 & 1 \end{bmatrix}$$

So the line tangency equation becomes

$$1^T\mathbf{Q}^*1 = \begin{bmatrix} 0 & 1 & -y_H \end{bmatrix} \begin{bmatrix} -1 & 0 & 0 \\ 0 & -1 & 0 \\ 0 & 0 & 1 \end{bmatrix} \begin{bmatrix} 0 \\ 1 \\ -y_H \end{bmatrix} = y_H^2 - 1$$

The line is tangent to the circle if $y_H = \pm 1$. If $|y_H| < 1$, the line intersects the circle at two points and the expression $y_H^2 - 1$ is negative; if $|y_H| > 1$, the line does not intersect the circle anywhere and the expression is positive. We then have the punch line:

$$\text{If the product } 1^T\mathbf{Q}^*1 \text{ is} \begin{Bmatrix} \text{negative} \\ \text{zero} \\ \text{positive} \end{Bmatrix} \text{ the line} \begin{Bmatrix} \text{intersects} \\ \text{is tangent to} \\ \text{is disjoint from} \end{Bmatrix} \text{ the curve.}$$

We can turn this around to solve another useful problem, namely, finding the $y$ extent of an arbitrary curve. We do this by making our horizontal line tangent to the curve $\mathbf{Q}$:

$$\begin{bmatrix} 0 & 1 & -y_H \end{bmatrix} \mathbf{Q}^* \begin{bmatrix} 0 \\ 1 \\ -y_H \end{bmatrix} = 0$$

Multiplying this out gives a quadratic equation for $y_H$. The two solutions are the maximum and minimum $y$ extent of the curve.

The line tangency equation also allows us to check the categorization of conic sections into the familiar categories of ellipse, parabola, and hyperbola. The interpretation is that an ellipse is disjoint from the line at infinity, a parabola is tangent to the line at infinity, and a hyperbola intersects it in two locations. The line at infinity has the vector $\begin{bmatrix} 0 & 0 & 1 \end{bmatrix}^T$, so this product

$$\begin{bmatrix} 0 & 0 & 1 \end{bmatrix} \mathbf{Q}^* \begin{bmatrix} 0 \\ 0 \\ 1 \end{bmatrix}$$

will simply equal the bottom-right element of $\mathbf{Q}^*$, which in terms of the original definition of the elements of $\mathbf{Q}$ equals $AD - B^2$. You can check that this works by referring to the $\mathbf{Q}$ matrices of the first three entries in Table 1.3.

## Normal Vectors

You can form a vector normal to a general algebraic curve $f(x, y, w) = 0$ by taking partial derivatives of the function:

$$\mathbf{n} = \begin{bmatrix} \dfrac{\partial f}{\partial x}, & \dfrac{\partial f}{\partial y} \end{bmatrix}$$

Simply evaluate the derivatives at the point at which you need the normal vector. This vector is not necessarily of unit length and must be appropriately scaled if this is a requirement.

For practice, let's look at a first-order surface

$$f(x, y, w) = ax + by + cw = \begin{bmatrix} x & y & w \end{bmatrix} \begin{bmatrix} a \\ b \\ c \end{bmatrix}$$

The normal vector is simply $\mathbf{n} = \begin{bmatrix} a & b \end{bmatrix}$. That is, the first two components of a homogeneous line form a vector perpendicular to the line.

For a second-order surface, the components of the normal vector come from the product rule for derivatives and the fact that $\mathbf{Q}$ is symmetric:

$$\frac{\partial f}{\partial x} = \begin{bmatrix} 1 & 0 & 0 \end{bmatrix} \mathbf{Q} \begin{bmatrix} x \\ y \\ w \end{bmatrix} + \begin{bmatrix} x & y & w \end{bmatrix} \mathbf{Q} \begin{bmatrix} 0 \\ 0 \\ 1 \end{bmatrix} = 2 \begin{bmatrix} x & y & w \end{bmatrix} \mathbf{Q} \begin{bmatrix} 1 \\ 0 \\ 0 \end{bmatrix}$$

$$\frac{\partial f}{\partial y} = \begin{bmatrix} 0 & 1 & 0 \end{bmatrix} \mathbf{Q} \begin{bmatrix} x \\ y \\ w \end{bmatrix} + \begin{bmatrix} x & y & w \end{bmatrix} \mathbf{Q} \begin{bmatrix} 0 \\ 1 \\ 0 \end{bmatrix} = 2 \begin{bmatrix} x & y & w \end{bmatrix} \mathbf{Q} \begin{bmatrix} 1 \\ 0 \\ 0 \end{bmatrix}$$

In other words, we get the components of the normal vector to curve $\mathbf{Q}$ at point $\mathbf{p}$ by multiplying $\mathbf{p}$ by the first two columns of $\mathbf{Q}$.

## Polar Lines and Points

Poor old **Q** is now sitting there singing, "Why not take all of me?" What happens if we go whole hog and multiply **p** times all of **Q**? We get a three-element vector:

$$\mathbf{Qp}^T = \mathbf{l}$$

If we dot this vector with **p**, we get 0 since **p** lies on the curve:

$$\mathbf{p} \cdot \mathbf{l} = \mathbf{p} \cdot \mathbf{Qp}^T = 0$$

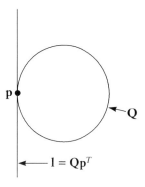

**p**

**Q**

**l = Qp**$^T$

**Figure 1.1**  *Polar line of point on curve*

In other words, we can interpret **l** as a line going through the point **p**. And since the normal to this line is also normal to the curve, the line is tangent to **Q**. The line so constructed is the tangent to the curve at **p**. Nifty. This line is called, by the cognoscenti, the *polar line* to curve **Q** at **p**. See Figure 1.1.

Now what happens if we try this with a point that is outside of **Q**? The quantity **Qp**$^T$ is still a perfectly reasonable line; it just no longer goes through point **p**. The polar line will intersect the curve in two points. If we connect these points to **p**, we find that the two lines formed are the two tangents from **p** to the curve. See Figure 1.2.

If the point **p** is inside the curve **Q**, the polar line will not intersect it. Instead, consider *all* lines **m** through **p**. Each **m** will intersect **Q** at two points. Find the two tangent lines at these points. The intersection of these two tangent lines will trace out the polar line **l** as **m** rotates about **p**. See Figure 1.3.

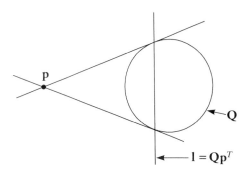

**p**

**Q**

**l = Qp**$^T$

**Figure 1.2**  *Polar line of point outside curve*

The dual form of "a polar *line* of a *point*" is a "polar *point* of a *line*." We form this by the expression

$$\mathbf{l}^T\mathbf{Q}^* = \mathbf{p}$$

If **l** is tangent to the curve, **p** is the point of that tangency (see Figure 1.1 and pretend that **l** was the input and **p** was the derived point). If **l** intersects the curve, **p** is the intersection of the two lines tangent to the curve at those points (see Figure 1.2 again). If **l** is disjoint from the curve, **p** is inside it (see Figure 1.3).

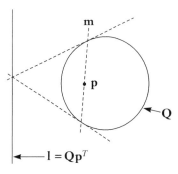

**m**

**p**

**Q**

**l = Qp**$^T$

**Figure 1.3**  *Polar line of point inside curve*

## The Tangent Quadric

How can we find the equations of the two tangent lines in Figure 1.2? Let's do this by remembering that a set of two intersecting lines is itself a (degenerate) second-order curve. We want to construct, given $\mathbf{p}$ and $\mathbf{Q}$, the degenerate quadric matrix $\mathbf{R}$ for these two intersecting tangent lines. First form the doubly degenerate quadric representation of the polar line $\mathbf{l}$ by forming the outer product, $\mathbf{l} \cdot \mathbf{l}^T$:

$$\mathbf{l} \cdot \mathbf{l}^T = \begin{bmatrix} a \\ b \\ c \end{bmatrix} \begin{bmatrix} a & b & c \end{bmatrix} = \begin{bmatrix} a^2 & ab & ac \\ ab & b^2 & bc \\ ac & bc & c^2 \end{bmatrix}$$

This symmetric matrix is an example of a "coincident lines" quadric, as shown in Table 1.3.

We now have two quadrics, $\mathbf{Q}$ and $\mathbf{l} \cdot \mathbf{l}^T$, which pass through the two points of tangency. Therefore, any linear combination of these two matrices must also pass through these two points:

$$\mathbf{R} = \alpha \left( \mathbf{l} \cdot \mathbf{l}^T \right) + \beta \mathbf{Q}$$

In particular, we wish to find that linear combination that passes through point $\mathbf{p}$ and thus satisfies:

$$\mathbf{p} \left[ \alpha \left( \mathbf{l} \cdot \mathbf{l}^T \right) + \beta \mathbf{Q} \right] \mathbf{p}^T = 0$$

We want to find any two values of $(\alpha, \beta)$ that cause this equality to hold. Inserting the definition $\mathbf{l} = \mathbf{Q}\mathbf{p}^T$ into the above and factoring, we get

$$\alpha \left( \mathbf{p}\mathbf{Q}\mathbf{p}^T \right)^2 + \beta \left( \mathbf{p}\mathbf{Q}\mathbf{p}^T \right) = 0$$

A reasonable choice for $(\alpha, \beta)$ would be

$$\alpha = 1$$
$$\beta = -\mathbf{p}\mathbf{Q}\mathbf{p}^T$$

So the net degenerate quadric forming the two tangent lines is

$$\mathbf{R} = \mathbf{l}\mathbf{l}^T - \left( \mathbf{p}\mathbf{Q}\mathbf{p}^T \right)\mathbf{Q}$$
$$= \mathbf{Q}\mathbf{p}^T\mathbf{p}\mathbf{Q} - \mathbf{p}\mathbf{Q}\mathbf{p}^T\mathbf{Q}$$

If the point $\mathbf{p}$ is outside the curve $\mathbf{Q}$, the quadric $\mathbf{R}$ will be an "intersecting lines" quadric consisting of the two tangents to the curve. If the point $\mathbf{p}$ is on the curve $\mathbf{Q}$, then $\mathbf{p}\mathbf{Q}\mathbf{p}^T$ is zero and $\mathbf{R}$ is just $\mathbf{l} \cdot \mathbf{l}^T$, the coincident-line quadric that is the tangent line $\mathbf{l}$ coincident with itself. If point $\mathbf{p}$ is inside the curve, there are no tangent lines. The quadric **R** indicates this by being a degenerate single-point curve—that point being **p** itself.

# Second-Order Surfaces

The generalization of the machinery above from two dimensions to three dimensions is mostly pretty simple. The general second-order equation in 3D is

$$0 = Ax^2 + 2Bxy + 2Cxz + 2Dxw$$
$$+ Ey^2 + 2Fyz + 2Gyw$$
$$+ Hz^2 + 2Izw$$
$$+ \mathcal{J}w^2$$

Rewriting this in matrix notation:

$$\begin{bmatrix} x & y & z & w \end{bmatrix} \begin{bmatrix} A & B & C & D \\ B & E & F & G \\ C & F & H & I \\ D & G & I & \mathcal{J} \end{bmatrix} \begin{bmatrix} x \\ y \\ z \\ w \end{bmatrix} = 0$$

I'll again call the 4×4 symmetric matrix **Q**. We can categorize the types of possible surfaces by looking at the signs of the eigenvectors. See Table 1.5.

Again, the classifications do not distinguish between shapes that are different only due to transformations (possibly including perspective). There are three distinct, perspectively equivalent, types of nondegenerate surfaces: null, ellipsoid and friends, and saddle point and friends. It is not possible to transform, say, a hyperboloid of two sheets into a hyperboloid of one sheet.

The ellipsoid, paraboloid, and hyperboloid of two sheets are the same shape as far as projective geometry is concerned. Like their 2D counterparts, you can think of a paraboloid as an ellipsoid that is tangent to the plane at infinity and a hyperboloid as an ellipsoid that intersects the plane at infinity, pokes through, and wraps around the other side. You can, with a perspective transformation, change any one of these to the other. These are the surfaces we are going to draw. We must realize, then, that our perspectivized sphere might become a hyperboloid on the screen.

As another intuition exercise, look at the equivalence of cylinders and cones. Consider a cylinder around the $x$ axis. All points on the cylinder very far away in the $x$ direction converge to the same single point at infinity [1, 0, 0, 0]. In other words, a cylinder is a cone with its apex at infinity.

**Table 1.5** *Types of second-order surfaces via eigenvalue sign*

| Eigenvalue signs | Curve type |
| --- | --- |
| **Nondegenerate** | |
| $(+,+,+,+)$ or $(-,-,-,-)$ | Null curve |
| $(+,+,+,-)$ or $(-,-,-,+)$ | Ellipsoid |
| | Paraboloid |
| | Hyperboloid of two sheets |
| $(+,+,-,-)$ | Hyperboloid of one sheet |
| | Hyperbolic paraboloid (saddle point) |
| **Degenerate** | |
| $(+,+,+,0)$ or $(-,-,-,0)$ | A single point (sphere with radius = 0) |
| $(+,+,-,0)$ or $(-,-,+,0)$ | Cylinder |
| | Cone |
| **Doubly degenerate** | |
| $(+,+,0,0)$ or $(-,-,0,0)$ | A single line (cylinder with radius = 0) |
| $(+,-,0,0)$ | Two intersecting planes |
| **Triply degenerate** | |
| $(+,0,0,0)$ or $(-,0,0,0)$ | Two coincident planes |

## Transformations

Given a 4×4 homogeneous transformation matrix $\mathbf{T}$ for transforming points, we transform a quadric surface by

$$\mathbf{Q'} = \mathbf{T}^*\mathbf{Q}\mathbf{T}^{*T}$$

## Plane Tangency and Intersection

Plane $\mathbf{l}$ is tangent to surface $\mathbf{Q}$ if

$$\mathbf{l}^T\mathbf{Q}^*\mathbf{l} = 0$$

If this quantity is negative, the plane intersects $\mathbf{Q}$; if positive, the plane is disjoint from $\mathbf{Q}$.

## Normal Vectors

You get the vector normal to surface $\mathbf{Q}$ at point $\mathbf{p}$ by multiplying $\mathbf{p}$ by the first three columns of $\mathbf{Q}$:

$$\mathbf{n} = \begin{bmatrix} x & y & z & w \end{bmatrix} \mathbf{Q} \begin{bmatrix} 1 & 0 & 0 \\ 0 & 1 & 0 \\ 0 & 0 & 1 \\ 0 & 0 & 0 \end{bmatrix}$$

## Polar Planes and Silhouettes

The plane tangent to surface $\mathbf{Q}$ at point $\mathbf{p}$ is

$$\mathbf{Q}\mathbf{p}^T = 1$$

If point $\mathbf{p}$ is outside of surface $\mathbf{Q}$, you will get a plane that intersects the surface instead of being tangent to it (see Figure 1.4). The geometric interpretation of this polar plane is as follows: take all the lines through $\mathbf{p}$ that are tangent to surface $\mathbf{Q}$. These form a cone. All the points of tangency will lie on the polar plane.

An interesting use of the polar plane construction is the silhouette plane. The silhouette edge of an object is formed of all points where the line of sight from the eye is tangent to the surface. This silhouette will lie in the polar plane of the eye point with respect to $\mathbf{Q}$.

The 2D construction of the two tangents from a point to a curve generalizes easily to three dimensions. The degenerate quadric surface

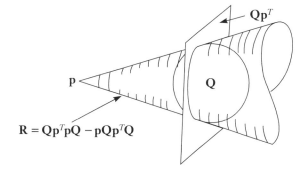

**Figure 1.4**  *Cone from point **p** to quadric **Q***

$$\mathbf{R} = \mathbf{Q}\mathbf{p}^T\mathbf{p}\mathbf{Q} - \mathbf{p}\mathbf{Q}\mathbf{p}^T\mathbf{Q}$$

is simply the cone with apex at point $\mathbf{p}$ and tangent to surface $\mathbf{Q}$. The perceptive reader will note that this is identical to the 2D equation of the two tangents to a conic from the previous section. In this case, the vectors have four elements and the matrices are 4×4, while previously they were 3-vectors and $3 \times 3$ matrices. Again look at Figure 1.4 for a geometric view.

The cone of Figure 1.4 is useful in calculating shadows. If the point $\mathbf{p}$ represents a light source, the surface $\mathbf{Q}$ will cast a shadow across all points that are both within the cone and on the opposite side of the polar plane $\mathbf{Q}\mathbf{p}^T$ from $\mathbf{p}$.

## Summary

So . . . we now have a bunch of geometric problem-solving techniques using matrix algebra under our belt. In the next chapter, we'll apply them to the rendering problem.

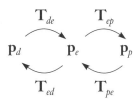

# CHAPTER TWO

# How to Draw a Sphere Part II, Coordinate Systems

MARCH 1995

This chapter continues my discussion about how to render a single arbitrarily transformed sphere. In Chapter 1, I tantalized you by describing what the inner loop is going to look like. Then I listed a whole bunch of vector/matrix algebra operations and the geometric constructions they represent. Now I'll start out to derive the inner loop of the rendering algorithm, and you will see all the matrix algebra in action. Most of our time, however, will be spent picking the correct coordinate system to make the inner loop fast and accurate. Even if you never have occasion to write a special-purpose sphere-rendering program, this will be an excellent illustration of the workings of the homogeneous perspective transform and geometric interpretations of the various other transformation matrices. This chapter will firmly establish my inexhaustible enthusiasm for matrices. You'll see so many matrices here your eyes will fall out.

## Coordinate Systems

In Chapter 14, "Pixel Coordinates," of *Jim Blinn's Corner: A Trip Down the Graphics Pipeline*, I described several different coordinate systems that an object implicitly passes through on its way to the screen, all related by simple 4×4 homogeneous matrix multiplications. Three of these coordinate systems will be of particular interest here, so let's review them.

### Definition Space

This is the coordinate system in which our sphere is defined. The sphere is centered at the origin and has a unit radius. This is the coordinate system in which we will derive texture coordinates for texture mapping.

### Eye Space

In this system, the eye is at the origin and is looking down the positive $z$ axis, a left-handed coordinate system. The sphere has been rotated, scaled, and translated to wherever the model and camera position dictate. Distances and angles in this system have real-world geometric meaning, so this is the coordinate space in which we will do lighting calculations. Even though we start out with a perfect sphere in definition space, we might perfectly well transform it into an ellipsoid in eye space, so our algorithm will actually render an arbitrarily oriented ellipsoid.

### Pixel Space

This is the coordinate system we're in after a homogeneous perspective projection has been performed, and after the $x$ and $y$ coordinates have been scaled so that integer values of $x$ and $y$ refer to pixel coordinates.

# Naming Conventions

We'll be dealing with algebraic constructions relating points, transformed spheres, and planes in each of these three coordinate systems, so let's devise some conventions to keep from getting lost. All this is summarized in Figure 2.1.

### Points

I'll use subscripts to distinguish between the coordinate systems so that, for example, $\mathbf{p}_d$ is a point in the definition space, $\mathbf{p}_e$ is the same point in eye space, and $\mathbf{p}_p$ is the same point in pixel space. All points are four-element homogeneous row vectors.

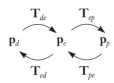
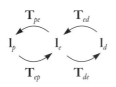

**Figure 2.1**  *Points, planes, and their transforms*

## Planes

Likewise, $\mathbf{l}_d$ is an arbitrary plane in definition space, $\mathbf{l}_e$ is the same plane in eye space, and $\mathbf{l}_p$ is the same plane in pixel space. All planes are four-element homogeneous column vectors.

## Transformations

I'll write transformations between the systems with double subscripts so that

$$\mathbf{p}_d \mathbf{T}_{de} = \mathbf{p}_e \text{ and } \mathbf{p}_e \mathbf{T}_{ep} = \mathbf{p}_p$$

and, of course, you can multiply the matrices themselves so that

$$\mathbf{T}_{de} \mathbf{T}_{ep} = \mathbf{T}_{dp}$$

The two matrices $\mathbf{T}_{de}$ and $\mathbf{T}_{ep}$ are the inputs to our algorithm. Matrix $\mathbf{T}_{de}$ contains rotations, scalings, and translations but probably doesn't have a perspective component. Matrix $\mathbf{T}_{ep}$ contains a homogeneous perspective and the appropriate $x$ and $y$ scalings to map the sphere to integer screen pixels.

## Adjoints

We will also use the inverses of these matrices, both to shove points "backward" up the pipeline and to transform planes forward down the pipeline. (Actually the adjoint, denoted by a superscript asterisk, is good enough and is easier to calculate.) We'll have to keep careful watch over these to keep from getting confused. Here are a few typical such operations:

$$(\mathbf{T}_{de})^* = \mathbf{T}_{ed}$$
$$\mathbf{p}_e \mathbf{T}_{ed} = \mathbf{p}_d$$

Given a plane $\mathbf{l}$, we can transform it by postmultiplying by the adjoint of the point transformation matrix. For example,

$$(\mathbf{T}_{de})^* \mathbf{l}_d = \mathbf{T}_{ed} \mathbf{l}_d = \mathbf{l}_e$$

Notice the nice way the subscripts work out; compare the two equations

$$\mathbf{p}_d \mathbf{T}_{de} = \mathbf{p}_e$$

and

$$\mathbf{T}_{ed} \mathbf{l}_d = \mathbf{l}_e$$

## Quadrics

Finally, the representation of our sphere as a 4×4 matrix in definition space looks like

$$\mathbf{Q}_d = \begin{bmatrix} 1 & 0 & 0 & 0 \\ 0 & 1 & 0 & 0 \\ 0 & 0 & 1 & 0 \\ 0 & 0 & 0 & -1 \end{bmatrix}$$

and in other coordinate systems it will look like

$$\mathbf{Q}_e = \mathbf{T}_{de}{}^* \mathbf{Q}_d \left( \mathbf{T}_{de}{}^* \right)^T$$

Remember that we transform a quadric surface by multiplying by the adjoint and the adjoint transpose of the point transformation matrix.

# Code and Indexing Conventions

I will ultimately translate all these calculations into C++ code using the simple vector/matrix classes listed in the Appendix, which define all the typical mathematical operations that vectors and matrices undergo. There is, however, a clash between indexing conventions of typical mathematical notation and C++, which as I described in Chapter 0, I will resolve by doing all mathematical matrix/vector indexing starting at zero. I will also predefine some constants so that retrieving specific components of a vector can be done symbolically.

```
const int a=0,b=1,c=2,d=3;
const int x=0,y=1,z=2,w=3;
Vector4 P; // can access elts by P[x],P[y],P[z],P[w]
Vector4 L; // can access elts by L[a],L[b],L[c],L[d]
```

# The Basic Algorithm

The basic idea of the whole algorithm is to calculate, in pixel space, the $z$ value for each $x$, $y$ pixel value. In other words, for a given pixel coordinate $\begin{bmatrix} x_p & y_p \end{bmatrix}$, we substitute into the equation

$$\begin{bmatrix} x_p & y_p & z_p & 1 \end{bmatrix} \mathbf{Q}_p \begin{bmatrix} x_p \\ y_p \\ z_p \\ 1 \end{bmatrix} = 0$$

This will give a quadratic equation in $z_p$, which we solve via the quadratic formula. Then we transform the resulting 3D point back up the pipe to the $e$ and $d$ coordinate systems in order to calculate normal vectors and texture coordinates, respectively. Do this for each pixel and, voila, you have a picture. Now let's look at some of the things that can go wrong with this quadratic equation.

# Why Space Is Scary

*Space is big. Really big. You just won't believe how vastly hugely, mind-boggling big it is.*

   —Hitchhiker's Guide to the Galaxy

Right-o. And the moons and planets are real small and real far apart. This can get us into nasty precision problems in some situations when we try to draw pictures of them. To see why, let's review what goes on in a typical transform.

The transformation from definition to eye space $\mathbf{T}_{de}$ contains no perspective, so it looks like

$$\mathbf{T}_{de} = \begin{bmatrix} * & * & a & 0 \\ * & * & b & 0 \\ * & * & c & 0 \\ * & * & z_c & 1 \end{bmatrix}$$

where the asterisks mark matrix elements we aren't particularly interested in for the time being, and $z_c$ is the $z$ coordinate of the center of the sphere (in eye space).

The transformation from eye to perspective space $\mathbf{T}_{ep}$ does contain perspective, defined by the field-of-view angle $f$ and the locations of the desired near and far clipping planes (in eye space) denoted by $z_n$ and $z_f$. We first precalculate the values

$$s = \sin\left(f/2\right)$$

$$Q = \frac{s}{1 - z_n/z_f}$$

Then we have

$$\mathbf{T}_{ep} = \begin{bmatrix} * & * & 0 & 0 \\ * & * & 0 & 0 \\ * & * & Q & s \\ * & * & -Qz_n & 0 \end{bmatrix}$$

The net transformation from definition space to pixel space is then

$$\mathbf{T}_{dp} = \mathbf{T}_{de}\mathbf{T}_{ep} = \begin{bmatrix} * & * & aQ & as \\ * & * & bQ & bs \\ * & * & cQ & cs \\ * & * & (z_c - z_n)Q & z_c s \end{bmatrix}$$

Typically, users won't *want* close-by objects to be clipped off, so they set the value of $z_n$ to be something very small (near the eye). But if $z_n$ is very small, the right-hand two columns of this matrix are almost the same (except for a scale factor). This is bad, baaaad. It means that any point transformed to pixel space is going to have its $z$ coordinate equal to something times $Q$ and its $w$ coordinate equal to the same something times $s$. After the homogeneous division, the sphere is squashed almost flat against the $Z_p = Q/s$ plane. And since

$$\frac{Q}{s} = \frac{1}{1 - z_n/z_f} = \frac{z_f}{z_f - z_n}$$

the smaller $z_n$ is, the closer this is to 1.

It's important to realize that this problem is really independent of the clipping process. Even if we're not going to do any $z$ clipping (which we, in fact, won't bother to do when rendering shaded images), the $z_d$ coordinate is going to have to map *somewhere* in $z_p$. The $z_n$ and $z_f$ values are just convenient handles on what the $z$'s transform to.

The solution to the resolution problem, of course, is to make $z_n$ as big as possible. Like maybe, $z_c - r$, with $r$ the radius of the sphere (in eye space). Good and bad values of $z_n$ are shown in Figure 2.2.

## Family Portraits

Now how about if we are looking at both a planet and a moon. For example, the moon Callisto orbits Jupiter at a distance of about 26.394 Jupiter radii and has a radius of about 0.034 Jupiter radii. Let's view this scene straight on from a distance of 50 Jupiter radii. The best we can do for the near clipping planes is $z_n = 50 - 26.394 - 0.034 = 23.572$. While drawing Jupiter, the matrix is

$$\mathbf{T}_{dp} = \begin{bmatrix} * & * & 0 & 0 \\ * & * & 0 & 0 \\ * & * & Q & s \\ * & * & 26.428Q & 50s \end{bmatrix}$$

The front and back of Jupiter transform to $\begin{bmatrix} 0 & 0 & 25.428Q & 49s \end{bmatrix}$ and $\begin{bmatrix} 0 & 0 & 27.428Q & 51s \end{bmatrix}$. After the homogeneous division, the $z_p$ coordinates will be $0.519\,Q/s$ and $0.537\,Q/s$; the entire sphere is squashed between these values. This is not too good for precision.

For this reason I don't even try to render multiple spheres in the same $z$ depth coordinate system. My sphere renderer only takes care of one sphere. I generate multiple spheres by the painter's algorithm, draw the whole farthest-away sphere first (with its own private $z_n$ and $z_f$), and then overlay the nearest sphere on top of it (with *its* own $z_n$ and $z_f$).

## Telescopic Views

Putting the near and far clipping planes snugly around our model is our best strategy, but it is not always easy. Suppose you wanted to generate a view of Callisto as seen from the Earth (simulating a telescopic view). The distance from Earth to Callisto is about 257231.27 times the radius of Callisto. Here we run into another problem, $z_c = 257231.27$, and the optimal $z_n = 257230.27$. To construct the matrix, we must subtract these two almost equal numbers and we lose precision.

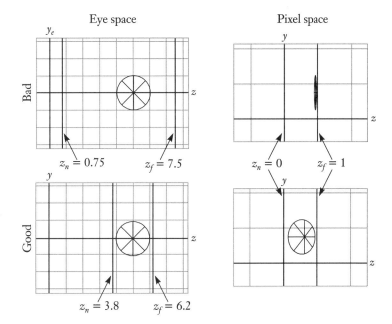

**Figure 2.2** *Good and bad choices for near and far clipping planes*

# Optimizing the Depth Transformation

It turns out that we can arrange for a post-facto repair of any roundoff errors in the matrix. We simply take the location of the $z_n$ and $z_f$ "clipping" planes out of the hands of the user and calculate an optimal matrix our-selves. To figure out how to do this, we have to get cozy with the matrix and find out what it really means geometrically.

Let's take a look at $\mathbf{T}_{dp}$. This transforms points from definition space to pixel space, but it also transforms planes from pixel space to definition space. One particularly interesting plane is the eye plane, which I'll call $\mathbf{v}$. In eye space, this is the $z_e = 0$ plane, or $\mathbf{v}_e = \begin{bmatrix} 0 & 0 & 1 & 0 \end{bmatrix}^T$. In perspec-tivized pixel space, this becomes the plane at infinity, $\mathbf{v}_p = \begin{bmatrix} 0 & 0 & 0 & 1 \end{bmatrix}^T$. And in definition space, we get

$$\mathbf{v}_d = \mathbf{T}_{dp}\mathbf{v}_p = \mathbf{T}_{dp} \begin{bmatrix} 0 \\ 0 \\ 0 \\ 1 \end{bmatrix}$$

This means that we can interpret the rightmost column of $\mathbf{T}_{dp}$ as the eye plane in definition space. I'll give this column the name $\mathbf{t}_{dpW}$. (Note that I use a lowercase $\mathbf{t}$ here to emphasize that this is a vector. The subscript now contains two pieces of information: the $dp$ designation for the matrix this column is a part of and the $W$ to indicate which column. I've used an up-percase $W$ here just to make it more visually separable from the $dp$.)

Next, consider the desired near clipping plane $\mathbf{n}$. In pixel space, this is the plane $z_p = 0$, whose vector representation is $\mathbf{n}_p = \begin{bmatrix} 0 & 0 & 1 & 0 \end{bmatrix}^T$. Taking this back to definition space, we get

$$\mathbf{n}_d = \mathbf{T}_{dp}\mathbf{n}_p = \mathbf{T}_{dp} \begin{bmatrix} 0 \\ 0 \\ 1 \\ 0 \end{bmatrix}$$

This means that column 2 (starting from zero) of $\mathbf{T}_{dp}$ is the near clipping plane in definition space. I'll call this column $\mathbf{t}_{dpZ}$.

Next, we realize that any $x$, $y$ coordinates on the sphere only depend on columns 0, 1, and 3 of $\mathbf{T}_{dp}$. If we change column 2, we don't change the placement of points in $x$, $y$ on the screen. We can then change this column, after the fact, to put the near plane wherever we want. What we would like is for $\mathbf{n}_d$ to be parallel to $\mathbf{v}_d$ and tangent to the sphere. The orientation of a plane is specified by the first three elements of its vector, and the distance from the origin is proportional to the fourth. So, if we name the elements of the fourth column of $\mathbf{T}_{dp}$ as follows:

$$\mathbf{t}_{dpW} = \mathbf{v}_d = \begin{bmatrix} a \\ b \\ c \\ d \end{bmatrix}$$

we can construct

$$\mathbf{t}_{dpZ} = \mathbf{n}_d = \begin{bmatrix} a \\ b \\ c \\ r \end{bmatrix}$$

and pick $r$ to make $\mathbf{n}_d$ tangent to $\mathbf{Q}_d$. The equation for tangency is

$$\begin{bmatrix} a & b & c & r \end{bmatrix} \mathbf{Q}_d^* \begin{bmatrix} a \\ b \\ c \\ r \end{bmatrix} = 0$$

and solving for $r$ gets us

$$r = \pm\sqrt{a^2 + b^2 + c^2}$$

Which sign do we pick for the root? We want planes $\mathbf{v}_d$ and $\mathbf{n}_d$ to be on the same side of the origin. Otherwise, our near plane will be tangent to $\mathbf{Q}_d$ on its far side. Dotting these vectors with the origin, $\begin{bmatrix} 0 & 0 & 0 & 1 \end{bmatrix}$, gives just their fourth components, $d$ and $r$. So we want $d$ and $r$ to have the same sign. The value of $d = z_c s$ is positive if the sphere is in front of us, so we must pick the positive root for $r$.

Now, we could just stuff in $\begin{bmatrix} a & b & c & r \end{bmatrix}^T$ for the third column of $\mathbf{T}_{dp}$, but there is a homogeneous subtlety here that we must be careful of. Remember that any scalar multiple of a column vector represents the same plane. So $\mathbf{t}_{dpZ}$ can be any scalar multiple of our result:

$$\mathbf{t}_{dpZ} = \begin{bmatrix} ka \\ kb \\ kc \\ kr \end{bmatrix}$$

The scale factor of the column *is* important. What does it mean? Well, it won't change where $\mathbf{T}_{dp}$ puts the planes $\mathbf{v}_d$ or $\mathbf{n}_d$, but it will change where it puts other planes parallel to these two. We can use it to adjust things so that the far clipping plane $\mathbf{f}$ is tangent to the back side of the sphere.

The far plane in pixel space is $Z_f = 1$, so the column vector for $\mathbf{f}_p$ is $\begin{bmatrix} 0 & 0 & 1 & -1 \end{bmatrix}^T$. In definition space, it is

$$\mathbf{f}_d = \mathbf{T}_{dp}\mathbf{f}_p = \mathbf{T}_{dp} \begin{bmatrix} 0 \\ 0 \\ 1 \\ -1 \end{bmatrix} = \mathbf{t}_{dpZ} - \mathbf{t}_{dpW} = \begin{bmatrix} ka - a \\ kb - b \\ kc - c \\ kr - d \end{bmatrix}$$

We want this to be tangent to $\mathbf{Q}_d$ so

$$(\mathbf{f}_d)^T \mathbf{Q}^* \, \mathbf{f}_d = 0$$

Plugging in and multiplying out leads to

$$(a^2 + b^2 + c^2)(k-1)^2 - (kr - d)^2 = 0$$

Solve for $k$

$$k = \frac{d+r}{2r}$$

Both $d$ and $r$ are positive numbers, so the addition creates no precision problems. And what if $r = 0$? This means that $\mathbf{v}_d$ is the plane at infinity, which means that the perspective transformation was not formed correctly. I disallow this.

What have we done here? We have constructed a whole new column 2 for $\mathbf{T}_{dp}$ without even looking at the old column 2, or how much the roundoff error might have messed it up. And this works even if, for some bizarre modeling purposes, we had happened to have a perspective component in $\mathbf{T}_{de}$.

## The Algorithm
The code for optimizing transformation $\mathbf{T}_{dp}$ is a lot simpler than the mathematical derivation. Translating it into C++ gives

```
// Replace column z of Tdp with a better one

Vector4 Vd = Tdp.Col(w); // eye plane in definition space
float  r    = sqrt(Vd[a]*Vd[a] + Vd[b]*Vd[b] + Vd[c]*Vd[c]);
Vector4 Nd = Vector4(Vd[a],Vd[b],Vd[c],r); //near plane, defn space
float  k    = (r+Vd[d])/(2*r);
Tdp.setCol(z, k*Nd);
```

# Milking the Perspective Transformation

As long as we're messing with the $z$ coordinate, let's go a bit further and do something really useful. Because we are going to solve a lot of quadratic equations to get $z_p$ values at each pixel, we'll do another transform to make these equations a lot simpler.

Take a look at a side view of the situation in eye and pixel space in Figure 2.3. As I described in Chapter 1, the visible outline of the sphere, the silhouette edge, lies in the polar plane from the eye point, **e,** to the sphere. We can calculate this plane, **s,** simply:

$$\mathbf{Q}\mathbf{e}^T = \mathbf{s}$$

If the center of the sphere is exactly on the $z_p$ axis, this plane will be parallel to the screen. But in general the center can be off the axis, the silhouette plane will be at some angle, and the silhouette outline will be an ellipse. In pixel space, the eye is at infinity, $\mathbf{e}_p = \begin{bmatrix} 0 & 0 & 1 & 0 \end{bmatrix}$, and the sight lines to the silhouette are all parallel. If we were to do a *shearing* operation in the $z$ direction, it would not change the visible outline of the sphere at all. Let us, then, postmultiply our pixel space by a transformation that shears the sphere so that its silhouette plane coincides with the $z = 0$ plane. This will create yet another coordinate space, to which I'll give the subscript $s$.

We want to generate the matrix $\mathbf{Q}_s$ for the sphere in our new sheared space to be something special. Marking nonzero values with asterisks, we want

$$\mathbf{T}_{sp}\mathbf{Q}_p(\mathbf{T}_{sp})^T = \mathbf{Q}_s = \begin{bmatrix} * & * & 0 & * \\ * & * & 0 & * \\ 0 & 0 & * & 0 \\ * & * & 0 & * \end{bmatrix}$$

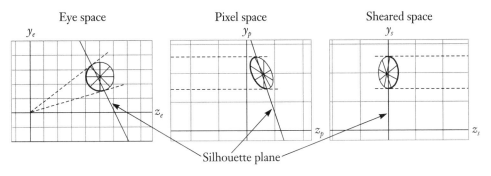

**Figure 2.3** *Shearing the silhouette plane to $z_s = 0$*

Why would this be nice? Because when we plug in a given pixel coordinate $\begin{bmatrix} x_s & y_s \end{bmatrix}$, we get

$$\begin{bmatrix} x_s & y_s & z_s & 1 \end{bmatrix} \begin{bmatrix} \star & \star & 0 & \star \\ \star & \star & 0 & \star \\ 0 & 0 & Q_{s22} & 0 \\ \star & \star & 0 & \star \end{bmatrix} \begin{bmatrix} x_s \\ y_s \\ z_s \\ 1 \end{bmatrix} = 0$$

(I've written the specific matrix element $Q_{s22}$ with italic type since it's a scalar.) We can rewrite this as

$$-\frac{1}{Q_{s22}} \begin{bmatrix} x_s & y_s & 1 \end{bmatrix} \begin{bmatrix} \star & \star & \star \\ \star & \star & \star \\ \star & \star & \star \end{bmatrix} \begin{bmatrix} x_s \\ y_s \\ 1 \end{bmatrix} = z_s^2$$

We can now solve for $z_s$ with just a square root, about as simple a quadratic equation as you could hope for. For future reference, I'll give the name $\tilde{Q}$ to the matrix

$$\tilde{Q} = -\frac{1}{Q_{s22}} \begin{bmatrix} \star & \star & \star \\ \star & \star & \star \\ \star & \star & \star \end{bmatrix}$$

So, what do we use for $\mathbf{T}_{sp}$ to make this happen? An arbitrary shearing transformation has the form

$$\mathbf{T}_{sp} = \begin{bmatrix} 1 & 0 & a & 0 \\ 0 & 1 & b & 0 \\ 0 & 0 & c & 0 \\ 0 & 0 & d & 1 \end{bmatrix}$$

(I'm recycling the variables $a$, $b$, $c$, $d$ here.) Why is this a shearing transformation? Multiply in any point and you see that you don't change the $x$, $y$, or $w$ components. And as long as the value of $c$ is not zero, the matrix is nonsingular.

Now what do we use for $a$, $b$, $c$, and $d$? Well, symbolically grunting through the matrix product $\mathbf{T}_{sp} \mathbf{Q}_p (\mathbf{T}_{sp})^T$ will tell us. I'm game if you are (grunt, grunt). The result is

$$Q_{s02} = c\left(Q_{p02} + aQ_{p22}\right)$$
$$Q_{s12} = c\left(Q_{p12} + bQ_{p22}\right)$$
$$Q_{s32} = c\left(Q_{p32} + dQ_{p22}\right)$$

We want these all to be zero so

$$a = -Q_{p02}/Q_{p22}$$
$$b = -Q_{p12}/Q_{p22}$$
$$d = -Q_{p32}/Q_{p22}$$

What if $Q_{p22} = 0$? It means that the eye point [0, 0, 1, 0] lies on the surface of the sphere. Ouch. Disallow this.

We don't get an explicit condition for $c$; it simply represents a $z$ scale factor applied to the sheared sphere. We don't really care what it is, so by analogy to the equations for $a$, $b$, $d$, I simply picked

$$c = -Q_{p22}/Q_{p22} = -1$$

But wait a minute. Since $c$ is negative, it means that our transformation $\mathbf{T}_{sp}$ contains a mirror reflection about the $z_s = 0$ plane. Isn't that bad?

Well, it happens that I kind of like this. A nonreflecting shear transformation would transform the front (visible) side of the sphere to the negative $z$ side of $s$ space. Now, since we are also reflecting about $z$, the visible side is on the positive $z$ side. In other words, when we go to take the square root of $z_s^2$ as calculated above, we want the positive square root.

## The Algorithm

The simplest implementation of this is

```
Matrix44 Tpd = Tdp.Adjoint();
Matrix44 Qp  = (Tpd * Qd).TimesTranspose(Tpd);//Q, pixel space
Matrix44 Tsp = Matrix44::Identity;
Tsp.setCol(z ,-Qp.Col(z)/Qp(z,z));
Matrix44 Tsd = Tsp * Tpd;
Matrix44 Qtemp = -(1/Qp(z,z)) *
                (Tsp * Qp).TimesTranspose(Tsp);
Matrix33 Qtilde(Qtemp(0,0), Qtemp(0,1), Qtemp(0,3),
               Qtemp(1,0), Qtemp(1,1), Qtemp(1,3),
               Qtemp(3,0), Qtemp(3,1), Qtemp(3,3));
```

Implementing it this way is simple, but I did it a bit differently. I took advantage of all the zeros in **Qd** and **Tsp** to write explicit expressions for the elements of **Qp** and **Tsd**. Also, the two matrix multiplications in the calculation of **Qtilde** can be removed by doing the product symbolically (more grunt, grunt). Some stuff cancels out, and you will find simply that

$$\tilde{\mathbf{Q}} = -\frac{1}{Q_{p22}} \begin{bmatrix} Q_{p00} - aQ_{p02} & Q_{p01} - bQ_{p02} & Q_{p03} - dQ_{p02} \\ \star & Q_{p11} - bQ_{p12} & Q_{p13} - dQ_{p12} \\ \star & \star & Q_{p33} - dQ_{p32} \end{bmatrix}$$

You can get the remaining starred elements from the fact that $\tilde{\mathbf{Q}}$ is symmetrical.

# Another Use for Shearing

While the main topic of Chapters 1 through 3 is shaded image rendering of spheres, I'll digress briefly here to discuss another tricky use of the $z$ shearing technique that is useful for line drawings. A normal line drawing of a sphere is confusing since both the front and back halves of the sphere are visible. We would like to turn off any lines on the back side of the silhouette plane. If we do a slight variant of the previous $z$ shearing, we can put the silhouette plane at the far clipping plane, $z_s = 1$. The standard line-clipping process will slickly slice off the back half of the sphere. But we need to make sure the rest of the sphere remains inside the clipping region (i.e., in front of the $z_s = 0$ plane). A good way to ensure this is to make the front of the sheared sphere tangent to the $z_s = 0$ plane.

We start with the (nonoptimized) $\mathbf{T}_{dp}$ and we want to calculate a new $\mathbf{T}_{ds}$. Again these differ only in their third columns. This time, instead of specifically finding the shear between them, we'll go straight for the desired new third column and stuff it in to $\mathbf{T}_{dp}$ to make $\mathbf{T}_{ds}$ directly. Our two requirements are that the silhouette plane coincides with the far clip plane and that the near clip plane is tangent to the front of the sphere.

For the first requirement, look at the far plane in definition space:

$$\mathbf{f}_d = \mathbf{T}_{ds}\mathbf{f}_s = \mathbf{T}_{ds}\begin{bmatrix} 0 \\ 0 \\ 1 \\ -1 \end{bmatrix} = \mathbf{t}_{dsZ} - \mathbf{t}_{dsW}$$

We make this equal to the silhouette plane in definition space, which is the polar of the eye point $\mathbf{e}$:

$$\mathbf{Q}_d \mathbf{e}_d^{\ T} = \mathbf{s}_d$$

Where do we get $\mathbf{e}_d^{\ T}$ from? We know where the eye is at in pixel space ... infinity. So, in definition space it's at

$$\mathbf{e}_d = \mathbf{e}_p \mathbf{T}_{dp}{}^* = \begin{bmatrix} 0 & 0 & 1 & 0 \end{bmatrix} \mathbf{T}_{dp}{}^*$$

But we don't really have to do a whole adjoint calculation. We can also express this as

$$\mathbf{e}_d \mathbf{T}_{dp} = \begin{bmatrix} 0 & 0 & 1 & 0 \end{bmatrix}$$

We can consider each column of $\mathbf{T}_{dp}$ as a plane in space. We want the dot product of the eye point with columns (planes) 0, 1, and 3 to be zero. In other words, we want to find the 3D intersection of these three planes. There is a specific formula for intersecting three planes that is a 4D analog of the 3D cross product; I call it the 4D cross product, and it's defined as follows:

$$cross \left( \begin{bmatrix} a_0 \\ b_0 \\ c_0 \\ d_0 \end{bmatrix}, \begin{bmatrix} a_1 \\ b_1 \\ c_1 \\ d_1 \end{bmatrix}, \begin{bmatrix} a_2 \\ b_2 \\ c_2 \\ d_2 \end{bmatrix} \right) = \begin{bmatrix} x & y & z & w \end{bmatrix}$$

where

$$x = \det \begin{bmatrix} b_0 & b_1 & b_2 \\ c_0 & c_1 & c_2 \\ d_0 & d_1 & d_2 \end{bmatrix}, \quad y = -\det \begin{bmatrix} a_0 & a_1 & a_2 \\ c_0 & c_1 & c_2 \\ d_0 & d_1 & d_2 \end{bmatrix},$$

$$z = \det \begin{bmatrix} a_0 & a_1 & a_2 \\ b_0 & b_1 & b_2 \\ d_0 & d_1 & d_2 \end{bmatrix}, \quad w = -\det \begin{bmatrix} a_0 & a_1 & a_2 \\ b_0 & b_1 & b_2 \\ c_0 & c_1 & c_2 \end{bmatrix},$$

So we just apply this to columns 0, 1, and 3 of $\mathbf{T}_{dp}$ (named below as $\mathbf{t}_{dpX}$, $\mathbf{t}_{dpY}$, $\mathbf{t}_{dpW}$) and get

$$\mathbf{e}_d = cross \left( \mathbf{t}_{dpX}, \mathbf{t}_{dpY}, \mathbf{t}_{dpW} \right)$$

Once we have the eye point in definition space, we can solve for $\mathbf{t}_{dsZ}$. But first we must remember that any scalar multiple of the silhouette plane is the same plane, so we must include a scale factor $\alpha$:

$$\alpha \mathbf{s}_d = \alpha \mathbf{Q}_d \mathbf{e}_d{}^T = \mathbf{t}_{dsZ} - \mathbf{t}_{dsW}$$

Solving for $\mathbf{t}_{dsZ}$ gets us

$$\mathbf{t}_{dsZ} = \alpha \mathbf{Q}_d \mathbf{e}_d{}^T + \mathbf{t}_{dsW}$$

We can use the factor $\alpha$ to give us the freedom to satisfy the first requirement, that the near plane be tangent to the sphere. The near plane in definition space is $\mathbf{t}_{dsZ}$ itself since

$$\mathbf{n}_d = \mathbf{T}_{ds}\mathbf{n}_s = \mathbf{T}_{ds}\begin{bmatrix} 0 \\ 0 \\ 1 \\ 0 \end{bmatrix} = \mathbf{t}_{dsZ}$$

We want this to be tangent to $\mathbf{Q}_d$. Tangency occurs if

$$0 = \mathbf{n}_d{}^T\mathbf{Q}_d{}^*\mathbf{n}_d$$
$$= \left(\alpha\mathbf{Q}_d\mathbf{e}_d{}^T + \mathbf{t}_{dsW}\right)^T\mathbf{Q}_d{}^*\left(\alpha\mathbf{Q}_d\mathbf{e}_d{}^T + \mathbf{t}_{dsW}\right)$$

Boiling this down a bit, and using the fact that $\mathbf{Q}_d\mathbf{Q}_d{}^* = -\mathbf{I}$ we get

$$0 = -\alpha^2\mathbf{e}_d\mathbf{Q}_d\mathbf{e}_d{}^T - 2\alpha\mathbf{e}_d\cdot\mathbf{t}_{dsW} + \mathbf{t}_{dsW}{}^T\mathbf{Q}_d{}^*\mathbf{t}_{dsW} \qquad (2.1)$$

Now, what is the geometric meaning for $\mathbf{t}_{dsW}$? The *ds* and *dp* transformations differ only in column 2 (z), so $\mathbf{t}_{dsW}$ is the same as our old friend $\mathbf{t}_{dpW}$; it's the eye plane in definition space $\mathbf{t}_{dpW} = \mathbf{v}_d$. The dot product with $\mathbf{e}_d\cdot\mathbf{t}_{dpW} = \mathbf{e}_d\cdot\mathbf{v}_d$ is zero, so the middle term in Equation (2.1) goes away and we can solve for

$$\alpha = \pm\sqrt{\frac{\mathbf{e}_d\mathbf{Q}_d\mathbf{e}_d{}^T}{\mathbf{t}_{dsW}{}^T\mathbf{Q}_d{}^*\mathbf{t}_{dsW}}}$$

Whew. Almost done.

Which sign, pray tell, of $\alpha$ do we use? Pick the wrong sign and you get the back side of the sphere instead of the front side. You know how I really did this: I tried both. It turns out that you need the negative root. Now let's be good boys and girls and go back and justify this. We can calculate the point of tangency of the near clip plane, $\mathbf{n}_d$, with the sphere in *d* space by the product

$$\left(\mathbf{n}_d\right)^T\mathbf{Q}_d{}^* = \left(\mathbf{t}_{dsZ}\right)^T\mathbf{Q}_d{}^*$$
$$= \left(\alpha\mathbf{Q}_d\mathbf{e}_d{}^T + \mathbf{t}_{dsW}\right)^T\mathbf{Q}_d{}^*$$
$$= -\alpha\mathbf{e}_d + \mathbf{t}_{dsW}{}^T\mathbf{Q}_d{}^*$$

We want this point to be on the same side of the silhouette plane as the eye point. So we want the dot product $\mathbf{e}_d\cdot\mathbf{s}_d$ to have the same sign as the dot product $\left(\mathbf{n}_d{}^T\mathbf{Q}_d{}^*\right)\cdot\mathbf{s}_d$. The first of these boils down to

$$\mathbf{e}_d\mathbf{Q}_d(\mathbf{e}_d)^T$$

and the second is

$$-\alpha\mathbf{e}_d\mathbf{Q}_d(\mathbf{e}_d)^T$$

How to make these have the same sign? Make $\alpha$ negative. And there you are.

### Making This an Algorithm

Implementing this in code, we first define a function to calculate $\mathbf{v}\mathbf{Q}_d\mathbf{v}^T$

```
//Multiply vector on both sides of sphere matrix

float VQV(Vector4& V) {
    return V[x]*V[x]+V[y]*V[y]+V[z]*V[z]-V[w]*V[w];}
```

The calculation of the new matrix is then

```
//      Calculate Tds from Tdp

Vector4 Ed = Cross(Tdp.Col(x),Tdp.Col(y),Tdp.Col(w));
float    d1 =   VQV(Ed);
float    d2 = -VQV(Tdp.Col(w));
float alpha = -sqrt(d1/d2);
Vector4 Sd(Ed[x],Ed[y],Ed[z],-Ed[w]); //Sd = Qd * Ed^t
Matrix44 Tds = Tdp;
Tds.setCol(z,  alpha * Sd + T.Col(w));
```

The results appear in Figure 2.4. Note that this works for an arbitrary ellipsoid at an arbitrary location in perspective.

# The Result

Anyway, back to shaded sphere rendering. We now have two vital pieces of information. We have the matrix $\tilde{\mathbf{Q}}$ to convert pixel coordinates $\begin{bmatrix} x_s & y_s \end{bmatrix}$ into $z_s^2$, and we have the sheared optimized matrix $\mathbf{T}_{sd}$ to transform $\begin{bmatrix} x_s & y_s & z_s \end{bmatrix}$ back to definition space. Though the matrix operations seem a bit intimidating at first, they are much easier to implement than to derive. And they only have to be performed once per picture.

(a)                    (b)

**Figure 2.4** *Clipping the back half of the sphere with the far clip plane: no shearing (a) and silhouette plane sheared to far clip plane (b)*

In the next chapter, I'll talk about how to actually construct the rendering loops. The final program, with a few antialiasing tricks, worked just fine for drawing the moons and planet for the two *Voyager* Jupiter encounter films. And the special-purpose sphere drawing code replaces a whole raft of polygon transforming, sorting, and tiling. That was especially nice since it had to run on a machine with 64 Kbytes of memory.

Then came Saturn.

Tune in next time to see why Saturn broke the program. (Hint: It has something to do with the rings.)

## Deleted Scene

As an example, let's generate the degenerate quadratic matrix for an arbitrary desired single point. We begin with the matrix that represents the quadratic that is only satisfied by the single point at the origin $\begin{bmatrix} 0 & 0 & 1 \end{bmatrix}$:

$$\begin{bmatrix} x & y & w \end{bmatrix} \begin{bmatrix} 1 & 0 & 0 \\ 0 & 1 & 0 \\ 0 & 0 & 0 \end{bmatrix} \begin{bmatrix} x \\ y \\ w \end{bmatrix} = x^2 + y^2 = 0$$

Now translate this to the required coordinates. The result will be

$$\begin{bmatrix} 1 & 0 & 0 \\ 0 & 1 & 0 \\ -x & -y & 1 \end{bmatrix} \begin{bmatrix} 1 & 0 & 0 \\ 0 & 1 & 0 \\ 0 & 0 & 0 \end{bmatrix} \begin{bmatrix} 1 & 0 & -x \\ 0 & 1 & -y \\ 0 & 0 & 1 \end{bmatrix} = \begin{bmatrix} 1 & 0 & -x \\ 0 & 1 & -y \\ -x & -y & x^2 + y^2 \end{bmatrix}$$

## Deleted Scene

Note that the condition of inside/outside makes sense in the second-order curve case although it does not for first-order curves (lines). This is because a conic section divides the plane into two disjoint regions, while a line doesn't (recall that points on each side of the line still connect through the plane at infinity). This condition can be defined in a manner consistent with the homogeneous philosophy; a point is inside a curve if *all* lines through it intersect the curve; it is outside if there are *some* lines through it that don't intersect the curve.

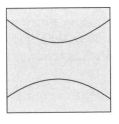

# CHAPTER THREE

# How to Draw a Sphere Part III, The Hyperbolic Horizon

S E P T E M B E R   1 9 9 5

## Our Story So Far

We want to draw a sphere. Actually, we want to draw an arbitrarily scaled and oriented ellipsoid. In Chapter 1, I showed some matrix algebra for describing, transforming, and intersecting points, planes, and quadric surfaces (of which a sphere is a special case). In Chapter 2, I defined some useful coordinate systems and transformations. I'll use the same notation conventions defined there. Let's list what we have done so far.

### Inputs

We are given the following:

■ $\mathbf{Q}_d$—A matrix describing a unit radius sphere in its definition coordinate system:

$$\mathbf{Q}_d = \begin{bmatrix} 1 & 0 & 0 & 0 \\ 0 & 1 & 0 & 0 \\ 0 & 0 & 1 & 0 \\ 0 & 0 & 0 & -1 \end{bmatrix}$$

- $\mathbf{T}_{de}$—The viewing transform: a transformation matrix to go from definition space to eye space (eye at origin, looking down $+z_e$). This can contain arbitrary scales and rotations, and thus could transform our sphere into an arbitrarily oriented ellipsoid.
- $\mathbf{T}_{ep}$—The perspective transform: a transformation matrix to go from eye space to pixel space (including perspective and $x$, $y$ scales necessary to place pixels at integer coordinates).

## Preprocessing

We first multiplied the transformations to get $\mathbf{T}_{dp}$. We then diddled the third column of $\mathbf{T}_{dp}$ to scale and translate the depth ($z$) coordinate to fully utilize the precision of the range between $z_d = 0$ and $z_d = 1$, without changing the $x$, $y$ appearance of the shape.

Emboldened by this, we realized that we could further mangle $\mathbf{T}_{dp}$ by shearing, as well as translating and scaling, in $z$. This defines a variant of pixel space (denoted by the subscript $s$) that doesn't change the $x$, $y$ shape of the sphere (or rather the ellipsoid) but makes it straddle the $z_s = 0$ plane with the silhouette outline embedded in the plane. We calculated the matrix $\mathbf{T}_{sd}$ to go between our new sheared pixel space and definition space. Algebraically, this makes the matrix for the ellipsoid have the following simple form (with asterisks marking nonzero elements):

$$\mathbf{T}_{sd}\mathbf{Q}_d\left(\mathbf{T}_{sd}\right)^T = \mathbf{Q}_s = \begin{bmatrix} * & * & 0 & * \\ * & * & 0 & * \\ 0 & 0 & Q_{s33} & 0 \\ * & * & 0 & * \end{bmatrix}$$

Since a point $\begin{bmatrix} x_s & y_s & z_s \end{bmatrix}$ is on this surface, if

$$\begin{bmatrix} x_s & y_s & z_s & 1 \end{bmatrix}\mathbf{Q}_s \begin{bmatrix} x_s \\ y_s \\ z_s \\ 1 \end{bmatrix} = 0$$

we can define the matrix

$$\tilde{\mathbf{Q}} = -\frac{1}{Q_{s33}}\begin{bmatrix} * & * & * \\ * & * & * \\ * & * & * \end{bmatrix}$$

so that

$$z_s^2 = \begin{bmatrix} x_s & y_s & 1 \end{bmatrix} \tilde{\mathbf{Q}} \begin{bmatrix} x_s \\ y_s \\ 1 \end{bmatrix} \tag{3.1}$$

This means that, for the pixel coordinates $\begin{bmatrix} x_s & y_s \end{bmatrix}$, solving for $z_s$ is particularly easy.

# My Goal

The general algorithm is just to scan the pixels on the screen, solve for $z_s$, multiply $\begin{bmatrix} x_s & y_s & z_s \end{bmatrix}$ by a transform to get to eye space, find a normal vector in eye space, and do lighting calculations. We can optionally further transform to definition space to get texturing coordinates.

My intent in this chapter is to squeeze as much air out of this process as possible to avoid doing a lot of unnecessary arithmetic in the inner loop. This is basically a game of doing arithmetic in the most convenient coordinate system, and of factoring calculations out of loops.

# Gross Clipping

Let's hold off for a second, though. One obvious question to ask before beginning to draw the sphere is whether it appears on the screen at all. So let's first devise a test to detect situations where the sphere is totally outside the visual screen area. This is useful primarily to get rid of the case where the sphere is behind us (otherwise, it would project through the eye upside down onto the screen).

We can reject the sphere if it is outside any one of the clipping planes defined by the edges of the screen. We'll name the clipping boundaries $X_L$, $X_R$, $Y_T$, and $Y_B$. In pixel space, these have the values

$$X_L = -0.5, \quad X_R = N_x - 0.5,$$
$$Y_T = -0.5, \quad Y_B = N_y - 0.5$$

where $N_x$ and $N_y$ are the number of pixels in $x$ and $y$, respectively. Note the use of the fact that pixel coordinate 0 covers the range $(-0.5, +0.5)$ and coordinate $N_x - 1$ covers the range $(N_x - 1.5, N_x - 0.5)$.

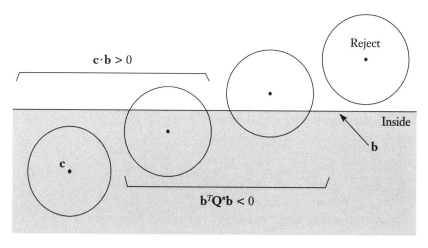

**Figure 3.1** *Four cases of sphere near boundary*

We represent the clipping planes as the column vectors:

$$Left = \begin{bmatrix} 1 \\ 0 \\ 0 \\ X_L \end{bmatrix}, \ Right = \begin{bmatrix} -1 \\ 0 \\ 0 \\ X_R \end{bmatrix}, \ Top = \begin{bmatrix} 0 \\ 1 \\ 0 \\ Y_T \end{bmatrix}, \ Bottom = \begin{bmatrix} 0 \\ -1 \\ 0 \\ Y_B \end{bmatrix}$$

I've defined these planes so that a point on the visible side of the plane yields a positive value when multiplied by the vector.

Considering any one of these planes, which I'll generically call $\mathbf{b}$, we can identify the four cases shown in Figure 3.1. For a particular plane, the reject condition is: the center $\mathbf{c}$ of the sphere is outside plane $\mathbf{b}$ *and* the sphere does not intersect plane $\mathbf{b}$. Algebraically, the test is

$$\text{reject if } (\mathbf{c} \cdot \mathbf{b} < 0) \text{ and } (\mathbf{b}^T \mathbf{Q}^* \mathbf{b} > 0)$$

Now, what coordinate system do we do this calculation in? We know $\mathbf{Q}$ and $\mathbf{c}$ in the definition coordinate system, and we know $\mathbf{b}$ in the pixel coordinate system. We'll have to convert one to the other. It is a nice illustration of the correctness of our transformation matrix mechanism that it looks the same both ways. For example, we must calculate the expression $\mathbf{c} \cdot \mathbf{b}$ as

$$\mathbf{c}_d \mathbf{T}_{dp} \mathbf{b}_p$$

We can think of this as either

$$(\mathbf{c}_d \mathbf{T}_{dp}) \mathbf{b}_p = \mathbf{c}_p \cdot \mathbf{b}_p$$

or

$$c_d\left(\mathbf{T}_{dp}\mathbf{b}_p\right) = \mathbf{c}_d \cdot \mathbf{b}_d$$

Similarly, we must calculate $\mathbf{b}^T\mathbf{Q}^*\mathbf{b}$ as

$$\mathbf{b}_p^{Tr}\mathbf{T}_{dp}^T\mathbf{Q}_d^*\mathbf{T}_{dp}\mathbf{b}_p$$

which we can think of as

$$\left(\mathbf{b}_p^T\mathbf{T}_{dp}^T\right)\mathbf{Q}_d^*\left(\mathbf{T}_{dp}\mathbf{b}_p\right) = \mathbf{b}_d^T\mathbf{Q}_d^*\mathbf{b}_d$$

or

$$\mathbf{b}_p^T\left(\mathbf{T}_{dp}^T\mathbf{Q}_d^*\mathbf{T}_{dp}\right)\mathbf{b}_p = \mathbf{b}_p^T\mathbf{Q}_p^*\mathbf{b}_p$$

## The Algorithm

Let's turn this into code. For actual calculations, let me remind you that

$$\mathbf{c}_d = \begin{bmatrix} 0 & 0 & 0 & 1 \end{bmatrix}$$

$$\mathbf{Q}_d^* = \begin{bmatrix} -1 & 0 & 0 & 0 \\ 0 & -1 & 0 & 0 \\ 0 & 0 & -1 & 0 \\ 0 & 0 & 0 & 1 \end{bmatrix}$$

We would like to have a helper function that calculates $\mathbf{b}_d^T\mathbf{Q}_d^*\mathbf{b}_d$. We already do have VQV from the previous chapter that calculates this same product for $\mathbf{Q}_d$. We can use that if we recall that $\mathbf{Q}_d^* = -\mathbf{Q}_d$.

The gross visibility test starts with an array of pixel-space bounding planes, **Bp[i]**. I convert the **b** vectors into definition (*d*) space and do calculations there. It looks like this:

```
bool AnyVisible(const Matrix44& Tdp ,
                const Vector4 Bp[4])
{
    for (int i=0; i!=4; ++i)
        {
        Vector4 Bd = Tdp * Bp[i];
        if ( Bd[d]<0 && -VQV(Bd)>0 ) return false;
        }
    return true;
}
```

Notice that for each test I checked $\mathbf{c}_d \cdot \mathbf{b}_d = \mathbf{Bd[d]}$ first since it's the easiest one to calculate. If this test fails, $\mathbf{VQV}$ isn't even called. This basic graphics culling trick probably doesn't make much difference here since we're in an initialization routine, but it's good to stay in practice.

# Inside the Rendering Loop

Now that we know that the sphere is at least partially visible, we can construct the basic rendering loop. For a given pixel, we calculate

$$z_s^2 = \begin{bmatrix} x_s & y_s & 1 \end{bmatrix} \tilde{\mathbf{Q}} \begin{bmatrix} x_s \\ y_s \\ 1 \end{bmatrix}$$

If the product is negative, it means that the sphere doesn't cover that pixel. If the product is positive, take its square root.

Once we have the coordinates $\begin{bmatrix} x_s & y_s & z_s & 1 \end{bmatrix} = \mathbf{p}_s$, it's then a simple matter of matrix multiplication to get normal vectors and texture coordinates. And which matrices do we multiply?

## Texture Coordinates

Texture coordinates come from positions on the unit sphere in definition space. To get here, simply multiply

$$\mathbf{p}_s \mathbf{T}_{sd} = \mathbf{p}_d$$

You can get texture-mapping coordinates by converting $\mathbf{p}_d$ to spherical coordinates. This requires nasty arctangents. I've streamlined this by doing a reasonable polynomial approximation to arctangent after doing a binary search on the signs of the coordinates to get to the primary octant. But this turned out to have the same speed as the library arctangent routine. One nice thing, though—arctangents only depend on ratios of $x$, $y$, and $z$. Therefore, you don't have to calculate the $w$ component of $\mathbf{p}_d$.

## Normal Vectors

We can get the normal vector (in eye space) from the first three components of the plane tangent to the viewed point. Getting the right matrix to convert $\mathbf{p}_s$ to this plane is a bit tricky. Take a deep breath. Go . . .

■ Transform $\mathbf{p}_s$ to definition space (we already did this):

$$\mathbf{p}_s \mathbf{T}_{sd} = \mathbf{p}_d$$

- Find the tangent plane to the unit sphere at this point. (Note that the normal vector of this plane points toward the outside of the sphere):

$$l_d = \mathbf{Q}_d \mathbf{p}_d^T$$

- Transform this plane forward to eye space. We're transforming planes, so we must multiply by the inverse of the point transform matrix $\mathbf{T}_{de}$, which we are writing as $\mathbf{T}_{ed}$:

$$l_e = \mathbf{T}_{ed} l_d$$

The net result is

$$l_e = \mathbf{T}_{ed} \mathbf{Q}_d (\mathbf{p}_s \mathbf{T}_{sd})^T$$

We can rewrite this as

$$l_e^T = \mathbf{p}_s \left( \mathbf{T}_{sd} \mathbf{Q}_d \mathbf{T}_{ed}^T \right)$$

(I've slipped in the fact that $\mathbf{Q}_d = \mathbf{Q}_d^T$.) We of course calculate the product of the three matrices in parentheses once outside the rendering loop, and give it a name.

$$\mathbf{T}_{sd} \mathbf{Q}_d \mathbf{T}_{ed}^T = \mathbf{M}$$

Note that the matrix $\mathbf{M}$ is not a transformation matrix. In the language of Chapter 9, "Uppers and Downers, Part I" of *Jim Blinn's Corner: Dirty Pixels* (and in Chapter 20 of this book), it is called *covariant tensor*. It takes a point (contravariant row vector) and produces a plane (a covariant column vector).

One thing . . . I use the inverse of $\mathbf{T}_{de}$ instead of the adjoint to transform the plane from definition to eye space. Normally, this doesn't matter since the adjoint differs from the inverse by a scalar factor of the determinant of the matrix. But here, if the determinant is negative, the calculated $\mathbf{M}$ matrix will flip the sign of the normal vector, making it point toward the inside of the sphere. We want to make the normal vector consistently point outward for proper lighting calculations.

## The Algorithm
Since $\mathbf{Q}_d$ is mostly zeros, you can do all calculation most easily in special case code. Furthermore, we only need the first three components of the tangent plane vector, and thus only the first three columns of matrix $\mathbf{N}$.

```
Matrix44 Ted = Tde.Inverse();
Matrix44 M;
for (int j=0; j!=3; ++j)
```

```
for (int i=0; i!=4; ++i)
   M(i,j)=Tsd(i,0)*Ted(j,0)
          +Tsd(i,1)*Ted(j,1)
          +Tsd(i,2)*Ted(j,2)
          -Tsd(i,3)*Ted(j,3);
```

# Range Calculations

Of course we're not going to scan the whole screen. Rather, we want to find the range in $x_s$ and $y_s$ that the sphere covers and only do calculations there. We can get this by considering another interpretation of the matrix $\tilde{\mathbf{Q}}$; it's a 2D curve. If a point $\begin{bmatrix} x_s & y_s \end{bmatrix}$ is on this curve, then the $z_s$ value is zero and we are on the silhouette. So $\tilde{\mathbf{Q}}$ represents the 2D silhouette curve for the sphere.

### y Range

How do we determine from $\tilde{\mathbf{Q}}$ what area to scan out on the screen? The $y_s$ range comes from finding what value of $y_H$ makes the horizontal line $y_s = y_H$ tangent to the curve. We represent this line by the 2D homogeneous column vector $\begin{bmatrix} 0 & -1 & y_H \end{bmatrix}^T$, and test tangency by multiplying by the adjoint of $\tilde{\mathbf{Q}}$:

$$\begin{bmatrix} 0 & -1 & y_H \end{bmatrix} \tilde{\mathbf{Q}}^\star \begin{bmatrix} 0 \\ -1 \\ y_H \end{bmatrix} = 0$$

(If this value is negative instead of zero, the scan line intersects the silhouette curve.) This expands out to the following quadratic equation (recall that $\mathbf{Q}^\star$ is symmetrical):

$$\left( \tilde{Q}^\star_{22} \right) y_H{}^2 - 2\left( \tilde{Q}^\star_{12} \right) y_H + \left( \tilde{Q}^\star_{11} \right) = 0 \tag{3.2}$$

where, by the definition of adjoint

$$\tilde{Q}^\star{}_{22} = \tilde{Q}_{00}\tilde{Q}_{11} - \tilde{Q}_{01}\tilde{Q}_{10}$$
$$\tilde{Q}^\star{}_{12} = \tilde{Q}_{01}\tilde{Q}_{20} - \tilde{Q}_{00}\tilde{Q}_{21}$$
$$\tilde{Q}^\star{}_{11} = \tilde{Q}_{00}\tilde{Q}_{22} - \tilde{Q}_{02}\tilde{Q}_{20}$$

Just solve for the two roots of the quadratic to get the floating point maximum and minimum $y$ range.

## X Range

A scan line algorithm is a successive reduction in dimensionality. For a given scan line, $y_s$ is constant and we can collapse any expressions containing it down by one dimension. In particular, the expression for $z_s^2$ becomes

$$z_s^2 = dx_s^2 + ex_s + f \qquad (3.3)$$

where

$$d = \tilde{Q}_{00}$$
$$e = 2\left(\tilde{Q}_{01}y_s + \tilde{Q}_{02}\right)$$
$$f = \tilde{Q}_{11}y_s^2 + 2\tilde{Q}_{12}y_s + \tilde{Q}_{22}$$

To determine the desired range for the inner $(x)$ loop, we can just solve this quadratic to find the two $x_s$ coordinates where $z_s = 0$. This will have real solutions if $e^2 - 4df > 0$. I'll leave it as an exercise for you to determine that this expression is just the negative of the left-hand side of Equation (3.2). In other words, our $y_s$ range calculation gives us just those scan lines for which the $x_s$ quadratic has real roots. How nice.

## Integer Subrange

For both $x$ and $y$, we want to scan out the integer coordinate range that fits within the calculated floating point range and that also fits within the screen pixel coordinate range. I'll define a routine to clamp a floating point range **(fmin, fmax)** to an integer range **(0, N)**, returning the integer range in **(imin, imax)**.

```
IRange(float fmin,float fmax,
       int* imin,int* imax, int N){
   if(fmin>N) return OutsideScreen;
   if(fmax<0) return OutsideScreen;
   if(fmin<0)   *imin=0;
   else         *imin=fmin+1; // round up
   if(fmax>N)   *imax=N;
   else         *imax=fmax; // round down
   return OK;}
```

Note that this can return an outside-screen condition. This should never happen in the $y$ direction, since our gross clipping algorithm would have caught it. This could happen in the $x$ direction if the sphere were partially off the screen to the side. The $x$ range of some of the scan lines near the

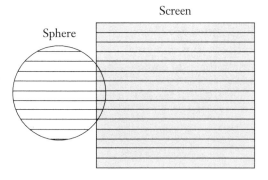

**Figure 3.2** *Some sphere scan lines offscreen*

top and bottom of the sphere could be completely off the screen. See Figure 3.2.

# The Rendering Loop

**n** ow that we've calculated all the appropriate conversion matrices and the *y* and *x* ranges to loop over, let's see what the main body of the program looks like. Pseudocode for the two nested loops looks like this:

```
calculate Qstar(2,2),Qstar(1,2),Qstar(1,1)
solve for ymin,ymax
IRange(ymin,ymax, &iymin,&iymax, Ny-1);
for (int ys=iymin; ys<=iymax; ++ys)
     {
     calculate d, e, f
     solve for xmin,xmax
     if(IRange(xmin,xmax, &ixmin,&ixmax, Nx-1)
               ==OutsideScreen) continue; // next y
     PrepareXCalc
     for (int xs=ixmin; xs<=ixmax; ++xs)
          {
          DoXCalc
          }
     }
```

I'll defer the details of solving for the min and max of *x* and *y* until the next section. Right now we'll set up a typical forward difference calculation for $z_s^2$, for the normal vector **n**, and for the definition space point **p**. Insert the following code in the spot labeled *PrepareXCalc*:

*PrepareXCalc*

```
int xs = ixmin;
float zSqrd = (d*xs + e)*xs + f; //value at xs
float dzSqrd = 2*d*xs + d + e;   //first difference at xs
float ddzSqrd = 2*d;             //secnd difference at xs
Vector3 Nx,Nz,NxXplusN0;   // only need 3 dim
Vector3 Px,Pz,PxXplusP0;   // only need 3 dim
for (int i=0; i!=3; ++i) {
     Nz[i] = M(z,i);
     NxXplusN0 [i] = M(x,i) *xs +M(y,i) *ys + M(w,i);
     Nx[i] = M(x,i);
```

```
    Pz[i] = Tsd(z,i);
    PxXplusP0 [i] = Tsd(x,i) *xs + Tsd(y,i)*ys + Tsd(w,i);
    Px[i] = Tsd(x,i);
    }
```

The innards of the *x* loop are then

*DoXCalc*

```
float zs = sqrt(zSqrd); zSqrd += dzSqrd; dzSqrd += ddzSqrd;
Vector3 P = zs*Pz + PxXplusP0; PxXplusP0 += Px;
Vector3 N = zs*Nz + NxXplusN0; NxXplusN0 += Nx;
```
*draw pixel using* **P** *and* **N**

as advertised in Chapter 1.

Don't forget to rescale the resulting normal vector to unit length since it doesn't come out that way automatically. This is known in the clever mathematical jargon as "normalizing the normal."

**Figure 3.3** *Nice picture of Jupiter*

# Results

So I used this fine algorithm in 1978 to crank out many pictures of Jupiter and its moons for the *Voyager* flybys in 1979. A sample picture appears in Figure 3.3.

Also in 1979, the *Pioneer 11* spacecraft made it out to Saturn. The interesting feature of Saturn, of course, is the rings. Drawing rings called for a special program in its own right, one I won't get into here. The spacecraft's trajectory took it on a very dramatic path under the rings, so when I tooled up to make a movie of this encounter, it was interesting to pan away from the planet to see the rings better. The disturbing thing is that when I panned over to look at the nifty rings, the planet disappeared. See Figure 3.4. Having major planets disappear is always a bad sign.

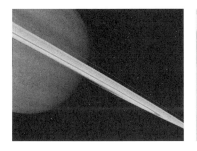 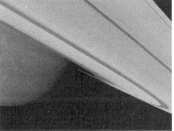 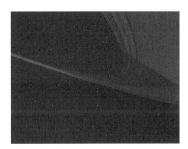

**Figure 3.4** *Sequence of Saturn pictures. Oops, where did Saturn go?*

# The Hyperbolic Horizon

The solution to this problem came to me from a question my thesis advisor, Martin Newell, once asked: "If you stand on the Earth and look at the horizon, what shape is it?" Give up? It's a hyperbola. Why?

The spherical shape of the Earth in eye space becomes a hyperboloid

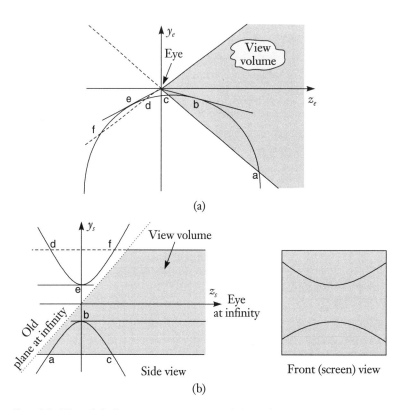

(a)

(b)

**Figure 3.5** *Hyperbolic horizon: eye space (a) and sheared pixel space (b)*

of two sheets in pixel space. This is because the plane containing the eye and perpendicular to the line of sight (the $z_e = 0$ plane) intersects the sphere. This plane is transformed to the plane at infinity in screen space (see Figure 3.5). Recall our earlier observation that a circle that intersects the line at infinity in 2D is a hyperbola. Similarly, a sphere that intersects the plane at infinity becomes a hyperboloid. The silhouette of such a shape is a hyperbola. Thus, the maximum and minimum $y_s$ values in the solution of Equation (3.2) might not necessarily define the $y_s$ range that is visible; they may define the complement of it.

The hyperbolic problem may also occur during the $x$ loop. For example, the original problem of flying around the side of Saturn gives this. This situation also implies an infinite range in $y$ (see Figure 3.6).

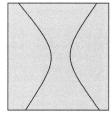

**Figure 3.6** *Hyperbolic in x, infinite in y*

## A Better Range Calculation

What we really want for the $y$ range calculation is the range over which the left-hand side of Equation (3.2) is negative. And what we really want for the $x$ range calculation is the range over which the right-hand side of Equation (3.3) is positive. Let's unify things a bit by flipping the sign of Equation (3.2), making it

$$ay_H^2 + by_H + c = 0$$

where

$$a = -\tilde{Q}_{22}^*$$
$$b = 2\tilde{Q}_{12}^*$$
$$c = -\tilde{Q}_{11}^*$$

Now we just write a general quadratic solver that returns not just the roots of a quadratic, but also the range over which the quadratic is positive. We can apply this to both the $y$ and $x$ range calculation.

There are several situations:

- There are two roots, and the quadratic is positive between them. Return the roots.

- There are no real roots, but the quadratic is always positive. The routine must return an infinite range. I do so by using the large values −32000 and 32000 as flags to represent minus and plus infinity. Later, when the range is clamped to the screen range, these infinity flag coordinates will be trimmed back to the proper screen boundary values.

- There are no real roots, and the quadratic is always negative. Return a failure indication.

- The quadratic degenerates into a linear equation. Return the semi-infinite range over which the linear equation is positive.

- The quadratic degenerates to a constant. Return an infinite range if it's positive and a failure if it's negative.

- There are two roots, and the quadratic is negative between them. The two positive ranges (say, for $y$) are then $\left[-\infty, y_{min}\right]$ and $\left[y_{max}, +\infty\right]$. I indicate this by swapping the min and max values and cleaning up later.

The code is

```
PosRange(float a, float b, float c,
         float* pymin, float* pymax)
{
    if(a!=0.) {
        float ba = b/(2*a);
        float ca = c/a;
        float discr = ba*ba - ca;
        if(discr<0) {
            if(c<0) return NeverPos;
```

```
                    *pymin = -32000;
                    *pymax = +32000;
                    return OK;}
            float d = sqrt(discr);
            if(a>0) d = - d; // signal that it's hyperbolic
            *pymax = -ba + d;
            *pymin = -ba - d;
            return OK; }
        if(b!=0) {
            if(b>0) {*pymin=-c/b  ; *pymax=32000;}
            else    {*pymin=-32000; *pymax=-c/b ;}
            return OK;}
        if(c<0) return NeverPos;
        *pymin = -32000;
        *pymax = 32000;
        return OK;
    }
}
```

## Selecting the Proper Piece

In the case where our root solver returns two ranges (indicated by the condition $y_{max} < y_{min}$), we would not actually expect to see two distinct sections of the planet visible. In fact, one of the two branches comes from that portion of the surface behind the observer that "wraps around infinity" due to the perspective transformation. The wrapped-around branch is the one we wish to eliminate.

Wrapped-around points are those that undergo a change of sign of their $w$ component due to the perspective transformation. Algebraically, a condition for a wrapped-around point is to start with a positive $w$ and end with a negative one. We can think of this as converting the point to definition space and testing its $w$:

$$\left( \begin{bmatrix} x_s & y_s & z_s & 1 \end{bmatrix} \mathbf{T}_{sd} \right) \begin{bmatrix} 0 \\ 0 \\ 0 \\ 1 \end{bmatrix} < 0$$

or we can think of it as transforming the definition-space plane at infinity to a local plane in pixel space:

$$\begin{bmatrix} x_s & y_s & z_s & 1 \end{bmatrix} \left( \mathbf{T}_{sd} \begin{bmatrix} 0 \\ 0 \\ 0 \\ 1 \end{bmatrix} \right) < 0$$

Either way, the result is the same: we take the dot product of the pixel space point with the fourth column of $\mathbf{T}_{sd}$. A negative result means it's a wrapped-around point. We update the inside-out range $[y_{min}, y_{max}]$ to a correctly ordered half-infinite range by simply updating $y_{min} \leftarrow -\infty$ to keep $[-\infty, y_{max}]$, or by updating $y_{max} \leftarrow +\infty$ to keep $[y_{min}, +\infty]$.

## New Y Range Calculation

To decide between two ranges for $y$, find a point on one branch and see if it has been wrapped around. I'll use the point on the silhouette at $y_s = y_{min}$. We find the $x_s$ value by substituting $y_0 = y_{min}$ into Equation (3.3). Since we are at a local extremum of the curve, we expect to get two coincident solutions for the $x_s$ range; that is, $e^2 - 4df = 0$ in Equation (3.3). Therefore the $x_s$ value at $y_{min}$ will be

$$x_{min} = -\frac{e}{2d} = -\frac{\tilde{Q}_{01} y_{min} + \tilde{Q}_{02}}{\tilde{Q}_{00}}$$

$z_s$ is, of course, zero since we're on the silhouette.

Here is the code for the beefed-up $y$ range calculation. We assume that Qtilde has been calculated as described in the previous chapter.

```
calculate a, b, c
PosRange(a,b,c, &ymin, &ymax);
if(ymin>ymax){           //signal for hyperbolic silhouette
    if( Qtilde(0,0)==0 )
        exit;            //sphere not visible
    float xmin = -(Qtilde(0,1)*ymin+Qtilde(0,2))/Qtilde(0,0);
    if (xmin*Tsd(0,3)+ymin*Tsd(1,3)+Tsd(3,3)<0)
        ymin=-32000; // keep [-inf,ymax] branch
    else ymax=+32000; // keep [ymin,+inf] branch
}
```

## New X Range Calculation

The analogous test for a potentially hyperbolic $x$ range is even simpler since we know the $y$ of the current scan line.

```
calculate d, e, f
PosRange(d,e,f, &xmin, &xmax);
if(xmin>xmax){
    if(xmin*Tsd(0,3)+ys*Tsd(1,3)+Tsd(3,3)<0)
        xmin=-32000;    // keep [-inf,xmax] branch
    else xmax=+32000;    // keep [xmin,+inf] branch
}
```

# Saturn Returns (Mostly)

So, this better $x$ and $y$ range finding worked fine, and Saturn came back. But . . . there was just one frame where there was a transition from an elliptical silhouette to a hyperbolic silhouette that the program still choked on. Here the silhouette should be a parabola. There is no inherent reason why this shouldn't fit into our generalization, but the program died anyway. I simply didn't have time to chase down the problem; I had to resort to analog techniques. I took a pair of scissors and physically cut the bad frame out of the film.

# Saturn Returns (Always)

When writing this column, I finally had time to go back and figure out the parabolic silhouette problem. It comes from our method of optimizing the $z$ range generated by the $\mathbf{T}_{dp}$ matrix. The parabolic silhouette happens if the eye plane is just tangent to the sphere. If you go back and look at what our highly clever optimization technique would do in that case, you find that it will generate a singular matrix for $\mathbf{T}_{dp}$. Bummer.

In fact, if there is a hyperbolic silhouette (eye plane intersects the sphere), the $\mathbf{T}_{dp}$ optimization introduces an extra sign flip in $z_p$ that I had to correct for. I won't go into this since I now have a better way to do the whole thing.

The new technique merges the two-step transformation preparation ($z$ optimization and $z$ shearing) into one step that doesn't have singularity or sign-flipping problems. It's also a good exercise in the geometric meaning of the matrices. The method is similar to the technique for finding a shearing matrix for back side clipping, described in Chapter 2. We turn the unoptimized $\mathbf{T}_{dp}$ into $\mathbf{T}_{ds}$ by replacing column 2. We want to find a new column that makes the silhouette plane in $s$ space be

$$\mathbf{s}_s = \begin{bmatrix} 0 \\ 0 \\ 1 \\ 0 \end{bmatrix}$$

In definition space, we have

$$\mathbf{s}_d = \mathbf{T}_{ds}\mathbf{s}_s = \mathbf{t}_{dsZ}$$

In other words, the desired column 2 of $\mathbf{T}_{ds}$ is just the silhouette plane in definition space.

# Color Plates

**Figure 3.3**  *Nice picture of Jupiter*

**Figure 3.4** *Sequence of Saturn pictures. Oops, where did Saturn go?*

Another way to get the silhouette plane is as the polar plane from the eye point:

$$\mathbf{s}_d = \mathbf{Q}_d \mathbf{e}_d^{\ T}$$

So . . . we need the eye point in definition space. It is

$$\mathbf{e}_d = \mathbf{e}_s \mathbf{T}_{sd} = \begin{bmatrix} 0 & 0 & 1 & 0 \end{bmatrix} (\mathbf{T}_{ds})^*$$

Last time I noted the fact that this expression, just row 2 of the adjoint of $\mathbf{T}_{ds}$, can easily be calculated using what I call the 4D cross product of columns 0, 1, and 3 of the matrix $\mathbf{T}_{ds}$. The desired new column 2 that turns $\mathbf{T}_{dp}$ into $\mathbf{T}_{ds}$ is then

$$\mathbf{t}_{dsZ} = \mathbf{Q}_d \mathbf{e}_d^{\ T}$$

But we're not quite done yet. Since we're in homogeneous land, we can include an arbitrary scale factor into this new, third column and still have it shear the silhouette plane the way we want. The scale factor simply represents a postshear scale in $z$. We can (in fact, we must) use this to make sure the front (visible) side of the sphere is on a predictable side of the $z_s = 0$ plane so that we know which sign of square root to take in Equation (3.1).

The original perspective transform, $\mathbf{T}_{ep}$, moves the eye $e_e = \begin{bmatrix} 0 & 0 & 0 & 1 \end{bmatrix}$ to

$$\mathbf{e}_p = \mathbf{e}_e \mathbf{T}_{ep} = \begin{bmatrix} 0 & 0 & - & 0 \end{bmatrix}$$

with the visible side of the sphere facing negative $z_p$ (the minus sign represents an arbitrary negative number). We want the new transform, $\mathbf{T}_{ds}$, to flip this around so that $\mathbf{e}_s = \begin{bmatrix} 0 & 0 & + & 0 \end{bmatrix}$, with the visible side of the sphere facing positive $z_s$. It turns out that we get this for free provided we do one thing. We must normalize the point $\mathbf{e}_d$ by dividing by its $w$ component. This is because the transform $\mathbf{T}_{de}$ contains no perspective and doesn't change $w$. Since $e_e = \begin{bmatrix} 0 & 0 & 0 & 1 \end{bmatrix}$, we want $\mathbf{e}_d$ to have a $w$ component of 1, too. We should always be able to do this since the eye point in definition space should be a local point, and thus have a nonzero $w$. (Actually, we only really need to flip the sign of $\mathbf{e}_d$ to make its $w$ component positive.)

The eye point in sheared pixel space will then be

$$\mathbf{e}_d \mathbf{T}_{ds} = \begin{bmatrix} 0 & 0 & z_s & 0 \end{bmatrix}$$

where

$$z_s = \mathbf{e}_d \mathbf{Q}_d \mathbf{e}_d^{\ T}$$

As long as the eye point is outside the sphere, $z_s$ is positive and the region between the eye and the silhouette plane in definition space will map to the region on the positive side of the $z_s = 0$ plane.

### The Algorithm

```
Vector4 Ed = Cross(Tdp.Col(x),Tdp.Col(y),Tdp.Col(w));
Ed /= Ed[w];
Vector4 Sd (Ed[x],Ed[y],Ed[z],-Ed[w]);// Sd = Qd*Ed^t
Matrix44 Tds = Tdp;
Tds.setCol(z)=Sd;
Tsd = Tds.Inverse();
```

Note that I got $\mathbf{T}_{sd}$ by taking an inverse instead of an adjoint. This is to prevent a negative determinant from confusing things later.

# Summary

There you have it. With the proper handling of hyperbolic silhouette curves, the program works for any sphere (or ellipsoid) viewed from any point and in any direction. Making the algorithm work properly seems to be mostly a game of minus-sign management since most of the tests hinge on the sign of some quantity. I've spent many hours chasing down rogue minus signs.

In the next chapter, I'll discuss some optimizations of the texturing process that were motivated by the planets.

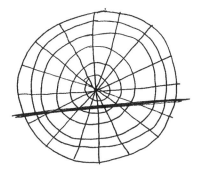

# CHAPTER FOUR

# The Truth about Texture Mapping

MARCH 1990

*This article was originally written in 1990 to document something I did in 1980. Since then, timing numbers have changed (computers are almost 1000 times faster now) and the names given to elements of the memory hierarchy have changed (for "disk" read "cache"), but the principle remains the same: locality of reference is good.*

Texture mapping is a good, cheap way to make a picture look more realistic than it really is. Most of my texture mapping has been devoted to making pictures of the outer planets. Astrologers tell us that the planets control our destinies. That may not be true for everyone, but the unique configuration of the planet Uranus has had its effect on me. It influenced me to take a close look at how the layout of a texture map in memory affects the performance of the rendering algorithm.

## A Trip to the Planets

My planet-rendering program basically calculates, for each occupied pixel on the screen, the latitude and longitude visible at that pixel. It uses this latitude and longitude to index into a texture map to get a surface color. The actual texture color comes from bilinearly interpolating the texture colors at the four texture map pixels that surround that latitude and longitude. This, along with the shading calculations, gives the net color of the pixel.

I use texture maps that are 512 pixels wide (east to west) by 256 pixels tall (north to south). So to look up a value in the map, the longitude is scaled to the range 0 to 512, and the latitude to the range 0 to 255. The integer parts of these numbers, call them $I_u$ and $I_v$, give the coordinates of the upper left of the $2 \times 2$ pixel region that must be fetched for interpolation. The interpolation amount comes from the fractional parts of the scaled $u$ and $v$ values.

So how do we lay the map out in memory? The most obvious thing is to lay out the map just as you do for a 2D matrix: by rows. Given a 9-bit $I_u$ value and an 8-bit $I_v$ value, the index of a map pixel can be found simply by concatenating the two values to give a 17-bit number:

8 bits $I_v$                    9 bits $I_u$

Originally, each pixel of the map consisted of one byte that encoded a 5-bit brightness and a 3-bit saturation (white to orange). Nowadays, I use 3-byte pixels for full color, so I must multiply this index by 3 to get the desired address in the texture map array.

# Virtual Memory

ow if you have gobs of memory, you can read the whole map into RAM and all accesses go lickety-split. RAM means just that—access to one random location is just as fast as access to some other random location.

But suppose you don't have enough memory for the whole pattern. Or suppose you have enough memory for one or two maps but you want to have *lots* of maps applied to the scene at once. (You can usually depend on an art director to want more texture maps than is convenient.) What do you do? You use virtual memory.

With virtual memory, you store the whole database on a disk file and only read parts of it into real memory as needed. The memory is divided, both on the disk and in RAM, into medium-sized chunks called *pages*. You have fewer RAM pages than disk pages. Each time a virtual memory location is accessed, some process looks at the high bits of the address (which select the page) and translates it either into the location in real memory where the data is stored or returns an indication that it is not there and must be read from disk. This latter event is called a *page fault*. When this occurs, one of the existing pages in real memory is recycled, usually the least recently used one, and the desired page of data is read into it. The tragedy is when you may later have to reread the page you threw out. But it can't be helped.

On big computers and workstations, this is all done with a combination of special CPU hardware and operating system code. On my small computer, I had to implement a simple virtual memory simulator that is used just for the texture memory.

With a virtual memory system (either hardware assisted or software simulated), you might think that you can just pretend you have zigabytes of real memory and everything will work out OK. Sorry, you lose. If you happen to access the memory in a truly random way, or even an unfortunately chosen ordered way, you can give the VM system fits. A classic example is the problem of zeroing out a very large matrix with two nested loops. If the matrix is laid out by rows and your loops are nested so that they access the memory by columns, you will likely get a page fault on every memory access. Bad idea.

The trick to minimizing the page fault rate is to keep your memory accesses within pages that are already in memory. You do this by keeping the memory accesses localized as much as possible. So a vital aspect of a texture map layout scheme is the addressing pattern it implies. Let's look at the memory access pattern for a specific example of the texture-mapping process.

Recall that we are storing the map by rows. I use a page size of 512 bytes, so each row takes three pages. I store the three RGB values consecutively, so the first 170 2/3 pixels are in the first page, and so forth. Figure 4.1 shows a schematic of the map with each rectangle standing for one memory page.

Let me digress for a moment and talk about this drawing. If I were to draw it completely to scale, there should be 256 rectangles vertically by 3 horizontally. It would look like a solid black blob. So the diagram is merely suggestive of the actual map. Now if I were to use my computer-

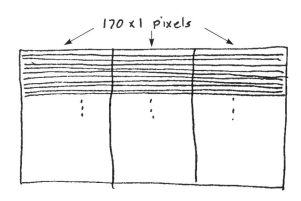

**Figure 4.1** *Row-ordered map*

enhanced drawing mechanism to draw the schematic diagram with perfectly regular lines, I think it would give the wrong impression about its literal accuracy. A schematic diagram should look sketchy to help you realize that it is indeed sketchy and should not be taken literally. For this reason, I have drawn it and all other such diagrams by hand using sketchy lines. I think this is a good idea in general for diagrams that are not meant to be geometrically precise. Take note, all you visualizers out there. End of digression.

Now, the first two planets I had occasion to draw were Jupiter and Saturn (and their moons). If we make a side view of the planet, as is usually the case with Jupiter and Saturn, this memory page pattern of Figure 4.1 wraps around the sphere, as sketched schematically in Figure 4.2(a). The scan lines more or less follow the horizontal stripes of the texture map. To see exactly how well this worked, I tricked up my planet renderer to dump out the page numbers for each texture access. Figure 4.2(b) shows the addressing pattern for two consecutive representative scan lines at $Y = 222$ and $Y = 223$ (indicated by the thicker horizontal line in Figure 4.2a). The vertical scale shows memory page numbers, and the horizontal scale shows the time sequence of the accesses. Seven different pages are accessed on the first scan line and eight on the next, with five of them common to both lines.

For the whole image, there were a total of 16,000 texture map accesses, each requiring a $2 \times 2$ array of pixels. The total number of virtual memory accesses turns out to be 33,028. (It's not 64,000 because I have in my code a test to see whether two texture pixels at $I_u$ and $I_{u+1}$ are in consecutive memory locations and make only one call to the virtual memory routines if so.) The 33,028 VM accesses generated 446 page faults. The whole image took 24.8 seconds to render. My profiler tells me that only 3.9 seconds of it were spent in the disk I/O for the page faults. Not too shabby. (Profilers are my favorite programming toy. I can spend days fiddling with code after examining the results of a profile test. If you haven't played with one, you are missing out on one of the great joys of programming.)

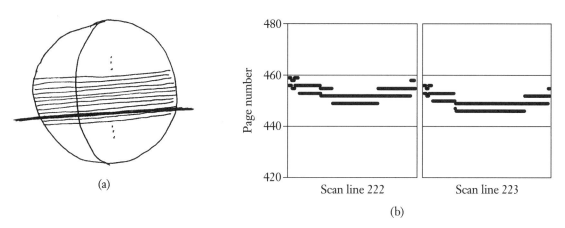

(a)

(b)

**Figure 4.2** *Row-ordered map, side view: geometry (a) and addressing pattern (b)*

# There's a Problem with Uranus

In 1980 and 1981, the two *Voyager* spacecraft went past Saturn and it was time to start drawing pictures of the next planet, Uranus. Uranus, as it happens, spins with its axis pointing almost directly toward the sun. The views from the spacecraft, and for my animations, required looking down at the pole. Now one scan line of the image could cover all the latitudes from the equator to the pole. If each latitude of the texture map came from a different memory page, it required accessing half the map for each scan line! This is very reminiscent of the zero-the-matrix problem done the wrong way.

For our explicit example, I took Figure 4.2 and rendered it with a 90-degree rotation of the planet. Figure 4.3(a) is a drawing of the sphere with texture pages sketched in. Figure 4.3(b) is a plot of the addressing pattern; note the change of vertical scale. Out of the 16,000 map accesses and 32,992 virtual memory accesses, there were 15,207 page faults! Ouch! The total run time was 144.4 seconds with fully 119.9 seconds devoted to paging. And that's using a RAM disk, so the actual I/O for disk accesses is negligible. (If I've got enough room for a RAM disk, you may ask, why am I using this virtual memory mechanism? The answer is flexibility. If I need more maps than will fit on the RAM disk, I can easily switch to getting the pages from a real disk.)

This might seem to be an extreme case, but a very similar thing happens when texture mapping any shape where the "grain" of the texture map is rotated 90 degrees to the direction of the inner loop of the rendering program.

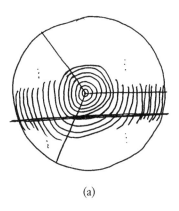

(a)

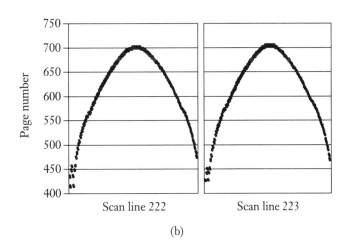

(b)

**Figure 4.3** *Row-ordered map, end view: geometry (a) and addressing pattern (b)*

# Tiles

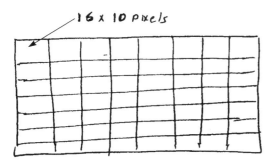

W e can give our poor disk some time off by using a better memory layout. With the by-rows layout, two pixels that are vertically adjacent are *always* in different memory pages. Let us instead try to store geometrically close texture pixels close together in address space. Let's break the map into a series of 16 by 32 pixel tiles. (For the productions I have done to date, I have used 32 by 32 pixel tiles, but while writing this column I realized that 16 by 32 works better.) Each tile requires three memory pages (16 × 32 × 3 bytes = 3 × 512 bytes). Within a tile the pixels are stored by rows, so each memory page covers a roughly square region 16 pixels wide by a little more than 10 pixels high. Finally, we store the tiles themselves by rows. The addressing of a pixel in the map is performed by interleaving the low bits of the $I_u$ and $I_v$ values with the high bits. The address is constructed as follows:

**Figure 4.4** *Tiled map*

| Hi 3 bits $I_v$ | Hi 5 bits $I_u$ | Lo 5 bits $I_v$ | Lo 4 bits $I_u$ |
|---|---|---|---|
| | | | |

Multiply this by 3 to get the net memory index. This arrangement gives the memory-page to map-region correspondence sketched in Figure 4.4. Figure 4.5(a) is a sketch of the planet with this map tiling wrapped around it. You can visually see that a lot fewer pages intersect a given scan line.

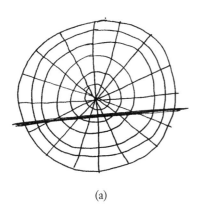

(a)

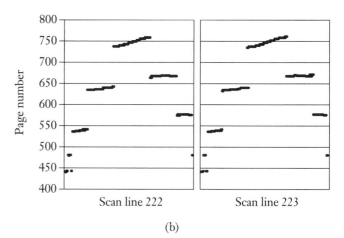

(b)

**Figure 4.5** *Tiled map, end view: geometry (a) and addressing pattern (b)*

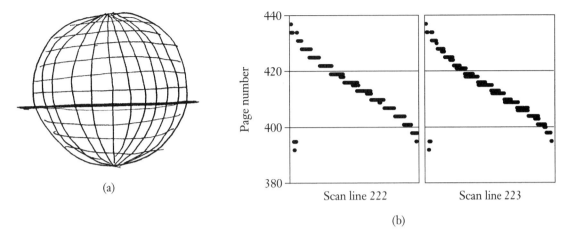

**Figure 4.6** *Tiled map, side view: geometry (a) and addressing pattern (b)*

Figure 4.5(b) is a plot of the addressing pattern. Tiling the map cut the total number of page faults down to 1492. The total run time was 33.7 seconds (over four times faster!) with 11.8 seconds of it being paging.

In fact, tiling even improved things for the side view. This is because, with the row layout, lots of pixels of the map from the back half of the planet were read in unnecessarily since they happened to be in the same memory page as pixels from the front of the planet. With tiling we only read in pixels that we have some chance of actually using. Figure 4.6(a) is a sketch of the geometry, and Figure 4.6(b) is the addressing pattern. The total number of page faults dropped to 356, and the total run time was slightly improved, 22.8 seconds with 2.6 seconds of it being paging.

# Address Generation

The address-bit shuffling can itself take up a bunch of time. (Address calculation for a row-ordered map is admittedly much faster, but remember you may just be generating page faults faster.) I have speeded address calculation for tiled maps by using a table lookup. I set up a 512-entry table for $I_u$, whose entries contain

| Hi 5 bits $I_u$ | | | | | Lo 4 bits $I_u$ |
|---|---|---|---|---|---|
| 0  0  0 | | | 0  0  0  0  0 | | |

and a 256-entry table for $I_v$, whose entries contain

| Hi 3 bits $I_v$ | | Lo 5 bits $I_v$ | |
|---|---|---|---|
| | 0  0  0  0  0 | | 0  0  0  0 |

Since we are ultimately going to need to multiply by 3, we can build this into the table, too. If you are using tables, you build as much arithmetic into the table as possible, so I also added a needed constant to the $I_v$ table entries to automatically skip over the header in the texture file. So when doing texture accessing, you only need to add the table values to get the net address:

```
Address = Utable[Iu] + Vtable[Iv]
```

# Some Analysis

There are two related things going on that improve matters when you lay out your pattern in tiles. First, you minimize the total number of pages that need to be accessed for a given scan line. The tile layout does this by effectively not reading in those parts of the pattern we won't be using for this scan line. For the end view and the two scan lines I monitored, this reduces the number of needed pages from 158 to 33.

Second, it increases our chances that the set of pages we read in for one scan line will be almost the same set that we need for the next scan line. And if you have enough real memory to hold one scan line's worth of texture, you will be less likely to need to read a particular page more than once. The advantages are substantial. The minimum number of page-ins possible happens when you read in each necessary page only once. (A necessary page is one that contains some visible bit of the texture.) Because of perspective, this will be a bit less than half of the whole map, a bit less than 384 for our test image. Compare this with 446 and 15,207 for the row-ordered map, side and end views. For the latter, this meant that each page had to be reread about 40 times. No wonder it was so slow. Now compare this with 356 and 1492 for the tiled map, side and end views.

Total rendering times appear in Figure 4.7. The dark gray bars are times spent actually calculating pixels, and the light gray bars are times spent doing paging.

# Other Ideas

I've described this whole thing using very specific numbers for page sizes, RAM size, and so on. But how does this work with hardware virtual memory environments? What if there are lots of RAM pages available but you also have lots of simultaneous texture maps? How about using an

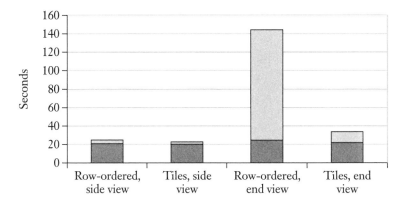

**Figure 4.1** *Dark bars are processing; light bars are paging*

addressing pattern that totally interleaves the bits for $u$ and $v$? This would make a set of tiles within tiles within tiles, a sort of fractal addressing scheme. This could improve locality even more, but I haven't tried it myself. Any sort of tiling of the map will almost certainly improve matters, but your mileage, as they say, may vary.

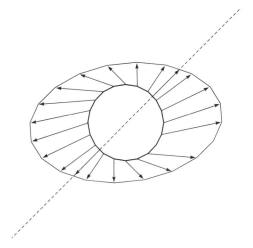

# CHAPTER FIVE

# Consider the Lowly 2×2 Matrix

MARCH 1996

If you're into computer graphics you gotta love matrices. But sometimes matrices are so . . . complicated. They have determinants, eigenvalues, and singular value decompositions. What does all this stuff really *mean*? What does it mean, for example, to take the square root of a matrix? How about the logarithm of a matrix?

I have built up my intuition about matrices by playing extensively with the simplest form, the lowly 2×2 matrix. These almost look too simple to be interesting, but they show off many of the properties of larger matrices. Better yet, we can write out explicit formulas for quantities that are hard to compute for larger matrices. This gives me a sense of concreteness about the relationships between the various matrix properties. Even so, some of the derivations here are probably at the limit of most people's appetite for algebra.

## Our Friend

OK. Here's the deal. A 2×2 matrix is simply the linear transformation of one 2D vector to another.

$$\begin{bmatrix} x & y \end{bmatrix} \begin{bmatrix} A & B \\ C & D \end{bmatrix} = \begin{bmatrix} x' & y' \end{bmatrix} \qquad (5.1)$$

An example of such a transformation appears in Figure 5.1. The arrows connect the input points to their transformed destination points. We start with points on a unit circle and find that they transform onto an ellipse at some orientation and eccentricity. Finding the eccentricity and orientation of the ellipse is an important part of understanding the matrix.

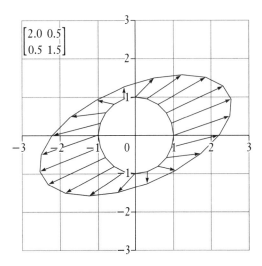

$$\begin{bmatrix} 2.0 & 0.5 \\ 0.5 & 1.5 \end{bmatrix}$$

**Figure 5.1**  *Example of transformation of unit circle*

# Basic Stuff

The basic matrix properties are easy to write for this matrix.

## The Trace

$$A + D$$

We'll see later why this is an interesting quantity to give a name to.

## The Determinant

$$\det \begin{bmatrix} A & B \\ C & D \end{bmatrix} \equiv \Delta = AD - BC$$

There is a simple geometric interpretation of the determinant. It's the amount by which the matrix scales the area of shapes. We can see this by looking at the transformation of the unit square in Figure 5.2. The point [1,0] transforms to [A,B], and the point [0,1] transforms to [C,D]. The area of the resulting parallelogram is

$$\tfrac{1}{2}CD + A\left(\frac{B+D+D}{2}\right) - C\left(\frac{B+B+D}{2}\right) - \tfrac{1}{2}AB = AD - BC$$

If the determinant is zero, it means, of course, that the parallelogram is squashed flat (zero area) along some line. If the determinant is negative, the square has turned inside out; the matrix has a mirror reflection.

As another geometric interpretation, we will see later that the determinant is the product of the semimajor and semiminor axes of the ellipse of Figure 5.1.

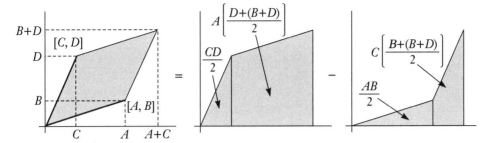

**Figure 5.2** *The transformation of the unit square*

## The Adjoint

$$\begin{bmatrix} A & B \\ C & D \end{bmatrix}^* = \begin{bmatrix} D & -B \\ -C & A \end{bmatrix}$$

## The Inverse

Only defined if $\Delta \neq 0$:

$$\begin{bmatrix} A & B \\ C & D \end{bmatrix}^{-1} = \frac{1}{\Delta}\begin{bmatrix} D & -B \\ -C & A \end{bmatrix}$$

## Factoring

Inverting matrices takes a lot of work for larger matrices. One basic tool for doing this is factorization. The idea is, given some matrix $\mathbf{M}$, to find matrices $\mathbf{L}$ and $\mathbf{N}$ whose product $\mathbf{LN} = \mathbf{M}$. If these new matrices have some simple structure, so that they can be inverted easily, we can get the inverse of $\mathbf{M}$ simply by

$$\mathbf{M}^{-1} = \mathbf{N}^{-1}\mathbf{L}^{-1}$$

The most common factorization of $\mathbf{M}$ is for $\mathbf{L}$ to be lower-triangular and $\mathbf{N}$ to be upper-triangular. For $2 \times 2$ matrices, this looks as follows (the *'s stand for values we must solve for):

$$\begin{bmatrix} A & B \\ C & D \end{bmatrix} = \begin{bmatrix} 1 & 0 \\ * & 1 \end{bmatrix}\begin{bmatrix} * & * \\ 0 & * \end{bmatrix}$$

It doesn't take much work to find the proper unknown values:

$$\begin{bmatrix} A & B \\ C & D \end{bmatrix} = \begin{bmatrix} 1 & 0 \\ C/A & 1 \end{bmatrix}\begin{bmatrix} A & B \\ 0 & (AD-BC)/A \end{bmatrix}$$

If $A$ is zero, this isn't much help. If that's the case, we can do partial pivoting, which, in the $2 \times 2$ case, is tantamount to rewriting our defining Equation (5.1) by swapping the $x$ and $y$ on the input vector, and correspondingly swapping the two rows of the matrix:

$$\begin{bmatrix} y & x \end{bmatrix} \begin{bmatrix} C & D \\ A & B \end{bmatrix} = \begin{bmatrix} x' & y' \end{bmatrix}$$

We can factor this new matrix into

$$\begin{bmatrix} C & D \\ A & B \end{bmatrix} = \begin{bmatrix} 1 & 0 \\ A/C & 1 \end{bmatrix} \begin{bmatrix} C & D \\ 0 & (BC - AD)/C \end{bmatrix}$$

If both $A$ and $C$ are zero, the matrix is singular and we're out of luck.

# Eigen Stuff

An *eigenvector* is a vector that does not change its direction when transformed by the matrix. It may, however, change its magnitude, and the factor by which that changes is called the *eigenvalue* $\lambda$. Algebraically, this means that

$$\begin{bmatrix} x & y \end{bmatrix} \begin{bmatrix} A & B \\ C & D \end{bmatrix} = \lambda \begin{bmatrix} x & y \end{bmatrix} \tag{5.2}$$

Notice that any scalar multiple of an eigenvector is also an eigenvector; only the direction of the eigenvector is important.

So let's find explicit formulas for $x$, $y$, $\lambda$ in terms of $A$, $B$, $C$, $D$. This is perfectly feasible for our simple $2 \times 2$ matrix even though it's virtually impossible for larger matrices. The trick, however, is making sure our formulas work for *all* possible values of $A$, $B$, $C$, $D$ without having to do unpleasant things like divide by zero.

### Eigenvalues

We start out by fiddling a bit with Equation (5.2) to turn it into

$$\begin{bmatrix} x & y \end{bmatrix} \begin{bmatrix} A - \lambda & B \\ C & D - \lambda \end{bmatrix} = \begin{bmatrix} 0 & 0 \end{bmatrix} \tag{5.3}$$

Since this new matrix squashes the eigenvector flat, it must be singular. This gives us a way to solve for the eigenvalues by solving the so-called *characteristic equation*:

$$\det\begin{bmatrix} A-\lambda & B \\ C & D-\lambda \end{bmatrix} = \lambda^2 - (A+D)\lambda + (AD - BC) = 0$$

The solutions are

$$\lambda_1 = \frac{A+D}{2} + \sqrt{\left(\frac{A+D}{2}\right)^2 - (AD - BC)}$$

$$\lambda_2 = \frac{A+D}{2} - \sqrt{\left(\frac{A+D}{2}\right)^2 - (AD - BC)}$$

(5.4)

You can easily verify that their sum is the trace of the matrix

$$\lambda_1 + \lambda_2 = A + D$$

and their product is the determinant

$$\lambda_1\lambda_2 = AD - BC$$

Since the eigenvalues are solutions to a quadratic equation, their reality and multiplicity depends on the sign of the discriminant of the characteristic equation. Since I'll be using this quantity a lot, I'll give it a name, $\rho$:

$$\rho \equiv \left(\frac{A+D}{2}\right)^2 - (AD - BC)$$

We then have three possibilities:

1. $\rho > 0$: two distinct real eigenvalues
2. $\rho = 0$: one real eigenvalue
3. $\rho < 0$: a complex conjugate pair of eigenvalues

If we fiddle with $\rho$ a bit, we can get it to look like

$$\rho = \left(\frac{A-D}{2}\right)^2 + BC$$

This makes it obvious that, if the matrix is symmetric ($B = C$), we have $\rho \geq 0$ and real eigenvalues are guaranteed. If not, the existence of real eigenvalues is more iffy.

## Eigenvectors

If an eigenvalue $\lambda$ is complex, there is no corresponding real eigenvector. This is the situation, for example, for rotation matrices; no vectors retain their same direction.

On the other hand, if we have a real eigenvalue $\lambda$, we can charge ahead and find its corresponding eigenvector. Start by plugging $\lambda$ into Equation (5.3). A little head scratching and we come to the conclusion that there are two possible candidates that satisfy this:

$$\begin{bmatrix} x & y \end{bmatrix} = \begin{bmatrix} C & \lambda - A \end{bmatrix} \quad \text{or} \quad \begin{bmatrix} \lambda - D & B \end{bmatrix} \tag{5.5}$$

The existence of these two possible eigenvector formulations is perfectly fine. Remember, it's only the direction of an eigenvector that's important, and these two vectors point in the same direction. You can see this by taking the ratios of their $x$ and $y$ coordinates. The condition that the $x$ and $y$ ratios are equal

$$\frac{C}{\lambda - D} = \frac{\lambda - A}{B}$$

is just the characteristic equation again.

The fact that we have these two choices will actually come in handy. For example, look at what happens if $C = 0$. The eigenvalues simplify down to $\lambda_1 = A$, $\lambda_2 = D$, and Equation (5.5) gives us the following candidates for the eigenvectors of $\lambda_1$:

$$\text{if } C = 0: \ \mathbf{v}_1 = \begin{bmatrix} 0 & 0 \end{bmatrix} \quad \text{or} \quad \begin{bmatrix} A - D & B \end{bmatrix}$$

Obviously, we prefer the second candidate. We can't just use the second choice all the time though; it will have its own problems if $B = 0$ and $A = D$. In that case, we still have $\lambda_1 = A$ but Equation (5.5) gives us the following candidates for the eigenvector:

$$\text{if } B = 0 \text{ and } A = D: \ \mathbf{v}_1 = \begin{bmatrix} C & 0 \end{bmatrix} \quad \text{or} \quad \begin{bmatrix} 0 & 0 \end{bmatrix}$$

Now we wish we'd picked the first candidate. There are similar problems with the choices for $\mathbf{v}_2$. What we need is a good algorithm for picking which of the two candidates to use. One algorithm would be to pick the choice that has the longest Euclidean length. That would work, but it generates a lot more arithmetic than the method I will show now.

As a first step, let's get the big picture by inserting the definition of $\lambda$ into our eigenvector candidates. The choices are

$$\text{for } \lambda_1 = \frac{A + D}{2} + \sqrt{\rho}$$

$$\mathbf{v}_1 = \begin{bmatrix} C, & -\dfrac{A - D}{2} + \sqrt{\rho} \end{bmatrix} \text{ or } \begin{bmatrix} \dfrac{A - D}{2} + \sqrt{\rho}, & B \end{bmatrix} \tag{5.6}$$

for $\lambda_2 = \dfrac{A+D}{2} - \sqrt{\rho}$

$$\mathbf{v}_2 = \left[ C, \quad -\dfrac{A-D}{2} - \sqrt{\rho} \right] \text{ or } \left[ \dfrac{A-D}{2} - \sqrt{\rho}, \quad B \right]$$

There are two key expressions in the choices above:

$$\dfrac{A-D}{2} + \sqrt{\rho} \text{ and } \dfrac{A-D}{2} - \sqrt{\rho}$$

We can make the candidate selection in such a way that we only need one of these values. We pick the one that makes sure we only need to add a positive number to a positive square root, or a negative number to a negative square root. This gives the following algorithm:

if $(A - D > 0)$

$$\text{use } \mathbf{v}_1 = \left[ \underbrace{\dfrac{A-D}{2} + \sqrt{\rho}}_{\text{positive+positive}}, \quad B \right] \text{ and } \mathbf{v}_2 = \left[ C, \quad -\underbrace{\left( \dfrac{A-D}{2} + \sqrt{\rho} \right)}_{\text{positive+positive}} \right]$$

if $(A - D < 0)$

$$\text{use } \mathbf{v}_1 = \left[ C, \quad -\underbrace{\left( \dfrac{A-D}{2} - \sqrt{\rho} \right)}_{\text{negative+negative}} \right] \text{ and } \mathbf{v}_2 = \left[ \underbrace{\left( \dfrac{A-D}{2} - \sqrt{\rho} \right)}_{\text{negative+negative}}, \quad B \right]$$

There is a third possibility: $A - D = 0$. To see what to do here, we first plug this condition into Equation (5.6) and simplify to get

$$\text{for } \lambda_1 = A + \sqrt{BC} , \quad \mathbf{v}_1 = \left[ C, \quad \sqrt{BC} \right] \text{ or } \left[ \sqrt{BC}, \quad B \right]$$

$$\text{for } \lambda_2 = A - \sqrt{BC} , \quad \mathbf{v}_2 = \left[ C, \quad -\sqrt{BC} \right] \text{ or } \left[ -\sqrt{BC}, \quad B \right]$$

We could only have gotten this far if the eigenvalues are real, so we know that $B$ and $C$ must have the same sign. Now, this can still mess up if either $B$ or $C$ are zero, but in each case there is a clear choice: if $B = 0$, take candidate one; if $C = 0$, take candidate two. Rather than making two tests for zero (always a dicy proposition with floating point numbers), I will make the decision based on which of $B$ or $C$ are smaller. Putting this all together, we get the algorithm in Table 5.1.

**Table 5.1** *Special cases for eigenvector calculation*

| Condition | | $v_1$ | $v_2$ |
|---|---|---|---|
| $A - D > 0$ | | $\left[\dfrac{A-D}{2} + \sqrt{\rho},\ B\right]$ | $\left[C,\ -\left(\dfrac{A-D}{2} + \sqrt{\rho}\right)\right]$ |
| $A - D = 0$ | $\|B\| > \|C\|$ | $\left[+\sqrt{BC},\ B\right]$ | $\left[-\sqrt{BC},\ B\right]$ |
| $A - D = 0$ | $B = C$ | $\left[B,\ B\right]$ | $\left[-B,\ B\right]$ |
| $A - D = 0$ | $\|B\| < \|C\|$ | $\left[C,\ +\sqrt{BC}\right]$ | $\left[C,\ -\sqrt{BC}\right]$ |
| $A - D < 0$ | | $\left[C\ -\dfrac{A-D}{2} + \sqrt{\rho}\right]$ | $\left[\dfrac{A-D}{2} - \sqrt{\rho}\ B\right]$ |

There is one final gotcha. What if $A = D$ and $B = C = 0$? In other words, the original matrix was

$$\begin{bmatrix} A & 0 \\ 0 & A \end{bmatrix}$$

The eigenvalue calculation gives us two equal real eigenvalues $\lambda = A$. According to Equation (5.5) both of our candidate eigenvectors are [0 0], obvious rubbish. Let's go back to the primary source. Putting $A = D$ and $B = C = 0$ into Equation (5.3), we find that the eigenvalue must satisfy

$$\begin{bmatrix} x & y \end{bmatrix} \begin{bmatrix} 0 & 0 \\ 0 & 0 \end{bmatrix} = \begin{bmatrix} 0 & 0 \end{bmatrix}$$

In this case, *any* vector is an eigenvector. Such cases are called *degenerate*.

There is an important thing to note here. There is no single global formula for calculating eigenvectors, even for $2 \times 2$ matrices. A proper algorithm must have "if" statements in it to choose between several different formulations that each only work for a subset of all the matrices. This gets even worse for larger matrices and is why eigenvalue calculation is typically done by some sort of numerical iteration.

## Orthogonality

For some further fun, let's take a look at the dot product between the two eigenvectors. Constructing this from Table 5.1, we get the results shown in Table 5.2.

**Table 5.2** *Dot product of eigenvectors*

| Condition | | $\mathbf{v}_1 \cdot \mathbf{v}_2$ |
|---|---|---|
| $A - D > 0$ | | $(C - B)\left(\dfrac{A-D}{2} + \sqrt{\rho}\right)$ |
| $A - D = 0$ | $\lvert B \rvert > \lvert C \rvert$ | $(C - B)(-B)$ |
| $A - D = 0$ | $B = C$ | $0$ |
| $A - D = 0$ | $\lvert B \rvert < \lvert C \rvert$ | $(C - B)C$ |
| $A - D < 0$ | | $(C - B)\left(\dfrac{A-D}{2} - \sqrt{\rho}\right)$ |

We can see immediately that if the matrix is symmetric ($C = B$), the dot product is zero; in other words, the eigenvectors are perpendicular. In fact, a little study reveals that the dot product is zero *only* when $C = B$.

## Examples

Let's look at some examples to see what sorts of things can happen with eigenvectors. Figures 5.3 through 5.8 show a collection of various matrix properties and what a representative transformation looks like. To make the source/destination arrows less cluttered, I have chosen sample matrices whose output ellipse happens to be larger than the input unit circle.

Figure 5.3 shows a uniformly scaled identity matrix. The eigenvalues are equal, the matrix is degenerate, and all vectors are eigenvectors. Figure 5.4 shows a uniformly scaled rotation. There are no real eigenvalues, and no eigenvectors. All vectors change direction when undergoing transformation.

Figure 5.5 shows a symmetric matrix with two real, unequal eigenvalues. The eigenvectors are perpendicular (all vectors on the dotted lines are eigenvectors).

Figure 5.6 shows a nonsymmetric matrix with two real eigenvalues, both positive but unequal. Note that the eigenvectors are not perpendicular. Figure 5.7 shows another nonsymmetric matrix with two real eigenvalues. This time one is positive and the other negative.

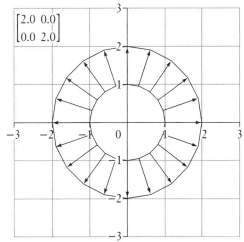

$$\begin{bmatrix} 2.0 & 0.0 \\ 0.0 & 2.0 \end{bmatrix}$$

**Figure 5.3** *Uniformly scaled identity*

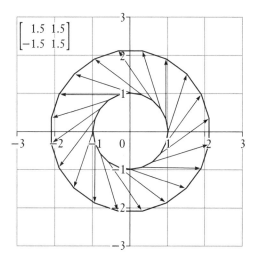

**Figure 5.4**  *Uniformly scaled rotation*

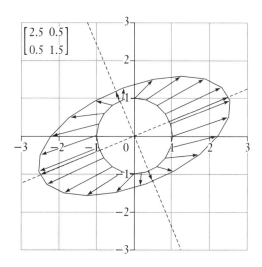

**Figure 5.5**  *Symmetric matrix with two different eigenvalues*

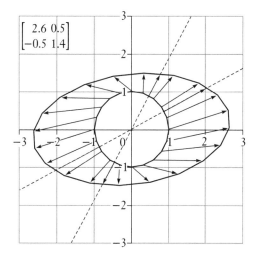

**Figure 5.6**  *Nonsymmetric matrix, unequal positive eigenvalues*

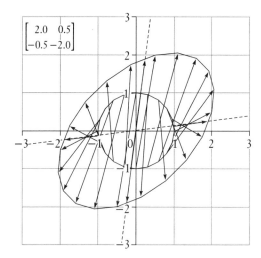

**Figure 5.7**  *Nonsymmetric matrix, one each positive and negative eigenvalues*

The horizontalish dashed line represents eigenvectors corresponding to the positive eigenvalue; the matrix reflects across this line. The verticalish dashed line represents the eigenvectors corresponding to the negative eigenvalue; vectors along this line reverse direction. Finally, Figure 5.8 shows a nonsymmetric matrix that has one real (double) eigenvalue and one eigenvector.

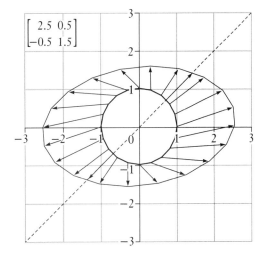

**Figure 5.8**  *Nonsymmetric matrix with one eigenvector*

# Definite Stuff

One of my favorite uses for symmetric matrices (where $B = C$) is to represent homogeneous polynomials:

$$\begin{bmatrix} x & y \end{bmatrix} \begin{bmatrix} A & B \\ B & D \end{bmatrix} \begin{bmatrix} x \\ y \end{bmatrix} = Ax^2 + 2Bxy + Dy^2 \qquad (5.7)$$

If this expression has no real roots, that is, it's positive (or negative) for all $[x\,y]$, the matrix is called *positive (negative) definite*. What condition on $A$, $B$, $D$ is necessary to guarantee this? Turn the question around. If a matrix is *not* positive/negative definite, there must be some real roots $[x\,y]$ that give

$$Ax^2 + 2Bxy + Dy^2 = 0$$

Use the quadratic formula to get

$$x = y \left\{ \frac{-B \pm \sqrt{B^2 - AD}}{A} \right\}$$

In order for this *not* to happen, we simply must make sure this has no real roots. That is,

$$\text{positive/negative definite} \Leftrightarrow B^2 - AD < 0 \qquad (5.8)$$

We can separate the positive and negative cases by plugging the vectors $[1,0]$ and $[0,1]$ into Equation (5.7) and noting the sign. We have

$$\text{positive definite} \Leftrightarrow (B^2 < AD) \text{ and } (A > 0) \text{ and } (D > 0)$$

$$\text{negative definite} \Leftrightarrow (B^2 < AD) \text{ and } (A < 0) \text{ and } (D < 0)$$

The condition of being positive definite is the same as the condition of having two positive eigenvalues, as in Figure 5.5. We can see this by putting $B = C$ into Equation (5.4) to get the eigenvalues of a symmetric matrix:

$$\lambda = \frac{A+D}{2} \pm \sqrt{\left(\frac{A+D}{2}\right)^2 - (AD - B^2)}$$

If the matrix is positive definite, then $(AD - B^2) > 0$ and the value of the square root is less than $(A+D)/2$. We are forming the two eigenvalues by adding and subtracting a smaller positive value from a larger positive value: presto, two positive eigenvalues.

Knowing that a matrix is positive definite is useful because it allows Cholesky factorization. This factors the matrix into

$$\begin{bmatrix} A & B \\ B & D \end{bmatrix} = \mathbf{G}\mathbf{G}^T$$

where $\mathbf{G}$ is a lower-triangular matrix. It's simple to show that

$$\mathbf{G} = \begin{bmatrix} \sqrt{A} & 0 \\ B/\sqrt{A} & (AD - B^2)/\sqrt{A} \end{bmatrix}$$

This is pretty trivial for 2×2 matrices, but of course, it's a bigger deal for larger matrices. A variant of this avoids square roots by making the lower-triangular matrix have 1s on the diagonal and including a separate diagonal matrix:

$$\begin{bmatrix} A & B \\ B & D \end{bmatrix} = \begin{bmatrix} 1 & 0 \\ B/A & 1 \end{bmatrix}\begin{bmatrix} A & 0 \\ 0 & (AD - B^2)/A \end{bmatrix}\begin{bmatrix} 1 & B/A \\ 0 & 1 \end{bmatrix}$$

Don't panic about the divisions or square roots. In a positive definite matrix, we always have $A > 0$.

# A New Orientation

Why is the trace of the matrix an interesting quantity? Why give a name to the sum of the diagonal elements? Why not choose the sum of the first column minus the square root of the upper-left element, or something? Here's why.

The matrix represents a transformation of one vector into another. The actual numbers for $x$ and $y$, however, are somewhat an accident of the coordinate system we use. We want to see what happens to the geometric form of the vector independent of the coordinate system. If we chose a different $x$ axis and a different $y$ axis, what would change about the transformation, and what would stay the same? If we chose the new vector $[p,q]$ as our $x$ axis and $[r,s]$ as our new $y$ axis, what should the elements in the transformation be to map an input vector into the same result vector? (This is similar to the derivation of a transformed matrix in Chapter 9, "Uppers and Downers, Part I" of *Jim Blinn's Corner: Dirty Pixels*). Our new input and output vectors would be

$$\begin{bmatrix} x_t & y_t \end{bmatrix} = \begin{bmatrix} x & y \end{bmatrix} \begin{bmatrix} p & q \\ r & s \end{bmatrix}$$

and

$$\begin{bmatrix} x_t' & y_t' \end{bmatrix} = \begin{bmatrix} x' & y' \end{bmatrix} \begin{bmatrix} p & q \\ r & s \end{bmatrix}$$

The vector transformation equation

$$\begin{bmatrix} x & y \end{bmatrix} \begin{bmatrix} A & B \\ C & D \end{bmatrix} = \begin{bmatrix} x' & y' \end{bmatrix}$$

becomes

$$\begin{bmatrix} x_t & y_t \end{bmatrix} \begin{bmatrix} p & q \\ r & s \end{bmatrix}^{-1} \begin{bmatrix} A & B \\ C & D \end{bmatrix} \begin{bmatrix} p & q \\ r & s \end{bmatrix} = \begin{bmatrix} x_t' & y_t' \end{bmatrix}$$

so that

$$\begin{bmatrix} A_t & B_t \\ C_t & D_t \end{bmatrix} = \frac{1}{ps - qr} \begin{bmatrix} s & -q \\ -r & p \end{bmatrix} \begin{bmatrix} A & B \\ C & D \end{bmatrix} \begin{bmatrix} p & q \\ r & s \end{bmatrix} \tag{5.9}$$

We can think of this the way mathematicians do—as representing the same vectors in a new coordinate system—or we can think of it the way computer graphicists do—as transforming the vector and the matrix within the current coordinate system.

Let's get adventurous and work this all the way out. We get

$$A_t = (psA + rsB - pqC - rqD)/(ps - rq)$$
$$B_t = (qsA + s^2B - q^2C - sqD)/(ps - rq)$$
$$C_t = (-prA - r^2B + p^2C + rpD)/(ps - rq)$$
$$D_t = (-rqA - rsB + pqC + psD)/(ps - rq)$$

Now let's play with it.

## General Invariants

Let's find the trace of the transformed matrix by adding the first and last equations above. Lo and behold, lots of stuff cancels out and we get

$$A_t + D_t = A + D$$

The trace doesn't change if we change coordinate systems. Of course, that is why the trace is an interesting quantity; it is *invariant* under transformation. I remember that it took me a long time to figure this out when I was first learning about matrices. The math books defined the trace, but it didn't immediately sink in why the sum of the diagonals was something worth giving a name to.

It so happens that the determinant of a matrix is also invariant. Proving this is a bit more grisly. But glutton for punishment that I am, I have actually done it even though I knew the answer in advance. I'll give you a hint on how to organize it. Write it out by first collecting the coefficients of $A^2$, then those of $AB$, and so on:

$$\begin{aligned} A_t D_t - B_t C_t = \{ &A^2(-psrq + psrq) + \\ &AB(-prs^2 - r^2qs + prs^2 + r^2qs) + \\ &... \\ &AD(p^2s^2 + r^2q^2 - rpqs - rpqs) + \\ &...\} / (ps - rq) \end{aligned}$$

Most terms cancel, and you finally get what you expected:

$$A_t D_t - B_t C_t = AD - BC$$

Now that we have determined the invariance of the trace and determinant, we can see that the eigenvalues, being simple functions of $A + D$ and $AD - BC$, also don't change when we change the coordinate system. The individual $x$ and $y$ components of the eigen*vectors*, however, do change with transformation.

If two real, nonequal eigenvalues exist, then there is a particularly interesting transform we can apply to the matrix, one that maps the eigenvectors to the coordinate axes. That is, given

$$\begin{bmatrix} x_t & y_t \end{bmatrix} \begin{bmatrix} p & q \\ r & s \end{bmatrix}^{-1} = \begin{bmatrix} x & y \end{bmatrix}$$

We want unit vectors in $[x_t, y_t]$ space to map to the eigenvectors in $[x,y]$ space. We can do this easily by making up the transformation matrix by

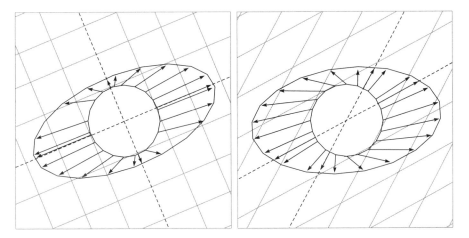

**Figure 5.9** *Special coordinate systems for matrices with nonequal real eigenvectors*

stacking the eigenvectors on top of each other. Using the formulas above for eigenvectors, the result is

$$\begin{bmatrix} p & q \\ r & s \end{bmatrix}^{-1} = \begin{bmatrix} C & -\frac{A-D}{2} - \sqrt{\rho} \\ \frac{A-D}{2} + \sqrt{\rho} & B \end{bmatrix}$$

A little refreshing algebra using this transform verifies that

$$\begin{bmatrix} A_t & B_t \\ C_t & D_t \end{bmatrix} = \begin{bmatrix} \lambda_1 & 0 \\ 0 & \lambda_2 \end{bmatrix}$$

In other words, if the eigenvalues exist, there is a coordinate system in which the transformation is just a scale along the two axes by the eigenvectors. Figure 5.9 shows this for the two matrices of Figures 5.5 and 5.6. Note that for the symmetric matrix, the new coordinate system is a simple rotation of the old one.

## Rotational Invariants

If we use a less general *pqrs* matrix, we can expect more quantities to be invariant. For example, if we only use pure rotations

$$\begin{bmatrix} p & q \\ r & s \end{bmatrix} = \begin{bmatrix} \cos\alpha & \sin\alpha \\ -\sin\alpha & \cos\alpha \end{bmatrix} \qquad (5.10)$$

we get

$$A_r = A\cos^2\alpha + (B+C)\sin\alpha\cos\alpha + D\sin^2\alpha$$
$$B_r = B\cos^2\alpha + (D-A)\sin\alpha\cos\alpha - C\sin^2\alpha$$
$$C_r = C\cos^2\alpha + (D-A)\sin\alpha\cos\alpha - B\sin^2\alpha$$
$$D_r = D\cos^2\alpha - (B+C)\sin\alpha\cos\alpha + A\sin^2\alpha$$

Subtracting the middle two equations gives us the new invariant:

$$B_r - C_r = B - C$$

The property of being symmetric ($B - C = 0$) or nonsymmetric ($B - C \neq 0$) is now invariant. Likewise, this means that the condition of being positive definite is a rotational invariant.

# A New Formulation

I'm now going to drop something on you that I've learned by long and hard toil in the matrix trenches, but that we've seen lots of hints of above—most 2×2 matrix operations are a lot easier to do algebraically if you write them in terms of the sum and difference of the matrix components. That is, we'll define $E$, $F$, $G$, and $H$ so that

$$\begin{bmatrix} A & B \\ C & D \end{bmatrix} = \begin{bmatrix} E+F & G+H \\ G-H & E-F \end{bmatrix} \tag{5.11}$$

One way of looking at this is to say that we are dividing up the matrix into the sum

$$\begin{bmatrix} A & B \\ C & D \end{bmatrix} = \begin{bmatrix} E & H \\ -H & E \end{bmatrix} + \begin{bmatrix} F & G \\ G & -F \end{bmatrix}$$

The first of these is a pure rotation by the angle $\tan^{-1}(H/E)$ times a uniform scale factor of $\sqrt{E^2 + H^2}$. The second is a mirror reflection times a uniform scale factor of $\sqrt{F^2 + G^2}$. By looking at its eigenvectors, we can find that the reflection is across a line at an angle of $\frac{1}{2}\tan^{-1}(G/F)$ with the $x$ axis.

## Even More Definite

One of the first benefits of our new notation is that it makes the condition of being positive (or negative) definite easier to understand. First, remember that we are dealing with symmetric matrices here, so $H = 0$. Now plug the new notation into Equation (5.8) and get, with some minor fiddling

$$\text{positive/negative definite} \Leftrightarrow \left(F^2 + G^2 < E^2\right)$$

We can get even more intuition about this by plugging our new notation into Equation (5.7), while rewriting the test vector $[x, y]$ in polar coordinates:

$$\begin{aligned}
\begin{bmatrix} r\cos\theta & r\sin\theta \end{bmatrix} &\begin{bmatrix} E+F & G \\ G & E-F \end{bmatrix} \begin{bmatrix} r\cos\theta \\ r\sin\theta \end{bmatrix} \\
&= (E+F)\,r^2\cos^2\theta + 2Gr^2\cos\theta\sin\theta + (E-F)\,r^2\sin^2\theta \\
&= r^2\big(E + F\big(\cos^2\theta - \sin^2\theta\big) + G\,(2\cos\theta\sin\theta)\big) \\
&= r^2\left(E + F\cos(2\theta) + G\sin(2\theta)\right)
\end{aligned}$$

In other words, we have the constant $E$ added to a sine wave of amplitude $\sqrt{F^2 + G^2}$. As long as $|E|$ is greater than the amplitude $\left(F^2 + G^2 < E^2\right)$, the net algebraic sign won't change. In this case, the condition of being positive definite versus negative definite just depends on the sign of $E$. Our new condition is then

$$\text{positive definite} \Leftrightarrow E > +\sqrt{F^2 + G^2}$$

$$\text{negative definite} \Leftrightarrow E < -\sqrt{F^2 + G^2}$$

## General Invariants

Let's now see what our general invariants look like in terms of this new notation. The trace is

$$A + D = 2E$$

The determinant is

$$\begin{aligned}
\Delta &= AD - BC \\
&= E^2 - F^2 - G^2 + H^2
\end{aligned}$$

The eigenvalue discriminant is also invariant since a little algebra can show that

$$\rho = \left(\frac{A-D}{2}\right)^2 + BC$$
$$= F^2 + G^2 - H^2 \qquad (5.12)$$
$$= E^2 - \Delta$$

The eigenvalues are

$$\lambda = \frac{A+D}{2} \pm \sqrt{\rho}$$
$$= E \pm \sqrt{F^2 + G^2 - H^2} \qquad (5.13)$$

If the matrix is symmetric, then $H = 0$, and we see another demonstration that real eigenvalues are guaranteed to exist. In general, real eigenvalues exist any time $\rho$ is positive. Combine this with a slight fiddling of Equation (5.12), and you get a simpler condition for real eigenvalues:

$$\Delta < E^2$$

This shows, for example, that a matrix with a negative determinant always has real eigenvalues.

## Rotational Invariants

The new invariant we got when we specialized to just rotations now looks like

$$B - C = 2H$$

Since $H$ and $F^2 + G^2 - H^2$ are invariant, $F^2 + G^2$ is invariant.

As another, more revealing way to see this, form the following difference and sum of the rotated matrix elements:

$$A_r - D_r = (A-D)\left(\cos^2\alpha - \sin^2\alpha\right) + (B+C)(2\sin\alpha\cos\alpha)$$
$$B_r + C_r = -(A-D)(2\sin\alpha\cos\alpha) \quad + (B+C)\left(\cos^2\alpha - \sin^2\alpha\right)$$

Applying double angle formulas and the definition of $F$ and $G$, this gives us

$$F_r = F\cos(2\alpha) + G\sin(2\alpha)$$
$$G_r = -F\sin(2\alpha) + G\cos(2\alpha)$$

So, in particular,

$$F_r^2 + G_r^2 = F^2 + G^2$$

If we start with a symmetric matrix ($H = 0$), we can perform a rotation to get $G_r = 0$ by solving

$$0 = -F \sin(2\alpha) + G \cos(2\alpha)$$

This means that we rotate by the angle

$$\alpha = \tfrac{1}{2} \tan^{-1}(G/F)$$

Now that $G_r = H_r = 0$, we have a diagonal matrix; that is, any symmetric matrix can be rotated to make it a diagonal matrix. This gives us a more elegant way of finding the eigenvectors (but only for symmetric matrices).

# Singular Value Decomposition

The matrix wizards[1] tell us that any matrix can be decomposed into a rotation, a nonuniform scale, and another rotation by another (possibly different) angle. For a $2 \times 2$ matrix, this looks like

$$\begin{bmatrix} A & B \\ C & D \end{bmatrix} = \begin{bmatrix} \cos\beta & \sin\beta \\ -\sin\beta & \cos\beta \end{bmatrix} \begin{bmatrix} w_1 & 0 \\ 0 & w_2 \end{bmatrix} \begin{bmatrix} \cos\gamma & \sin\gamma \\ -\sin\gamma & \cos\gamma \end{bmatrix} \tag{5.14}$$

In order to believe this, we must be able to solve for the angles and scales in terms of $A$, $B$, $C$, and $D$. Start by multiplying out the matrix above to get

$$A = w_1 \cos\beta \cos\gamma - w_2 \sin\beta \sin\gamma$$
$$B = w_1 \cos\beta \sin\gamma + w_2 \sin\beta \cos\gamma$$
$$C = -w_1 \sin\beta \cos\gamma - w_2 \cos\beta \sin\gamma$$
$$D = -w_1 \sin\beta \sin\gamma + w_2 \cos\beta \cos\gamma$$

Then we simply solve the four equations above for $w_1$, $w_2$, $\beta$, $\gamma$ and we're golden. After a bit of thrashing around, we remember our magic reformulation. We add and subtract elements and apply a few trigonometry addition formulas and voila:

$$2E = A + D = (w_1 + w_2) \cos(\gamma + \beta)$$
$$2F = A - D = (w_1 - w_2) \cos(\gamma - \beta)$$
$$2G = B + C = (w_1 - w_2) \sin(\gamma - \beta)$$
$$2H = B - C = (w_1 + w_2) \sin(\gamma + \beta)$$

---

1  Press, H., Teukolski, S., Vetterling, W., Flanners, B., *Numerical Recipes: The Art of Scientific Computing*, Cambridge University Press, 1992.

Now things look easier. One more crank turn gives us

$$\frac{w_1 + w_2}{2} = \sqrt{E^2 + H^2}$$

$$\frac{w_1 - w_2}{2} = \sqrt{F^2 + G^2}$$

$$\gamma - \beta = \tan^{-1}(G/F) \tag{5.15}$$

$$\gamma + \beta = \tan^{-1}(H/E)$$

You can take it from here.

There are two situations when this has a bit of a hiccup. The first is when $F = G = 0$. If we blindly stuff this into Equation (5.15), we get that $w_1 = w_2 = \sqrt{E^2 + H^2}$, but that $\gamma - \beta$ is undefined, or rather, that it can have *any* value. Further thought shows that in this situation, our original matrix was of form

$$\begin{bmatrix} A & B \\ C & D \end{bmatrix} = \begin{bmatrix} E & H \\ -H & E \end{bmatrix}$$

In other words, it is a uniformly scaled rotation. The formula for singular value decomposition degenerates into

$$\begin{bmatrix} \cos\beta & \sin\beta \\ -\sin\beta & \cos\beta \end{bmatrix} \begin{bmatrix} w_1 & 0 \\ 0 & w_2 \end{bmatrix} \begin{bmatrix} \cos\gamma & \sin\gamma \\ -\sin\gamma & \cos\gamma \end{bmatrix}$$

$$= w_1 \begin{bmatrix} \cos(\beta+\gamma) & \sin(\beta+\gamma) \\ -\sin(\beta+\gamma) & \cos(\beta+\gamma) \end{bmatrix}$$

So if the two singular values are equal, the angles are not unique. Any two values of $\beta$ and $\gamma$ that add up to $\tan^{-1}(H/E)$ will work.

The other hiccup is when $E = H = 0$. Here we find that $w_1 = -w_2 = \sqrt{F^2 + G^2}$ and that $\gamma + \beta$ is undefined. The original matrix must have been of the form

$$\begin{bmatrix} A & B \\ C & D \end{bmatrix} = \begin{bmatrix} F & G \\ G & -F \end{bmatrix}$$

This is our uniformly scaled mirror reflection about a line at an angle of $(\gamma - \beta)/2$ to the $x$ axis. Again, we get that the angles $\beta$ and $\gamma$ are not unique, but must simply satisfy $\gamma - \beta = \tan^{-1}(G/F)$.

We now believe that the factoring in Equation (5.14) is always possible. Now imagine what happens when we pass a unit circle through it. It will first rotate (no change in shape), then scale by the singular values (now it's an ellipse), and then rotate again (ellipse tilted at an angle). In other words, the semimajor and semiminor axes of the ellipses of Figures 5.1, 5.3, and 5.9 are the singular values of the matrices. And the angle of tilt of the ellipse equals $\gamma$.

## Invariants of SVD

How do the singular values fit into the matrix invariant picture? Putting the rotational invariants $(E, H, F^2 + G^2)$ into Equation (5.15), we can see that $(w_1, w_2, \gamma + \beta)$ are also rotationally invariant. We can also see this by noting that a rotation of a matrix will add an angle to $\beta$ while it subtracts the same angle from $\gamma$, all the while leaving $w_1$ and $w_2$ alone.

## Comparison with Eigenvalues

Compare the formulas for eigenvectors and singular values:

$$\lambda = E \pm \sqrt{F^2 + G^2 - H^2}$$
$$w = \sqrt{E^2 + H^2} \pm \sqrt{F^2 + G^2}$$

You can see that, though a matrix may or may not have real eigenvalues, it always has real singular values. The *product* of the eigenvalues and of the singular values is always the same (it's the determinant):

$$\lambda_1 \lambda_2 = w_1 w_2 = E^2 - F^2 - G^2 + H^2 = \Delta$$

Only if $H = 0$ (symmetric matrix) are the eigenvalues and singular values the same:

$$\lambda_1 = w_1, \lambda_2 = w_2$$

# Summary of Invariants

There are two independent general invariant quantities for a $2\times2$ matrix. For each of our four ways of expressing the matrix, they are

| | |
|---|---|
| $A + D$ | $AD - BC$ |
| $E$ | $F^2 + G^2 - H^2$ |
| $\lambda_1$ | $\lambda_2$ |
| $(w_1 + w_2)\cos(\gamma + \beta)$ | $w_1 w_2$ |

plus any algebraic combinations of them.

There are three independent rotational invariants, the above two plus one more. With some simple algebraic fiddling, the catalog can be more easily written as

| $A + D$ | $B - C$ | $AD - BC$ |
|---------|---------|-----------|
| $E$ | $H$ | $F^2 + G^2$ |
| $\lambda_1$ | $\lambda_2$ | Angle between eigenvectors |
| $w_1$ | $w_2$ | $\gamma + \beta$ |

plus any algebraic combinations.

Finding these invariants, as well as solving several other matrix problems, is easiest using the $E$, $F$, $G$, $H$ formulation of the matrix elements.

# Visualizations

I don't know about you, but to me all these formulas and properties are beginning to merge into a soft, gray blur. Let's try to make sense of this with a . . . wait for it . . . *visualization*. The $A$, $B$, $C$, $D$ values of an arbitrary 2×2 matrix generate a 4D space. We could draw a diagram of this 4D space and divide it up into regions for the various properties, but visualizing in 4D is kinda hard. Let's instead see if we can find a reasonable projection down into fewer dimensions. I've flailed around with this for a while, and here's my favorite projection.

Applying ancient wisdom, we first convert the matrix to the $E$, $F$, $G$, $H$ form. Then we realize that the first step of singular value decomposition, Equation (5.15), basically involves rewriting the two vectors $(E,H)$ and $(F,G)$ in polar coordinates. I'll give names to the lengths of these vectors:

$$\|EH\| = +\sqrt{E^2 + H^2}$$
$$\|FG\| = +\sqrt{F^2 + G^2}$$

We can diagram some basic matrix properties using just these two axes. For example, if $\|FG\| = 0$ and $\|EH\| = 1$, the matrix is a pure rotation. If $\|EH\| = 0$ and $\|FG\| = 1$, the matrix is a pure mirror reflection. And in any case, the determinant is

$$\Delta = \|EH\|^2 - \|FG\|^2$$

Figure 5.10 shows our first visualization of these properties. Each point on this chart represents many matrices, in fact, a two parameter set: the parameters being the angles $\tan^{-1}(G/F)$ and $\tan^{-1}(H/E)$.

Now let's visualize some other matrix properties. First, take a look at Table 5.3, a catalog of various properties written in terms of $E$, $F$, $G$, $H$.

Now recall that the three rotational invariants of a matrix are $E$, $H$, and $\|FG\|$ These, then, make good candidates for the axes of a 3D plot. Imagine rotating Figure 5.10 around the $\|FG\|$ axis, sweeping the $\Delta = 0$ line into a cone, and you get Figure 5.11. Matrices with negative determinants are inside the cone; those with positive determinants are outside. Each point in the $EH$ plane now represents a single matrix, one that is a uniformly scaled rotation. All the pure rotations lie on the unit circle on the $EH$ plane. Each point above the $EH$ plane (where $\|FG\| > 0$) still represents a multitude of matrices, those with various values of $\tan^{-1}(G/F)$. Applying a rotation to a matrix via Equations (5.9) and (5.10) will only change this angle, but will not change its $E$, $H$, $\|FG\|$ coordinates in this figure.

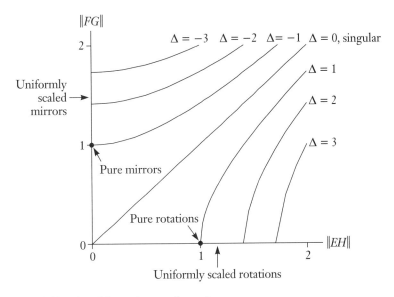

**Figure 5.10** *Plot of determinants of matrix*

Now let's add the various conditions on eigenvalues to make Figure 5.12. Here a V-shaped trough represents the zone of real eigenvalues; inside the trough there are two nonequal real eigenvalues, on the surface of the trough there is one unique real value, and outside the trough the eigenvalues are complex. See how the cir-

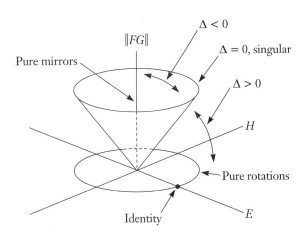

**Figure 5.11** *Cone of singularity*

cle of rotation matrices is in the complex eigenvalue region. See how the cone of singularity lies inside and tangent to the trough, so any matrix with a negative determinant has real eigenvalues. See how the plane of symmetric matrices, $H = 0$, is also inside the real eigenvalue trough. Degenerate matrices are on both the trough and the $H = 0$ plane; this is the $E$ axis. Positive and negative definite matrices are on the shaded portion of the $H = 0$ plane.

**Table 5.3** *Summary of matrix properties*

| | |
|---|---|
| Pure rotation | $\|FG\| = 0, \|EH\| = 1$ |
| Uniformly scaled rotation | $\|FG\| = 0$ |
| Pure mirror | $\|EH\| = 0, \|FG\| = 1$ |
| Uniformly scaled mirror | $\|EH\| = 0$ |
| Determinant | $\Delta = \|EH\|^2 - \|FG\|^2$ |
| Singular (determinant = 0) | $\|FG\| = \|EH\|$ |
| Symmetric | $H = 0$ |
| Eigenvalues | $\lambda = E \pm \sqrt{\|FG\|^2 - H^2}$ |
| Equal eigenvalues | $H = \pm\|FG\|$ |
| Real eigenvalues | $H^2 \le \|FG\|^2$ |
| Degenerate | $H = \|FG\| = 0$ |
| Singular values | $w = \|EF\| \pm \|FG\|$ |
| Equal singular values | $\|FG\| = 0$ |
| Positive definite | $H = 0, \;\; E > \|FG\|$ |
| Negative definite | $H = 0, \;\; E < -\|FG\|$ |

# Square Root of a Matrix

Now let's get back to one of the problems posed in the introduction to this chapter: find the square root of the matrix. That is, we want to find $a, b, c, d$ such that

$$\begin{bmatrix} a & b \\ c & d \end{bmatrix}^2 = \begin{bmatrix} a^2 + bc & b(a + d) \\ c(a + d) & d^2 + bc \end{bmatrix} = \begin{bmatrix} A & B \\ C & D \end{bmatrix}$$

The four matrix elements give four equations for the four unknowns. We just solve for $a$, $b$, $c$, and $d$. Just. Again, hack and bash on these got

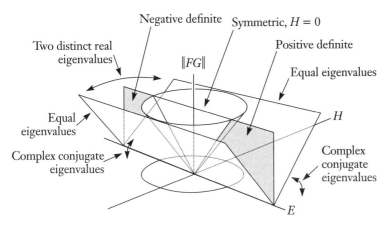

Negative definite   Symmetric, $H = 0$

Two distinct real eigenvalues

$\|FG\|$

Positive definite

Equal eigenvalues

Equal eigenvalues

$H$

Complex conjugate eigenvalues

Complex conjugate eigenvalues

$E$

**Figure 5.12** *Eigenvalues and symmetry*

me nowhere until I discovered the sum-and-difference reformulation; we want to find $e, f, g, h$ such that

$$\begin{bmatrix} e+f & g+h \\ g-h & e-f \end{bmatrix}^2 = \begin{bmatrix} E+F & G+H \\ G-H & E-F \end{bmatrix}$$

This gives

$$e^2 + 2ef + f^2 + g^2 - h^2 = E + F$$
$$e^2 - 2ef + f^2 + g^2 - h^2 = E - F$$
$$2e(g+h) = G + H$$
$$2e(g-h) = G - H$$

Add and subtract pairs of equations to get

$$e^2 + f^2 + g^2 - h^2 = E$$
$$2ef = F$$
$$2eg = G \qquad\qquad (5.16)$$
$$2eh = H$$

Now we can mash these together to get an equation for $e$:

$$e^4 - Ee^2 + \left( \frac{F^2 + G^2 - H^2}{2} \right) = 0 \qquad\qquad (5.17)$$

so that

$$e^2 = \frac{E \pm \sqrt{E^2 - F^2 - G^2 + H^2}}{2} = \frac{E \pm \sqrt{\Delta}}{2}$$

If the determinant is negative, we're dead; the matrix has no real square roots. Otherwise, there can be zero, two, or even four possible values for $e$, and hence four possible square roots of our matrix. It's a fascinating exercise to work out the various constraints on $E$, $F$, $G$, and $H$ that determine the number of roots.

If one of the roots of $e$ in Equation (5.17) equals zero, it means that we must have had

$$F^2 + G^2 - H^2 = 0$$

This is just the condition that the eigenvalues are equal. Looking at Equations (5.16), we can see that this double root at $e = 0$ further implies that we had to have started with the situation where $F = G = H = 0$. The original matrix had to have been

$$\begin{bmatrix} E & 0 \\ 0 & E \end{bmatrix}$$

There are a whole continuum of square roots; *any* matrix for which $f^2 + g^2 - h^2 = E$. The square root matrix looks like

$$\begin{bmatrix} f & g+h \\ g-h & -f \end{bmatrix}$$

As a check, square this and lo and behold:

$$\begin{bmatrix} f & g+h \\ g-h & -f \end{bmatrix}^2 = \begin{bmatrix} f^2 + g^2 - h^2 & 0 \\ 0 & f^2 + g^2 - h^2 \end{bmatrix}$$

On the other hand, for each nonzero $e$ root of Equation (5.17), we can easily solve for $f$, $g$, and $h$ using Equation (5.16), and from that get $a$, $b$, $c$, and $d$. I'm going to do a rabbit trick, however, and do this in a way that presents the result in a particularly amusing way. I'll factor out the quantity $1/2e$ from the desired matrix and then plug in the values from Equation (5.16):

$$\begin{bmatrix} e+f & g+h \\ g-h & e-f \end{bmatrix} \equiv \frac{1}{2e} \begin{bmatrix} 2e^2 + 2ef & 2eg + 2eh \\ 2eg - 2eg & 2e^2 - 2ef \end{bmatrix}$$

$$= \frac{1}{2e} \begin{bmatrix} E \pm \sqrt{\Delta} + F & G+H \\ G-H & E \pm \sqrt{\Delta} - F \end{bmatrix}$$

We find that the square root is

$$\begin{bmatrix} a & b \\ c & d \end{bmatrix} = \frac{1}{2e} \begin{bmatrix} A \pm \sqrt{\Delta} & B \\ C & D \pm \sqrt{\Delta} \end{bmatrix}$$

That is, the square root of a matrix is that same matrix plus or minus the square root of the determinant on the diagonals, times a global scale factor. The four roots come from the $\pm\sqrt{\Delta}$ and from the overall $\pm 1$ scale factor incurred when we get $e$ from $\sqrt{e^2}$.

How does finding the square root matrix relate to singular value decomposition? I originally thought that the square root of a matrix with singular value parameters $(w_1, w_2, \beta, \gamma)$ might be a matrix with the SVD $(\sqrt{w_1}, \sqrt{w_2}, \frac{1}{2}\beta, \frac{1}{2}\gamma)$. Then I had fantasies that a matrix to any arbitrary power $n$ could be constructed from the SVD parameters $(w_1^n, w_2^n, n\beta, n\gamma)$. Alas, this is not the case. For one thing, since

$$\frac{G}{F} = \frac{g}{f}$$

we know that the value of $\gamma - \beta$ must be the same for a matrix and its square root. Furthermore, you can show that it's the eigenvalues that get square-rooted, not the singular values. To see this, let's recall our definition of the eigenvector discriminant

$$F^2 + G^2 - H^2 = \rho$$
$$f^2 + g^2 - h^2 = \rho_{root}$$

Equation (5.16) then tells us that

$$e^2 + \rho_{root} = E$$
$$4e^2\rho_{root} = \rho$$

Then

$$\lambda = E \pm \sqrt{\rho}$$
$$= e^2 + \rho_{root} \pm \sqrt{4e^2\rho_{root}}$$
$$= \left(e \pm \sqrt{\rho_{root}}\right)^2$$

# Musings

What, then, is the logarithm of a matrix? Well, any function that has a Taylor series should be applicable to matrices, under some sort of convergence criterion. . . .

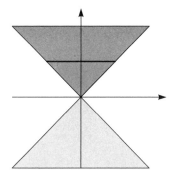

# CHAPTER SIX

# Calculating Screen Coverage

MAY 1996

When drawing a 3D object, it is sometimes useful to find a rectangle on the screen that completely encloses the object. This can be used to minimize screen-update and z buffer–clear regions. If the entire object is visible within the screen boundaries, this calculation is easy. You just find the minimum and maximum $x$ and $y$ screen coordinates. If the object extends outside the screen boundaries in one or more coordinates, this calculation is a little trickier. Simply extending the enclosing boundaries to the entire screen dimensions is overly conservative. This chapter describes a way to determine a reasonable screen extent enclosing an object even if some points are off the screen, or, even worse, behind the viewer's head. It's also a good exercise of your intuition about the homogeneous perspective transformation.

The calculations for this feat have much in common with those you are probably already doing for clip culling, so let's first review this technique.

## Review of Clip Culling

Culling is the process of making quick decisions about some geometric problem by first doing tests that are simple arithmetically, capable of identifying many commonly occurring situations, but not guaranteed to find a definitive answer. In other words, it can return three answers: yes, no, and maybe. If these simple tests fail, we go through progressively more complex tests to identify more involved but rarer situations.

When applied to the clipping of a geometric shape, culling can quickly place the shape into one of three categories: completely visible, completely invisible, or something more complex. (I'll use the word *visible* here to mean, "lies within the screen clipping boundaries.") I've described this clip-culling process in some detail in Chapter 13, "Line Clipping," of *Jim Blinn's Corner: A Trip Down the Graphics Pipeline*. I'll give a quick review here.

First of all, we don't need to test every vertex in the object. Instead, we will pick a (presumably small) set of points such that the object lies completely within their convex hull. The idea is that if all these hull points are within the screen region, then the whole object is, too. And if all the hull points are outside one of the screen boundaries, then the whole object is, too.

Then, for each frame, we transform all the hull points of our object by a homogeneous 4×4 matrix into a coordinate space in which it's convenient to do clipping. This transform includes the modeling, viewing, and homogeneous perspective transformations to map the viewing frustum to a parallel-sided rectangular brick after homogeneous division of all points by their $w$ values (though it won't do the homogeneous division unless it's absolutely necessary). It is common to define this brick-shaped clipping space as extending from −1 to 1 in both $x/w$ and $y/w$. However, in my column that became Chapter 13, "Line Clipping," of *Jim Blinn's Corner: A Trip down the Graphics Pipeline*, I made the case for including an extra scale and offset to scrunch this to the range 0 to 1. For purposes of this discussion, I'll generalize and use the symbolic value XL to represent the left clipping boundary and XR to represent the right boundary.

From now on, I'll only talk about the $x$ coordinates. You can do the calculations for the $y$ and $z$ coordinates in a similar manner.

The next step is, for each hull point, to calculate a value for each clip boundary that tells whether that point is inside or outside the boundary. For the left and right boundaries, these will be

$$L = x - XL * w$$
$$R = -x + XR * w$$

A point is visible if both $L$ and $R$ are positive. (We can see here why $XL = 0, XR = 1$ are beneficial.) The signs of $L$ and $R$ give flag bits for "outside to the left," Lout, and "outside to the right," Rout . We will combine these sign bits into one flag word `sLR`. I'll encapsulate these data and calculations in the following C++ class:

```cpp
const int Rout=1, Lout=2;
struct ClipPoint{
    float x,y,w;
    float L,R; int sLR;
    ClipPoint(float xx,float yy,float ww)
              : x(xx), y(yy), w(ww) {;}
    CalcCodes() {
        sLR=0;
        L =  x - XL*w; if (L<0) sLR|=Lout;
        R = -x + XR*w; if (R<0) sLR|=Rout;}
    };
```

The whole clip-culling operation then consists of going through an array of hull points, `P`, calculating their flag words, and forming a cumulative AND and OR of them. Again, more detail and justification is provided in the chapter on line clipping referenced above.

```cpp
int Ocumulate=0, Acumulate=~0;
for (int i=0; i!=NbrPts; ++i) {
    P[i].CalcCodes();
    Ocumulate |= P[i].sLR;
    Acumulate &= P[i].sLR; }
if(Ocumulate==0)
    {exit} //Trivial Accept, whole object visible
if(Acumulate!=0)
    {exit} //Trivial Reject, whole object not vis.
// Maybe visible.
```

If the calculation falls out the bottom, the object must be clipped by the full clipping algorithm.

# The Screen Extent

N ow let's see how to calculate the screen extent of these hull points. (Actually, we are going to get the clip space extent; a simple scale and offset can turn this into pixel space.) For reference, let's look at Figure 6.1 to see what's happening in homogeneous space. For a more intuitive feel, you could also interpret this diagram as representing the situation *before* the perspective transformation by thinking of the $w$ axis as the $z$ axis (a perspective transformation sets $w$ to the preperspective $z$ value).

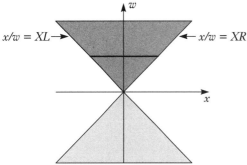

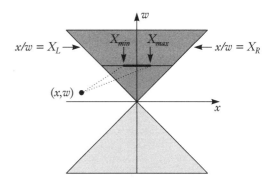

**Figure 6.1**  *Homogeneous clipping space*          **Figure 6.2**  *New hull point off screen to the left*

The darker gray region represents those points in front of the eye that project to the visible screen region (the dark line); this is where sLR==0. The lighter gray region represents the points that are behind the eye but would project into the screen region if we simply did the *x/w* divide. These points are, however, not visible.

We'll calculate the screen extent by maintaining a running coverage range, Xmin and Xmax, and looping through the hull points, extending this range as necessary.

If sLR==0 for the next hull point, the situation is trivial; just update the range if the new point extends outside it.

```
if((x/w)<Xmin) Xmin=x/w;
if((x/w)>Xmax) Xmax=x/w;
```

If sLR==Lout, the new point is in the left quadrant of the *x,w* plane (see Figure 6.2). All possible polygons connecting this new point with the current span will hit the left edge of the screen, so any points in this region should trigger an update of Xmin to push it out to the minimum value of XL. As an aside, note that if the point is in the negative *w* region of (sLR==Lout), then its projection will map to the right of the screen. This is an illusion of homogeneous perspective. All edges connecting it to the current range will only hit the left edge of the screen, and the update of Xmin=XL is still the correct thing to do.

The situation where sLR==Rout is symmetrical with sLR==Lout. Update Xmax to XR.

Now for the interesting situation: points in the light gray sLR==(Lout+Rout) region. There are three possible cases, depending on exactly where the new point is in the region.

In the first case, shown in Figure 6.3(a), the new hull point projects to a visible screen coordinate to the right of Xmax, but this is an illusion. In

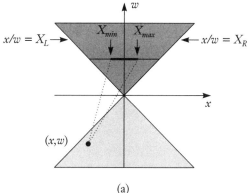

(a)

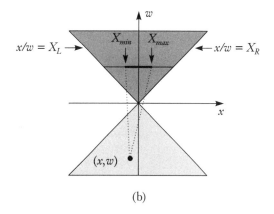

(b)

fact, all the visible points on the lines connecting the new point to the existing span will project to points to the left of `Xmin`. In this case, the appropriate action would be to extend `Xmin` to the left edge of the clip region, `XL`.

In the second case, Figure 6.3(b), all visible points connecting the new point to the existing span will project to points covering the whole screen. In this situation, the viewer is (potentially) inside the object. The appropriate action to take is to set `Xmin` to `XL` and to set `Xmax` to `XR`.

In the third case, Figure 6.3(c), all visible points connecting the new point to the existing span will project to points to the right of `Xmax`. So here we should set `Xmax` to `XR`.

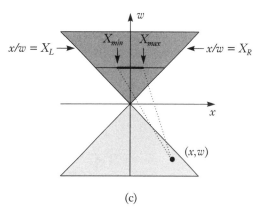

(c)

**Figure 6.3** *Update Xmin (a), update both Xmin, Xmax (b), and update Xmax (c)*

The boundaries between cases 1 and 2 are where the rightmost dotted line passes through the origin, that is, where x/w=Xmax. The boundaries between cases 2 and 3 are where the leftmost dotted line passes through the origin, that is, where x/w=Xmin. Transliterating this into C++, we get

```
if      (Xmax<x/w)          Xmin=XL;               // case 1
else if(Xmin<x/w<Xmax){Xmin=XL; Xmax=XR;} // case 2
else if      (x/w<Xmin) Xmax=XR;               // case 3
```

With a little fiddling, we can collapse this to actual legal C++.

```
if(Xmin<x/w) Xmin=XL; // case 1 and 2
if(x/w<Xmax) Xmax=XR; // case 2 and 3
```

# Putting It Together

Combining all four cases, we get a first cut at the algorithm. Note that for the **sLR==0** case, one or the other of the subsidiary if statements might be true, but not both. For the sLR==(Lout+Rout) case, at least one of the subsidiary if statements will be true and both might be.

```
if(sLR==0){
    if((x/w)<Xmin) Xmin=x/w;
    if((x/w)>Xmax) Xmax=x/w;  }
if(sLR==Lout)        Xmin=XL;
if(sLR==Rout)        Xmax=XR;
if(sLR==Lout+Rout){
    if((x/w)>Xmin) Xmin=XL;
    if((x/w)<Xmax) Xmax=XR;  }
```

Now we can make the following observation: whenever sLR==0, the value of $w$ must be positive, so we can calculate ((x/w)<Xmin) as (x<Xmin*w). But what's really interesting is that when sLR==Lout+Rout, the value of $w$ must be negative, so we can also calculate ((x/w)>Xmin) as (x<Xmin*w). This gives us our next iteration.

```
if(sLR==0){
    if(x<Xmin*w) Xmin=x/w;
    if(x>Xmax*w) Xmax=x/w;}
if(sLR==Lout)
                  Xmin=XL;
if(sLR==Rout)
                  Xmax=XR;
if(sLR==Lout+Rout){
    if(x<Xmin*w) Xmin=XL;
    if(x>Xmax*w) Xmax=XR;}
```

Finally, we can boil this down even further by first looking at Xmin and Xmax separately. For Xmin, the calculation is

```
if(sLR==0)
    if(x<Xmin*w)     Xmin=x/w;    // case a
if(sLR==Lout)        Xmin=XL;     // case b
if(sLR==Lout+Rout)
    if(x<Xmin*w)     Xmin=XL;     // case c
```

Figure 6.4 shows the three cases where Xmin changes. Notice that this only happens when x<Xmin*w and that in both cases b and c Xmin gets

the same value, `XL`. This means that we can reduce the complexity of the code by reversing the order of the tests:

```
if(x<Xmin*w){
    if(sLR&Lout==0) Xmin=x/w;    // case a
    else            Xmin=XL;}    // cases b and c
```

A similar analysis for the `Xmax` case gives

```
if(x>Xmax*w){
    if(sLR&Rout==0) Xmax=x/w;
    else            Xmax=XR;}
```

## Initialization of Xmin Xmax

What I have glossed over, however, is the initialization of the (`Xmin,Xmax`) screen range we are testing against. A tempting, but wrong, way to do this is to initialize `Xmin=XR` and `Xmax=XL`, that is, a turned-inside-out range. We would then expect the first point to set `Xmin` and `Xmax` to a reasonable value, and we could continue from there. Unfortunately, the first point might not be in a region that triggers update of the `Xmin` or `Xmax` value (for example, the white area in Figure 6.4). Figuring out a reasonable initial setting for `Xmin` and `Xmax` leads to enough weird special cases that I've resorted

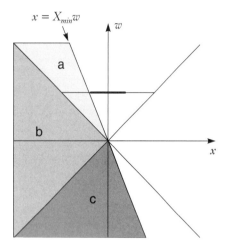

**Figure 6.4** *Three cases that update Xmin*

to doing the whole thing as a two-pass process: the first pass scans for visible hull points and finds the min/max coordinates for them; the second pass then scans for nonvisible hull points and extends the range to `XL` and/or `XR` as appropriate. Effectively, pass 1 finds points in case a of Figure 6.4, and pass 2 finds points in cases b and c. The good news is that pass 1 can be merged with the original loop that calculates L, R, and so on.

You can skip pass 2 if a trivial accept condition occurs. The accumulated (`Xmin,Xmax`) from pass 1 is correct in this case since all points are visible. You can also skip pass 2, of course, if a trivial reject occurs. Finally, you should skip pass 2 if *none* of the hull points are themselves visible—for example, if they straddle the screen on both the left and right. In this case, there may or may not be visible polygons in the final image; this algorithm won't be able to figure it out. We must be conservative and return the whole range (`XL,XR`) in this case. The net algorithm, in official C++, is

```
float Xmin=XR, Xmax=XL;
int Ocumulate=0, Acumulate=~0;
```

```
bool anyvis=false;
//////////////////// pass 1 ////////////////////////
for (int i=0; i!=NbrPts; ++i){
    ClipPoint& p=P[i];
    p.CalcCodes();
    Ocumulate |= p.sLR;
    Acumulate &= p.sLR;
    if(p.sLR==0) {
        anyvis=true;
        if(p.x - Xmin*p.w < 0)    Xmin=p.x/p.w;
        if(p.x - Xmax*p.w > 0)    Xmax=p.x/p.w;}
        }
if(Ocumulate==0) { . . . exit}
                    // Trivial Accept, use(Xmin,Xmax)
if(Acumulate!=0) { . . . exit}
                    // Trivial Reject
if(anyvis)         {
    Xmin=XL;
    Xmax=XR;
 . . . exit }     // no visible points, use whole range


//////////////////// pass 2 ////////////////////////
for (i=0; i!=NbrPts; ++i){
    ClipPoint& p=P[i];
    if((p.sLR&Lout) && (p.x - Xmin*p.w < 0)) Xmin=XL;
    if((p.sLR&Rout) && (p.x - Xmax*p.w > 0)) Xmax=XR;}
```

# Caveat

While this algorithm generates a rectangle that encloses the entire screen projection of the object, it sometimes generates a more conservative region than necessary. We must look at both $x$ and $y$ to see why. Suppose we have a tetrahedron whose base is in front of us but whose apex is behind us, say, to the right and downward. We can construct the screen region covered by the whole tetrahedron by projecting the apex through the eye onto the screen (now it's to the left and upward), and drawing edges away from that point off to infinity, as shown in Figure 6.5.

Now let's see what happens when we start with the Xmin and Xmax values from the visible base

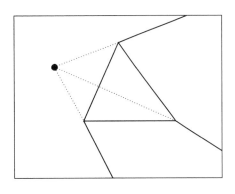

**Figure 6.5** *Tetrahedron with apex behind us*

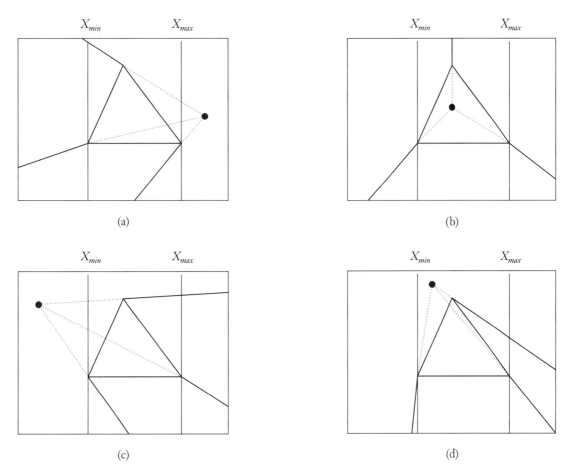

**Figure 6.6** *Algorithm correctly sets* Xmin *to* XL *(a),* Xmin *to* XL *and* Xmax *to* XR *(b), and* Xmax *to* XR *(c). Here's the catch (d)*

triangle and merge the apex point into the span. The three cases mentioned above are shown in Figures 6.6(a) through 6.6(c). In Figure 6.6(a) we have x/w>Xmin so Xmin is set to XL. This is fine. In Figure 6.6(b) we have x/w>Xmin so Xmin gets XL, and x/w<Xmax so Xmax gets XR. We are inside the tetrahedron. This is also fine. The situation in Figure 6.6(c) is basically symmetrical to that in 6.6(a): x/Xmax so Xmax gets XR. Also OK. The problem case is shown in Figure 6.6(d).

In Figure 6.6(d), since x/w is between Xmin and Xmax, both extents are extended to XL and XR. And, in fact, the polygon does stretch to infinity in the *x* direction. It is, however, clipped in *y* before it gets there. So, the region that is generated by the algorithm is more conservative than it needs to be. I'm not sure if this is a common situation though. And even if it is, things might not be so bad. Suppose that a hull point generates an

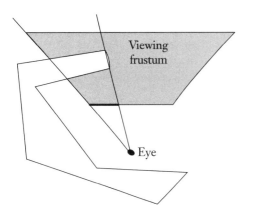

Viewing frustum

Eye

**Figure 6.7** *Concave object that generates pessimistic extent*

overly conservative estimate using the current algorithm, but that we had a more complicated algorithm that considered the above situation and makes a better estimate. A later point in the hull array could quite possibly come along and expand the Xmin value back out to XL anyway.

# Another Caveat

As another example of overconservativeness of the algorithm, recall that it finds the region covering the convex hull of the set of vertices. It is possible that concavities in the actual object might make for a situation where the covering rectangle is again too large. See Figure 6.7, which shows physical *x* and *y* in nonperspective space viewing a C-shaped structure. The algorithm would return the entire screen in this situation since the eye is inside the convex hull.

# Summary

The algorithm developed here always returns a screen rectangle that is guaranteed to completely enclose the image of the 3D object. Sometimes, however, the rectangle is larger than absolutely necessary. I believe these situations are rare, but I am still doing some experimentation with real objects and viewing positions to really see if this happens often enough to worry about.

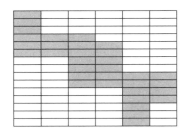

# CHAPTER SEVEN

# Fugue for MMX

*This exercise in parallel processing assumes that pixel values are encoded "linearly" as a function of pixel value. That situation is actually fairly rare. Applying this algorithm to gamma-corrected pixels will only return an approximation to the correct result. Make sure you look at Chapter 9 to see the tradeoffs involved in this approximation.*

One of my secret desires has always been to compose a symphony. The idea of getting about a hundred instruments cranking away playing different things at the same time and having the whole thing sound good seems totally miraculous to me.

When I was an undergraduate in a hardware architecture course, one of my instructors compared programming for parallel processors with writing a symphony. At the time, parallel processors were largely theoretical machines though, and there were none around for me to play with. I finally had occasion to actually try some parallel programming as a graduate student in 1975 at the University of Utah. We had an add-on to our PDP-11 made by a company called Floating Point Systems that did three pipelined floating add/multiplies per clock. Unfortunately, it was disconnected before I got to debug my program. Then in the summer of 1976 when I worked at NYIT, I was supposed to program a similar unit, but it never got delivered until just before I returned to Utah. That was the extent of my symphonic programming efforts until about a year ago, when I started playing with Pentium instruction pairing. Now MMX adds more instruments to the orchestra. This column documents some of my early experiences with programming a simple compositing routine for MMX and the lessons I've learned from it. It's not exactly a symphony, more like a fugue.

# The Problem

The program deals with pixels comprised of red, green, blue, and alpha (coverage) components, and with the assumption that the rgb components have already been multiplied by their own alpha component. In vector notation, a pixel is

$$\mathbf{F} = \begin{bmatrix} F_{red} & F_{green} & F_{blue} & F_{\alpha} \end{bmatrix}$$

The alpha component has a value from 0 to 1, so the color components have values from 0 to $F_{\alpha}$.

I will implement the most common image-compositing operation, the Porter-Duff *over* operator.[1] This takes a foreground pixel **F** and a background pixel **B** and calculates

$$\mathbf{F} \text{ over } \mathbf{B} = \mathbf{F} + (1 - F_a)\mathbf{B}$$

We must perform the same arithmetic (in parallel) on each of the four components.

# 8-Bit Arithmetic

We represent each component of the pixel as an 8-bit fixed-point quantity with the range of 0 to 1 mapped linearly to byte values 0 to 255. The arithmetic operations needed for the over operator translate as follows to 8-bit arithmetic.

### Addition

No big deal here, just add the byte values. Except . . . there is an often used trick in rendering that complicates things a bit. Glowing objects can be represented by pixels with zero coverage (alpha) but nonzero color components. If the alpha value of **F** is zero in the above definition of *over*, the operation reduces simply to **F** + **B**; that is, the color components of **F** (the glow) are added to the background, but the alpha component doesn't

---

1 Porter, T., and Duff, T., "Compositing Digital Images," *Computer Graphics, Proc. SIGGRAPH*, Vol. 18, No. 3, July 1984, pp. 253–259.

change (since $F_a = 0$). When we do this, however, it is quite possible to get a color value greater than 255. About the only reasonable thing to do in this case is to clamp the resulting summed color values at 255. Doing this using conventional machine instructions is a real time waster. Fortunately, the MMX instructions have such a clamped addition (which they call saturation) built in.

## Inversion

This is the calculation of $(1 - F_a)$. Translated into 8-bit arithmetic, the value 1 becomes the byte value 255. Subtracting an 8-bit quantity from 255 is the same as inverting all the bits in the original quantity. We can do this simply with an exclusive-or. In C notation:

$$1 - F_a = \texttt{F.a \^{} 0xFF}$$

## Multiplication

The product of two 8-bit numbers representing values from 0 to 1 should be another 8-bit number representing the same range. In other words, since each 8-bit quantity has a built-in scale of 255, we must divide their 16-bit product by 255 to get it to the correct 8-bit range. Including rounding into the mix gives, in C syntax:

```
prod(a,b)
    {return (a*b+128)/255;}
```

In Chapter 19, "Three Wrongs Make a Right," of *Jim Blinn's Corner: Dirty Pixels*, I discussed ways that you can avoid the explicit division. The basic idea is to use the fact that $1/255 \approx 257/65,536$ and do the division by 65,536 with a 16-bit right shift. This gives us

```
prod(a,b)
    {return ((a*b+128)*257)>>16;}
```

There are some subtleties about why this works. Look at the original article for details.

If you are operating on a machine where multiplies aren't cheap (like a Classic Pentium with its 10-cycle multiply) you can multiply by 257 (hexadecimal 101) with shifts and adds. This also allows the entire operation to fit into 16-bit arithmetic, a fact we will exploit later. The code is

```
prod(a,b)
    {temp = a*b+128;
     return (temp+(temp>>8))>>8;}
```

### All Together Now

The net calculation to be performed on each component is

```
temp = F.a^0xFF                 // calc 1-F.a
C.i=clamp(F.i+prod(temp,B.i))
```

# The MMX Implementation

Now let's see how the MMX hardware can do some of this in parallel. This is by no means a complete description of MMX. You can get more details from Intel's Web site.[2] You can also get a quick overview from a recent *CACM* article[3] that straight-facedly refers to the process we are doing here as "image compositing [sic]." True, I myself wrote a column called "Compositing" (IEEE *CG&A*, Nov. 1994) but that was a *joke*.

I'll describe here just those MMX instructions we need for this project. The MMX engine has eight 64-bit registers named mm0 through mm7. Instructions that operate on these registers (or on 8-byte memory quadwords) can treat them as either two independant 32-bit values (doublewords), four 16-bit values (words), or eight 8-bit values (bytes). This latter seems ideally suited to our needs. We can store two whole RGBα pixels in a single MMX register and perform arithmetic on these two pixels, with all four components, in one MMX instruction. This is despite the outrageous statement in Peleg, et al., that "MMX technology can process two of these complete pixels simultaneously but wastes the operations on alpha components." Pardon me, but arithmetic on alpha is *not* wasted.

### Addition

There are two addition opcodes we will use. One adds four 16-bit operands in parallel. We'll use it in the shift/add calculation. The opcode is

**paddw *dest,source***          add word

The other opcode adds eight 8-bit numbers. We will use this to do the final addition of two scaled background pixels to two foreground pixels. There are various versions, but we will use the one that does saturation clamping as described above. The opcode is

**paddusb *dest,source***          add byte saturated

2  *www.intel.com/design/MMX/manuals/INDEX.HTM*

3  Peleg, A., Wilkie, S., and Weiser, U., "Intel MMX for Multimedia PCs," *CACM*, Vol. 40, No. 1, January 1997, pp. 25–38.

By the way, the Peleg article comes up with another weird comment justifying saturation arithmetic for Gouraud shading: "calculations may start to overflow . . . a dark polygon being shaded toward black may suddenly start having white pixels." Well, it's my humble opinion that if you are getting overflow during Gouraud shading, you are doing something seriously wrong.

## Logical Operations

MMX has a typical complement of boolean and shift operations for each of the three data formats, as well as an 8-byte (quadword) move instruction. We will need the following:

| | | |
|---|---|---|
| **movq** | *dest,src* | move quadword |
| **pxor** | *dest,src* | exclusive-or |
| **psrld** | *dest,count* | shift doubleword right |
| **psrlw** | *dest,count* | shift word right |

## Multiplication

The scaled, rounded multiply operation represented by prod(a,b) is fundamental to any 8-bit pixel arithmetic. It would be nice if there were an 8-byte parallel multiply that did this directly. No such luck. The only multiply available in MMX operates on four 16-bit value pairs in parallel giving four 16-bit results. Since the result of each 16-bit multiply is a 32-bit value, there are actually two opcodes. One calculates the upper half of the result, and one calculates the lower half:

| | | |
|---|---|---|
| **pmulhw** | *dest,src* | multiply word, keep high |
| **pmullw** | *dest,src* | multiply word, keep low |

We must now build the prod(a,b) operation out of these existing instructions. Since the available multiply takes 16-bit inputs, we can operate on only one pixel at a time (unpacked from 8-bit to 16-bit components). I have found three ways to do this, but only two of them work.

The first, shortest, neatest—but nonworking—way uses the keep-high version of the multiply to do the division by 65,536:

```
ROUND=0x0080 0080 0080 0080
N257 =0x0101 0101 0101 0101
pmullw mm3,mm1        four products
paddw  mm3,ROUND      add 128
pmulhw mm3,N257       times 1/255
```

Unfortunately, this does not work because MMX only provides a *signed* multiply. Since pixel values are only positive, what we want is an *unsigned* multiply. This is a shame since this would be a *very* often used idiom.

The second technique simulates an unsigned multiply by subtracting a magic constant (0x8000) before the multiply and adding 257 times the constant (0x808000) after the multiply. But this latter value needs both the high and low result, which we don't get with one instruction. If we multiply by 257*2, the second constant becomes 0x1010000. Just keep the high part and then shift right. We can also merge adding the initial 0x8000 with the rounding constant. Confusing? Yes. But it works. The net result is the five instructions:

```
x8080=0x8080 8080 8080 8080
x0202=0x0202 0202 0202 0202
pmullw mm3,mm1          four products
paddw  mm3,x8080        add bias
pmulhw mm3,x0202        times 514
paddw  mm3,N257         plus bias*514
psrlw  mm3,1            over 2
```

I chose not to use this technique, however, since it makes the instruction pairing (to be done later) a *lot* harder.

The actual technique I used in the final code is the shift-and-add method from my earlier IEEE column, which conveniently can be done using 16-bit arithmetic. In MMX code:

```
ROUND=0x0080 0080 0080 0080
pmullw mm3,mm1          product
paddw  mm3,ROUND        product+128=Pr
movq   mm5,mm3          Pr
psrlw  mm5,8            Pr>>8
paddw  mm5,mm3          Pr+(Pr>>8)
psrlw  mm5,8            (Pr+(Pr>>8))>>8
```

## Packing/Unpacking

Finally, there are a whole bunch of instructions for converting back and forth between byte, word, and doubleword formats. Instead of a detailed description of exactly what each of these does, I'll refer you to the comments in the code in Listing 7.1 for a sort of diagrammatic description. I'll give a brief overview here.

To convert four of the eight 8-bit values in a register to four 16-bit values, you can use

```
punpcklbw     unpack low bytes to word
punpckhbw     unpack high bytes to word
```

To go the other way, converting two registers each containing four 16-bit values to one register containing eight 8-bit values, you use

**packuswb**          pack words to byte

Finally, we'll use a trick with the word-unpacking instructions. If the source and destination operands are the same, this replicates the alpha component through the register. The opcodes are

**punpcklwd**          unpack low words to doubleword
**punpckhwd**          unpack high words to doubleword

# The Base Code

Listing 7.1 shows my basic implementation of the *over* operation between two buffers of pixels. Each iteration through the loop processes two pixels. For later reference, I have numbered each loop instruction using a notation that shows the destination register, a dot, and an instruction sequence number.

Listing 7.1 Straightforward code

```
// Array Over
// operates on pairs of pixels at once
// each pair stored in a quadword
//   (C,D) = (G,F) over (A,B)
//
    xor ebx,ebx          // offset for the three pointers
    mov edx,GF           // edx -> destination
    mov edi,GF           // edi -> Foreground source
    mov esi,AB           // esi -> Background source
    mov ecx,cPxls        // ecx = loop count

    static __int64 ZERO =0x0000 0000 0000 0000;
    static __int64 ROUND=0x0080 0080 0080 0080;
    static __int64 MASK =0x0000 00FF 0000 00FF;

loopb:
    movq mm1,[edi+ebx]   // 1.01 mm1= Ga Gb Gg Gr Fa Fb Fg Fr
    psrld mm1, 24        // 1.02 mm1= 0000 00Ga 0000 00Fa
    pxor mm1,MASK        // 1.03 mm1= 0000 1-Ga 0000 1-Fa
    movq mm2,mm1         // 2.04 mm2= 0000 1-Ga 0000 1-Fa
    punpcklwd mm1,mm1    // 1.05 mm1= 0000 0000 1-Fa 1-Fa
```

```
punpckhwd mm2,mm2      // 2.05 mm2= 0000 0000 1-Ga 1-Ga
punpcklwd mm1,mm1      // 1.06 mm1= 1-Fa 1-Fa 1-Fa 1-Fa
punpcklwd mm2,mm2      // 2.06 mm2= 1-Ga 1-Ga 1-Ga 1-Ga
movq mm3,[esi+ebx]     // 3.04 mm3= Aa Ab Ag Ar Ba Bb Bg Br
movq mm4,mm3           // 4.05 mm4= Aa Ab Ag Ar Ba Bb Bg Br
punpcklbw mm3,ZERO     // 3.06 mm3= 00Ba  00Bb  00Bg  00Br
punpckhbw mm4,ZERO     // 4.06 mm4= 00Aa  00Ab  00Ag  00Ar
pmullw mm3,mm1         // 3.07 mm3= (1-Fa)*B
pmullw mm4,mm2         // 4.07 mm4= (1-Ga)*A
paddw mm3,ROUND        // 3.08 mm3= (1-Fa)*B+128=FBr
paddw mm4,ROUND        // 4.08 mm4= (1-Ga)*A+128=GAr
movq  mm5,mm3          // 5.09 mm5=  FBr
movq  mm6,mm4          // 6.09 mm6=  GAr
psrlw mm5,8            // 5.10 mm5=  FBr>>8
psrlw mm6,8            // 6.10 mm6=  GAr>>8
paddw mm5,mm3          // 5.11 mm5=  FBr+(FBr>>8)
paddw mm6,mm4          // 6.11 mm6=  GAr+(GAr>>8)
psrlw mm5,8          // 5.12 mm5= (FBr+(FBr>>8)>>8)= 00Sa 00Sb 00Sg 00Sr
psrlw mm6,8          // 6.12 mm6= (Gar+(GAr>>8)>>8)= 00Ta 00Tb 00Tg 00Tr
packuswb mm5,mm6       // 5.13 mm5= Sa Sb Sg Sr Ta Tb Tg Tr
paddusb mm5,[edi+ebx]// 5.14 mm5= Ca Cb Cg Cr Da Db Dg Dr
movq [edx+ebx],mm5    // 5.15 store
add ebx,8             //      increment index
dec ecx               //      decrement loop counter
jg  loopb             //      loop
```

# Squeezing Out the Air

Now for some real fun. In addition to the data parallelism of the MMX instructions, the Pentium CPU can execute two of these instructions simultaneously if certain constraints are met. Some of the necessary conditions for two instructions to be paired are

- The second does not depend on the results of the first.
- Only one shift instruction is allowed (this includes pack and unpack instructions).
- Only one memory reference is allowed, and it must be the first of the pair.
- Only one multiply is allowed.

Each instruction, paired or not, takes only one cycle unless some condition causes the pipeline to stall. Criteria for avoiding pipeline stalls include

- The result of a multiply cannot be referenced until the third clock cycle after the instruction.

- Storing a register to memory can only happen on the second clock cycle after it is calculated.

Keeping track of all these conditions is a real pain, but fortunately Intel has a wonderful tool called VTune[4] that can examine your code and inform you of pairing and stalling problems.

The next stage of the game, then, is to shuffle the order of the instructions to achieve maximum pairing and remove stalls. I also had some help from David Shade of Intel in this exercise. Simply passing the raw code through VTune is pretty discouraging. Part of the problem is that there are 12 pack/unpack/shift instructions in the loop that won't pair. Simply exchanging instructions that do not have data dependencies gives only limited improvement. We can get a real boost, however, by looking at the instruction sequence according to Table 7.1. This table correlates with the instruction numbering in Listing 7.1. Each column represents the contents of one register, and each row is one (potentially concurrent) step of the algorithm. The shaded regions indicate steps where the register contents are valid. The notation (*) stands for the previous contents of a register.

The unusually interesting shape of this table suggests that we can make the algorithm into a fugue. Musically, a fugue is like a round, as in "Row, row, row your boat." Algorithmically, we are going to make the loop operate on registers mm3 through mm6 for the current iteration while setting up mm1 and mm2 for the next iteration. Think of slicing Table 7.1 through the middle and overlaying the top half on the bottom half. The way I did this in practice was as follows: Take some instructions from the top of the loop and move them to the bottom, adjusted to index the next pixel (as well as putting another copy in an initialization prolog before the loop begins). Then percolate these bottom-of-loop instructions back earlier in the loop to fill in the holes left by unpairable or stalling instructions from the current iteration cycle. Keep passing this through VTune and moving more instructions until you fill in all the pipeline gaps.

Listing 7.2 is my best reshuffling of the 30 instructions to achieve maximum pairing and minimal stalls. Instructions that refer to the next loop have a + flag in the comment field. The pairing is complete; every successive pair of instructions executes in one cycle. The only slight snag is

---

4  *http://developer.intel.com/software/products/vtune/index.htm*

**Table 7.1** *Register history during algorithm*

| | mm1 | mm2 | mm3 | mm4 | mm5 | mm6 |
|---|---|---|---|---|---|---|
| 01 | (G,F) | | | | | |
| 02 | Ga    Fa | | | | | |
| 03 | 1-Ga   1-Fa | | | | | |
| 04 | *copy →* | 1-Ga   1-Fa | (A,B) | | | |
| 05 | 0,0,1-Fa,1-Fa | 0,0,1-Ga,1-Ga | *copy →* | (A,B) | | |
| 06 | 1-Fa *4 times* | 1-Ga *4 times* | Ba,Br,Bg,Bb | Aa,Ar,Ab,Ag | | |
| 07 | | | (1-Fa)*B | (1-Ga)*A | | |
| 08 | | | (*)+128=FBr | (*)+128=GAr | | |
| 09 | | | *copy →* | *copy →* | FBr | GAr |
| 10 | | | | | FBr>>8 | GAr>>8 |
| 11 | | | | | FBr+(*) | GAr+(*) |
| 12 | | | | | (*)>>8=S | (*)>>8=T |
| 13 | | | | | (S,T) | |
| 14 | | | | | (C,D) | |
| 15 | | | | | store | |

that instruction 5.15 has a one-cycle stall since it is storing a value to memory that was calculated on the previous cycle. More work might eliminate this but, as it stands, the loop theoretically takes 16 cycles, or 8 cycles per pixel. My best implementation using conventional instructions (albeit in optimized C) takes 37 cycles/pixel on a Pentium, and 19 on a Pentium Pro.

On a 200 MHz machine, MMX could theoretically composite 25 million pixels per second. That's the equivalent of compositing two full 1024×1024 screens 24 times per second. This sounds pretty good. *But...*

Listing 7.2 Final code

```
#include "pixel32.h"
///////////////////////////////////////////////////////
// Array Over
// operates on pairs of pixels at once
// each pair stored in a quadword
//   (C,D) = (G,F) over (A,B)
///////////////////////////////////////////////////////

void OverArrayMMX(Pixel32 F[], Pixel32 B[], int cPxls)
{
static __int64 MASK =0x000000FF000000FF;
static __int64 ROUND=0x0080008000800080;
```

```
__asm push ebx
__asm push ecx
__asm push edx

__asm xor ebx, ebx              // offset for the three pointers
__asm mov edx,F                 // edx -> destination
__asm mov edi,F                 // edi -> Foreground source
__asm mov esi,B                 // esi -> Background source
__asm mov ecx,cPxls             // ecx = loop count

//  prolog: prime the pump
//
__asm pxor mm0,mm0              // mm0 = 0000 0000 0000 0000
__asm movq mm7,MASK             // mm7 = 000000FF  000000FF

__asm movq mm1,[edi+ebx]        // 1.01 mm1= Ga Gb Gg Gr Fa Fb Fg Fr
__asm psrld mm1, 24             // 1.02 mm1= 0000 00Ga 0000 00Fa
__asm pxor mm1,MASK             // 1.03 mm1= 0000 1-Ga 0000 1-Fa
__asm movq mm2,mm1              // 2.04 mm2= 0000 1-Ga 0000 1-Fa
__asm punpcklwd mm1,mm1         // 1.05 mm1= 0000 0000 1-Fa 1-Fa
__asm punpckhwd mm2,mm2         // 2.05 mm2= 0000 0000 1-Ga 1-Ga
__asm punpcklwd mm1,mm1         // 1.06 mm1= 1-Fa 1-Fa 1-Fa 1-Fa
__asm punpcklwd mm2,mm2         // 2.06 mm2= 1-Ga 1-Ga 1-Ga 1-Ga

__asm movq mm3,[esi+ebx]        // 3.04 mm3= Aa Ab Ag Ar Ba Bb Bg Br
__asm movq mm4,mm3              // 4.05 mm4= Aa Ab Ag Ar Ba Bb Bg Br
__asm punpcklbw mm3,mm0         // 3.06 mm3=  00Ba  00Bb  00Bg  00Br

__asm shr ecx, 1 // divide loop counter by 2; pixels are processed in pairs
__asm dec ecx    //  do one less loop to correct for prolog/postlog
__asm jz skip    //      if original loop count=2

loopb:
__asm punpckhbw mm4,mm0         // 4.06 mm4=  00Aa  00Ab  00Ag  00Ar
__asm pmullw mm3,mm1            // 3.07 mm3=  (1-Fa)*B

__asm movq mm1,[edi+ebx+8]      //+1.01 mm1= Ga Gb Gg Gr Fa Fb Fg Fr
__asm pmullw mm4,mm2            // 4.07 mm4=  (1-Ga)*A

__asm psrld mm1, 24             //+1.02 mm1= 0000  Ga 0000  Fa
__asm add ebx,8                 //      increment offset
```

```
__asm paddw mm3,ROUND          // 3.08 mm3=   prod+128=FBr
__asm pxor mm1,mm7             //+1.03 mm1=  0000 1-Ga 0000 1-Fa

__asm paddw mm4,ROUND          // 4.08 mm4=   prod+128=Gar
__asm movq mm2,mm1             //+2.04 mm2=  0000 1-Ga 0000 1-Fa

__asm movq mm5,mm3             // 5.09 mm5=   FBr
__asm punpcklwd mm1,mm1        //+1.05 mm1=  0000 0000 1-Fa 1-Fa

__asm movq mm6,mm4             // 6.09 mm6=   GAr
__asm punpckhwd mm2,mm2        //+2.05 mm2=  0000 0000 1-Ga 1-Ga

__asm psrlw mm5,8              // 5.10 mm5=   FBr>>8
__asm dec ecx                  //        decrement loop counter

__asm psrlw mm6,8              // 6.10 mm6=   GAr>>8
__asm paddw mm5,mm3            // 5.11 mm5=   FBr+(FBr>>8)

__asm paddw mm6,mm4       // 6.11 mm6=   GAr+(GAr>>8)
__asm psrlw mm5,8         // 5.12 mm5= (FBr+(FBr>>8))>>8)= 00Sa 00Sb 00Sg 00Sr

__asm movq mm3,[esi+ebx] //+3.04 mm3= Aa Ab Ag Ar Ba Bb Bg Br
__asm psrlw mm6,8         // 6.12 mm6= (Gar+(GAr>>8))>>8)= 00Ta 00Tb 00Tg 00Tr

__asm movq mm4,mm3             //+4.05 mm4=  Aa Ab Ag Ar Ba Bb Bg Br
__asm packuswb mm5,mm6         // 5.13 mm5=  Ta Tb Tg Tr Sa Sb Sg Sr

__asm paddusb mm5,[edi+ebx-8]// 5.14 mm5=  Ca Cb Cg Cr Da Db Dg Dr
__asm punpcklwd mm1,mm1        //+1.06 mm1=   1-Fa  1-Fa  1-Fa  1-Fa

__asm movq [edx+ebx-8],mm5    // 5.15 store
__asm punpcklwd mm2,mm2        //+2.06 mm2=   1-Ga  1-Ga  1-Ga  1-Ga

__asm punpcklbw mm3,mm0        //+3.06 mm3=   00Ba  00Bb  00Bg  00Br
__asm jg  loopb                //        loop
//
// loop postlog, drain the pump
//
skip:
__asm punpckhbw mm4,mm0        // 4.06 mm4=  00Aa  00Ab  00Ag  00Ar
__asm pmullw mm3,mm1           // 3.07 mm3=  (1-Fa)*B
__asm pmullw mm4,mm2           // 4.07 mm4=  (1-Ga)*A
```

```
__asm paddw mm3,ROUND              // 3.08 mm3=  prod+128=FBr
__asm paddw mm4,ROUND              // 4.08 mm4=  prod+128=Gar
__asm movq  mm5,mm3                // 5.09 mm5=  FBr
__asm movq  mm6,mm4                // 6.09 mm6=  GAr
__asm psrlw mm5,8                  // 5.10 mm5=  FBr>>8
__asm psrlw mm6,8                  // 6.10 mm6=  GAr>>8
__asm paddw mm5,mm3                // 5.11 mm5=  FBr+(FBr>>8)
__asm paddw mm6,mm4                // 6.11 mm6=  GAr+(GAr>>8)
__asm psrlw mm5,8    // 5.12 mm5= (FBr+(FBr>>8)>>8)= 00Sa 00Sb 00Sg 00Sr
__asm psrlw mm6,8    // 6.12 mm6= (Gar+(GAr>>8)>>8)= 00Ta 00Tb 00Tg 00Tr
__asm packuswb mm5,mm6             // 5.13 mm5= Sa Sb Sg Sr Ta Tb Tg Tr
__asm paddusb mm5,[edi+ebx]        // 5.14 mm5= Ca Cb Cg Cr Da Db Dg Dr
__asm movq [edx+ebx],mm5           // 5.15 store
//
// really done now
//
__asm EMMS
__asm pop edx
__asm pop ecx
__asm pop ebx
}
```

# Not So Fast

The MMX loop doesn't really go that fast. The fly in the ointment is memory bandwidth. And tricks that allow us to ease this bottleneck are hard to do on MMX.

### Memory Bandwidth

The acronym RAM is supposed to mean random access memory. It doesn't anymore. Random access means that it should take the same amount of time to access *any* byte of memory. With modern memory hierarchies consisting of two-level caches and the like, memory access time strongly depends on whether the desired memory is already in the cache, and this depends on the addressing pattern of your accesses.

For MMX instructions, if the referenced memory is in the cache, the instruction takes no longer than if it was in a register. That's why I was able to access the ROUND constant with no extra delay. Memory accesses can introduce stalls for other reasons though. That's why I put the constants ZERO and MASK into registers mm0 and mm7.

If a memory location is not in cache, however, the CPU must wait for it to be brought in from main memory. In our case, this is the likely situation since frame buffer–sized blocks of memory won't fit into the cache. The bad news is that a memory access can take upwards of *100 cycles*. You do, however, retrieve 32 bytes per memory access, so the 100-cycle delay costs 12.5 cycles per pixel access. If the destination buffer is the same as one of the two source buffers, there are only two pixel accesses per loop, so the memory access overhead could be as much as 25 cycles per pixel. It's not quite that bad since there is some overlap between memory retrieval and CPU execution. Some rough timings I've done with the Listing 7.2 code indicate that the worst-case memory access overhead adds more like 10 cycles per pixel to the CPU cycle count. On large buffers, this narrows the gap between MMX and conventional processing. Per pixel, MMX takes about 20 cycles, conventional Pentium about 47 cycles, and Pentium Pro about 29. These numbers are only approximate though since my timing tests currently aren't very rigorous.

## Testing Special Cases

There is another way to speed up this calculation that I described in Chapter 16, "Compositing—Theory" of *Jim Blinn's Corner: Dirty Pixels*. It's based on the observation that, for a typical image being composited into a frame buffer, most of the pixels have an alpha of zero (the outer transparent region) or one (the inside of the object). Fractional values typically only occur around the antialiased edges of the object. It's therefore a big win mathematically to test for 0 and 1 and skip the arithmetic for these special cases. It's an even bigger win given our problems with cache coherence since parts of the background buffer sometimes don't need to be touched in the special cases.

There are various variants of this economization, depending on whether you are compositing front to back or back to front, and depending on whether you allow glowing pixels. The version I tested was back to front with no glows. The algorithm is

```
if      (F.a==1) B=F;
else if(F.a!=0) B=F+(1-F.a)*B;
//else           leave B alone
```

I coded this with non-MMX instructions and applied it to a buffer with mostly 1s and 0s for `F.a`. The result was a bit faster (an average of 15 cycles per pixel) than blindly applying the MMX code to the whole buffer (20 cycles). If the foreground object had a lot of transparency, though, the MMX version would win.

So how about the best of both worlds? Doing special-case testing with parallelized MMX instructions is a nuisance or downright impossible. The ultimate algorithm would preprocess the foreground object into spans of F.a=0, F.a=1, and F.a=*fraction* and apply the appropriate code to each span.

# Observations

MMX certainly helps, but only in very regular algorithms. Any sort of special-case testing dilutes its usefulness. Small, easily programmed loops provide little opportunity for instruction pairing and require clever programming.

Speeding up one part of a calculation just makes something else into the bottleneck. Using conventional Pentium instructions, the bottleneck was the 10-cycle multiply. With MMX and four multiplies in one cycle, it's memory bandwidth. If we can do more to the pixels once we've hauled them out of memory, we will win.

Too many of the instructions in the code are data format conversions; it spends most of its time packing and unpacking data. This is not unique to MMX code; conventional pixel processing code has a similar problem. This is an indication that the basic opcodes of the machine are not well matched to the problem.

I don't think we'll see compilers automatically generating MMX code any time soon, so there is still a need for human assembly language crafters. This makes me happy.

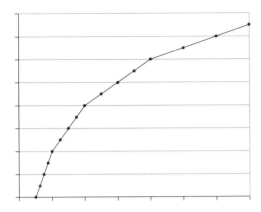

# CHAPTER EIGHT

# Floating-Point Tricks

JULY - AUGUST   1 9 9 7

"Oh, you work with computers? Gee, I can't even balance my checking account!"

Don't you just love it when some friend comes up with this one? So much of what we do with computers has nothing to do with arithmetic. Word processing, painting, stuff that even mathphobes can appreciate. But in the rendering game there's no substitute for nice juicy numbers. And what kinds of numbers are they?

There are basically two popular numeric types inside a computer, floating point and fixed point (which I have sometimes referred to as scaled integers). In my career of number crunching, I've oscillated back and forth between favoring each of them. My first available computer (a PDP-9) didn't have floating-point hardware, so I was motivated to use scaled integer representations. Then I played with an IBM 360 and floats were practical. When I got ahold of a PDP-11, floats were available but slow—back to integers. Then on to a VAX and floating point. When I moved to early PCs, it was back to scaled integers. Now that Pentia can do floating point fairly fast, it's float time. Finally, with MMX instructions, integers have come back into the fore. Gee, I wonder what will happen next?

Well, I recently learned about some interesting properties of the IEEE floating-point representation that sort of mixes the two. In order to see (and believe) how this works, I must first review this representation.

# IEEE Floating-Point Representation

The IEEE floating-point representation stores numbers in what amounts to scientific notation. Conventional scientific notation would write the number 3,485,000 in the form $3.485 \times 10^6$. This notation is not unique; we could, for example, use any of the following:

$$3,485,500 = 3.485 \times 10^6 = 0.3485 \times 10^7 = \text{etc.}$$

It is typical, however, to standardize on the version with one decimal digit to the left of the decimal point.

The IEEE floating-point version of scientific notation represents numbers similarly but with powers of two instead of ten. We would, for example, write

$$18_{10} = 1.001_2 \times 2^4$$
$$3.75_{10} = 1.111_2 \times 2^1$$

again standardizing on the version with one binary digit (bit) to the left of the binary point.

Next, being parsimonious about bits, the IEEE decided that it didn't necessarily need to store the 1 that is just to the left of the binary point since it's always 1. Only the fractional bits are stored in the low 23 bits of the floating-point value. The exponent of 2 is stored in the next 8 bits but offset with a bias of $127_{10}$. (This allows the exponent field to be treated as an unsigned integer but still be able to represent fractions less than one.) Finally, the sign bit takes up the remaining 1 bit. Some examples of this representation appear in Table 8.1.

# Opening the Box

Most programmers don't need to know about any of this detail. They can think of floating-point values as black boxes—subjects of mystery not to be tampered with by mere mortals. But we are not mere mortals, are we? Let's dive in.

### The Sign Bit

In Chapter 13, "Line Clipping," of *Jim Blinn's Corner: A Trip Down the Graphics Pipeline*, I opened the box for the first time. The operation in question was the creation of a bit mask that specifies which clipping planes need to be processed. This decision comes from calculating a floating-point value for each vertex and for each clipping plane. If the value is positive, the vertex is on the inside of the plane; if it's negative, it's on the

**Table 8.1** *Examples of IEEE floating point-representation*

| Float | Sign | Exponent | Fraction | Combined hexidecimal value |
|---|---|---|---|---|
| .625 | 0 | 01111110 | (1).01000000000000000000000 | 0x3F200000 |
| 1.0 | 0 | 01111111 | (1).00000000000000000000000 | 0x3F800000 |
| 2.0 | 0 | 10000000 | (1).00000000000000000000000 | 0x40000000 |
| 4.0 | 0 | 10000001 | (1).00000000000000000000000 | 0x40800000 |
| −13.75 | 1 | 10000010 | (1).10111000000000000000000 | 0xC15C0000 |

outside of the plane. A completely legal, nontricky way to generate the mask word would be

```
mask=0;
for (i=0,m=1; i<6;  ++i,m=m<<1)
    {if val[i]<0 mask |=m;}
```

This requires six floating-point tests, things that were unpleasantly slow on 1991 vintage PCs. Feeling brave, I constructed the six-bit mask by performing logical shifts on the sign bit of the floating-point words. I won't go into the details of the code, but I'll just scare you by saying that it required assembly language at that time. The important thing, though, is that no floating-point operations were required—just logical shifting and masking of the floating-point values as bit patterns. This sort of thing might seem exceedingly machine dependent, but let's face it, the IEEE isn't going to change their floating-point format any time soon. The only trap here is if a value happens to be minus zero (which has the perfectly reasonable representation 0x80000000) that should actually be treated as a positive number. I did get this to happen once due to some unfortuitous forward-differencing calculations. But on the whole the speed-up was worth the risk.

## The Rest of the Bits

Now let's get to the interesting part, tricky things we can do with the rest of the floating-point word. I am indebted to Steve Gabriel and Gideon Yuval here at MS Research for first pointing out to me the following amusing fact:

> If you only deal with positive numbers, the bit pattern of a floating-point number, interpreted as an integer, gives a piecewise linear approximation to the logarithm function.

**Table 8.2** *A 4-bit floating point number*

| Complete bit pattern | Exponent Bit field | Exponent Interpretation | Mantissa Bit field | Mantissa Interpretation | Floating-value represented |
|---|---|---|---|---|---|
| 0000 | 00 | $2^{-1}$ | 00 | $1.00_2 = 1.00_{10}$ | $1.00 \times 2^{-1} = 0.500$ |
| 0001 | | | 01 | $1.01_2 = 1.25_{10}$ | $1.25 \times 2^{-1} = 0.625$ |
| 0010 | | | 10 | $1.10_2 = 1.50_{10}$ | $1.50 \times 2^{-1} = 0.750$ |
| 0011 | | | 11 | $1.11_2 = 1.75_{10}$ | $1.75 \times 2^{-1} = 0.875$ |
| 0100 | 01 | $2^{0}$ | 00 | $1.00_2 = 1.00_{10}$ | $1.00 \times 2^{0} = 1.000$ |
| 0101 | | | 01 | $1.01_2 = 1.25_{10}$ | $1.25 \times 2^{0} = 1.250$ |
| 0110 | | | 10 | $1.10_2 = 1.50_{10}$ | $1.50 \times 2^{0} = 1.500$ |
| 0111 | | | 11 | $1.11_2 = 1.75_{10}$ | $1.75 \times 2^{0} = 1.750$ |
| 1000 | 10 | $2^{1}$ | 00 | $1.00_2 = 1.00_{10}$ | $1.00 \times 2^{1} = 2.000$ |
| 1001 | | | 01 | $1.01_2 = 1.25_{10}$ | $1.25 \times 2^{1} = 2.500$ |
| 1010 | | | 10 | $1.10_2 = 1.50_{10}$ | $1.50 \times 2^{1} = 3.000$ |
| 1011 | | | 11 | $1.11_2 = 1.75_{10}$ | $1.75 \times 2^{1} = 3.500$ |
| 1100 | 11 | $2^{2}$ | 00 | $1.00_2 = 1.00_{10}$ | $1.00 \times 2^{2} = 4.000$ |
| 1101 | | | 01 | $1.01_2 = 1.25_{10}$ | $1.25 \times 2^{2} = 5.000$ |
| 1110 | | | 10 | $1.10_2 = 1.50_{10}$ | $1.50 \times 2^{2} = 6.000$ |
| 1111 | | | 11 | $1.11_2 = 1.75_{10}$ | $1.75 \times 2^{2} = 7.000$ |

To show why this is true, I'll use a rather abbreviated version of the format with 2 bits for exponent and 2 bits for mantissa. See Table 8.2.

The first thing to notice about this is the fact that the bit pattern, interpreted as an integer, is a monotonic function of the floating-point value it represents. This means, for example, that when comparing two positive floating-point numbers, as floating-point numbers, you would get the same answer as comparing the two bit patterns as integers. In some situations, this could be handy, as for example, when floating-point comparisons are more expensive than integer comparisons (still the case on many machines), or when you have an integer parallel processor as with MMX. Remember that this only works when the numbers are positive. An article by Walt Donovan and Tim Van Hook in *Graphics Gems IV* explores doing this with negative numbers, too.[1]

---

1  Donovan, W., and Van Hook, T., "Direct Outcode Calculation for Faster Clip Testing," *Graphics Gems IV*, P. Heckbert, ed., AP Professional, Cambridge, Mass., 1994, pp. 125–131.

The next question to ask is, what is the monotonic function? Figure 8.1 plots our abbreviated numbers. Does this look familiar? It is, as I said, a piecewise linear approximation to a logarithm function. Each linear span connects two powers of two. By properly switching interpretations of a bit pattern between integer and float, we can come up with cheap but approximate exponential and logarithm functions.

Let's turn this into code. First, though, we will need to be able to swindle the compiler into changing the interpretation of a bit pattern between integer and float without actually doing a conversion. Two C functions that will work are

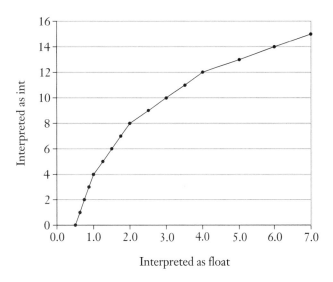

**Figure 8.1** *Integer vs. floating interpretation of bit pattern*

```
inline long int AsInteger(float   f) {return *(int  *)&f;}
inline float     AsFloat  (long int i) {return *(float*)&i;}
```

## Logarithm

Now let's do the logarithm function, in particular, the base 2 logarithm. This is essentially just **float(AsInteger(x))**, but there is a scale and offset we have to include to get it right. Referring to Table 8.3, we can see that if we subtract the bit pattern for 1.0 (as an integer), we will get the logarithm scaled up by 0x00800000. We simply need to divide by this quantity (as a floating value) and we're done. The code is

```
const long int OneAsInteger = AsInteger(1.0f);
const float     ScaleUp  = float(0x00800000);
const float     ScaleDwn = 1./ScaleUp;

float Alog2(float x){
    return float(AsInteger(x)-OneAsInteger) *ScaleDwn;}
```

**Table 8.3** *Bit patterns for base 2 logarithm*

| Float | Bit pattern | log₂ of float | Bit pattern − 0x3F800000 |
|-------|-------------|---------------|--------------------------|
| 1.0 | 0x3F800000 | 0.0 | 0x00000000 |
| 2.0 | 0x40000000 | 1.0 | 0x00800000 |
| 4.0 | 0x40800000 | 2.0 | 0x01000000 |

### Exponential (Power)

To get the exponential function—or, in this case, the function $y = 2^x$—we basically reverse the above calculation.

```
float Apow2(float x){
    return AsFloat(int(x*ScaleUp)+OneAsInteger);}
```

Note that this function works properly even for negative values of $x$.

Since the two factors **ScaleUp** and **ScaleDwn** are powers of two, it is possible to perform their multiplication by simply adding or subtracting from the exponent field of the floating-point number (again, in integer mode). I don't do this here because a typical application will actually require powers or logarithms to some base other than 2. The conversion formulas are

$$\frac{\log_2 x}{\log_2 y} = \log_y x$$

$$2^{x \log_2 y} = y^x$$

The conversion factor, $\log_2 y$, which is not a nice power of two, can be merged with the **ScaleUp** and **ScaleDwn** multiplication to generate functions for any desired base with the same number of operations as above.

### Fog

One typical graphics application where the exponential function approximation is likely to be accurate enough is fog simulation. In this case, the transparency of fog is given by

$$f = e^{-zd} = 2^{z(-d \log_2 e)}$$

where the fog density is $d$ and the distance from the eye is $z$. If the fog density is constant, this gives another case where the multiplication by the factor $(-d\log_2 e)$ can be merged with **ScaleUp**.

# Other Functions

**N**ow we can go nuts with approximations to many other functions that are popular in computer graphics. One general function that we like a lot is a simple power

$$x^p = 2^{p \log_2 x}$$

Express this with our approximation code and you get

```
float temp  = (AsInteger(x)-OneAsInteger)*ScaleDwn;
float power = AsFloat(int(p*temp*ScaleUp)+OneAsInteger);
```

The multiplications by **ScaleUp** and **ScaleDwn** cancel, and we can fold this together into

```
power = AsFloat( int(p*(AsInteger(x)-OneAsInteger))
            + OneAsInteger );
```

or

```
power = AsFloat(int(p*AsInteger(x)+(1-p)*OneAsInteger));
```

One could use this to evaluate the "cosine power" for Phong shading, but I think "cosine power" is such a bad way of modeling surface smoothness that I won't mention it further. Instead, let's see how this looks with several specific, but popular, values of $p$.

## Square Root

Here p = 1/2. This generates the code

```
sqrt = AsFloat((AsInteger(x)+OneAsInteger)/2);
```

In practice, however, we must guard against integer overflow in the above addition, so I divide by 2 (with a shift) before adding. Final code is

```
float Asqrt(float x){
    int i= (AsInteger(x)>>1)+(OneAsInteger>>1);
    return AsFloat(i);}
```

This is actually pretty weird. We are shifting the floating-point parameter, (exponent and fraction) right one bit. The low-order bit of the exponent shifts into the high-order bit of the fraction. But it works.

You can pull the expression (`OneAsInteger>>1`) out into a precalculated constant if your compiler is not smart enough to do it for you. I will not do that explicitly here or in the following code.

### Inverse

This is useful in doing perspective. In this case, $p = -1$. The code is

```
float Ainverse(float x){
    int i = -AsInteger(x) + 2*OneAsInteger;
    return AsFloat(i);}
```

This function also works properly for negative values of $x$.

### Inverse Square Root

This is useful to normalize vectors. Here $p = -1/2$. The raw code is

```
invsqt = AsFloat(int(-(1/2)AsInteger(x)+(3/2)*OneAsInteger));
```

Turning this into shifts gives us the code

```
float AinverseSqrt(float f){
    int i = (OneAsInteger +(OneAsInteger>>1)) -
(AsInteger(f)>>1);
    return AsFloat(i);}
```

You can polish this a bit by turning the **3/2*OneAsInteger** into a single compile-time constant, if the compiler doesn't do that for you already.

# Errors and Refinements

Well, how close are these approximations? Figure 8.2 gives a series of graphs of the relative error (correct minus approximation divided by correct). Each error curve will repeat itself at different horizontal scales to the right and left. We can see that worst-case relative error is about 10%.

One nice thing about these approximations is that they make good seeds for iterative refinement techniques. The most common such technique is Newton-Raphson iteration. Simply building one step of such an iteration into the function can improve the results considerably. Here are better versions of our three power functions using such a scheme.

```
float Binverse(float x){
    float y = Ainverse(x);
    return y*(2-x*y);}
```

```
float Bsqrt(float x){
    float y =   Asqrt(x);
    return (y*y+x)/(2*y);}

float BInverseSqrt(float x){
    float y = AInverseSqrt(x);
    return y*(1.5-.5*x*y*y);}
```

One might be tempted to replace the division in the square root refinement with a call to `Ainverse`. When I tried this, however, the error got worse than that from the original `Asqrt` function. The relative errors of these three improved functions are plotted as the lower curves in Figure 8.2.

I'll tantalize you a bit by mentioning that you can double the accuracy of the inverse square root function by modifying the correction calculation to

```
        return y*(1.47-.47*x*y*y);
```

That is what I actually showed in Figure 8.2. The explanation will have to wait for a later column though.

How about iterative improvement of the logarithm and exponential functions? Newton iteration effectively requires evaluation of the inverse of the function we are solving for, so it's really no help here. The following trick for the exponential function is due to Gideon Yuval. First, look at the relative errors in `Apow2` plotted in the upper curve of Figure 8.3. The maximum errors are at points halfway between integral parameter values. Near these points we could use the mathematical identity

$$2^x = 2^{x+1/2} \times 2^{-1/2}$$

That is, we could shift our evaluation to a region where the function is more

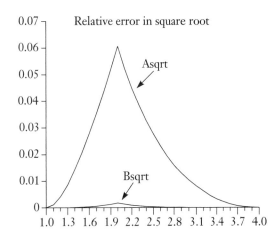

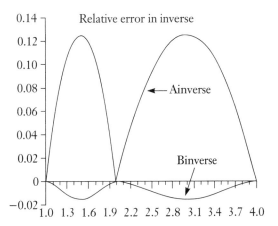

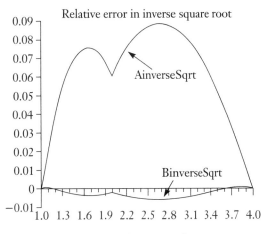

**Figure 8.2** *Relative errors for various functions*

accurate by adding one half to the parameter value and multiplying the result by a constant. But we don't really want to have to test parameter ranges and switch functions. A better plan is to calculate a sort of geometric mean between the two functions. This effectively uses the identity

$$2^x = 2^{x/2} \cdot 2^{(x/2+1/2)} \cdot 2^{-1/2}$$

Then approximate the right side with

$$2^x \approx \text{pow2}\left(x/2\right) \cdot \text{pow2}\left(x/2 + 1/2\right) \cdot c$$

and adjust the scale factor $c$ to spread the error fairly uniformly across the $x$ parameter range. Some numerical tests show that a good value is about 0.657. This gives the code

```
float Bpow2(float x) {
    return Apow2(x/2)*Apow2(x/2+.5)*.657;}
```

Of course, the halving of the parameter values can be absorbed into the ScaleUp constant within Apow2. The resultant relative error curve appears as the bottom curve in Figure 8.3.

A similar gimmick leads us to the improved version of the logarithm function:

```
float Blog(float x) {
    return .5*(Alog(x)+Alog(x*.6666))+.344;}
```

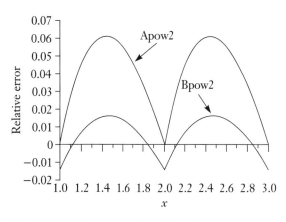

**Figure 8.3** *Relative errors of pow2 functions*

# Conclusion

For some quick-and-dirty approximations, it pays to be brave and open the magic floating-point box. There are also many other possible refinement techniques I haven't gone into here. You could, for example, try table lookups or other simple functions applied to the high few bits of the fraction. You just have to make sure your refined approximate solution doesn't wind up being slower than the original correct solution. I'm still interested in what other goodies can be extracted from this trick.

# CHAPTER NINE

# A Ghost in a Snowstorm

JANUARY - FEBRUARY 1998

There's a storm cloud growing on the horizon of the digital convergence between computer graphics and television/graphic arts. Computer graphics and image processing assume that pixel values are linearly related to light intensity. A typical video or paint image, however, encodes intensity nonlinearly. Most image manipulation software doesn't take this into account and just does arithmetic on the pixel values as though they were linearly related to light intensity. This is obviously wrong. The questions are how wrong, and for what pixel values is the problem worst and best?

Let's review the two basic concepts.

## Compositing

A full color pixel has four components: a transparency value, alpha, and three color primaries that are implicitly already multiplied by the alpha value:

$$\mathbf{F} = \begin{bmatrix} F_{red} & F_{green} & F_{blue} & F_{alpha} \end{bmatrix}$$

The most useful image-compositing operation, called *over*, simulates one partially transparent pixel in front of another. The *over* operation of a foreground **F** in front of a background **B** is defined as

$$\mathbf{F} \text{ over } \mathbf{B} \equiv \mathbf{F} + \left(1 - F_{alpha}\right)\mathbf{B}$$

Since each pixel component is treated identically, I will simplify by only dealing with the calculation of one component. I'll call a generic component of **F**, $f$; a generic component of **B**, $b$; and the alpha component of **F**, $a$. Our basic calculation is then

$$(f, a) \text{ over } b \equiv f + (1 - a)b$$

The parameters $a$ and $b$ can have values from 0 to 1. Since $f$ is premultiplied by $a$, we have $f \leq a$.

Some applications have occasion to composite images with nonpremultiplied colors. To distinguish this case, I'll call the generic *non*premultiplied color component $g$, with $g = f/a$. We then have another basic calculation:

$$(g, a) \text{ over } b \equiv ag + (1 - a)b$$

All these parameters, $f$, $g$, $a$, and $b$, are assumed linearly related to light intensity.

# Display Gamma

Light output from CRT display electronics is not linearly related to input voltage. The light intensity $I$ as a function of the voltage $V$ from the DACs on the display card is approximately

$$I = V^\gamma$$

This means that an 8-bit pixel value sent directly to a DAC does not encode intensity linearly.

Many people who generate images with painting programs just pick colors that look good in the final image, little knowing that they are implicitly generating pixel values with the gamma of their personal monitor burned into them. And different monitors have different values of gamma, explaining why an image created on one system might not look too good on another system. There are, however, standards for explicitly specifying the translation from linear light-intensity space to nonlinearly encoded pixel values. For example, for digital video, the algorithm to go from a "linear" representation f to a video pixel value p is

```
if(f<.018)    fTilde = f*4.50;
else          fTilde = 1.099*pow(f,.45) -.099;
p = round(fTilde*219 + 16);
```

On the computer side, a nonlinear encoding standard called *sRGB* uses a slightly different function. The exact algorithm is

```
if (f<.00304)     fTilde = f*12.92;
else              fTilde = 1.055*pow(f,1/2.4) -.055;
p = round(fTilde*255);
```

Both of these functions have small linear regions and shifted power function regions. The net result, however, is pretty close to a power function with a gamma of about 1/2.2 for sRGB, and 1/1.9 for video. See Figure 9.1.

Notice also that, in going to 8 bits, the video conversion uses a scale factor of 219, while sRGB uses a scale factor of 255. More information on this is available at *www.color.org/contrib/sRGB.html* or at *http://w3.hike.te.chiba-u.ac.jp/IEC/100/PT1966/parts/part2/1966_7a.pdf*.

This nonlinear encoding actually has an advantage in that it approximately models the perceptual space of the eye. When a nonlinearly encoded pixel is quantized into the typical 8-bit byte, the jumps between pixel values are roughly equal perceptually.

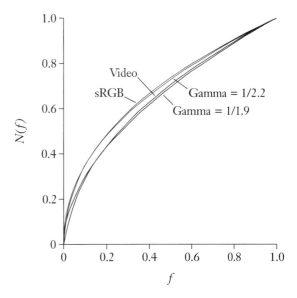

**Figure 9.1** *Typical nonlinearity functions*

# Linear/Nonlinear Notation

For notational convenience, I will use tildes ($\tilde{N}$) to identify stored pixel values that are nonlinearly related to light intensity. (Get it? A tilde is not a straight line.):

$$\tilde{f},\ \tilde{g},\ \tilde{a},\ \tilde{b}$$

This nonlinear encoding doesn't change the range of values of a pixel; all values, tilde or no, range in value from 0 to 1.

Referring to Figure 9.1, I will write the function that transforms a linear intensity value to a gamma-encoded value as $N$, for "Nonlinearize," so

$$\tilde{f} = N\left(f\right)$$

I will name the inverse of this function $L$, for "Linearize":

$$f = L\left(\tilde{f}\right)$$

Here are a few identities:

$$L(0) = 0; \; L(1) = 1$$
$$N(0) = 0; \; N(1) = 1$$

The following relation is precisely true only for pure power functions, but is close enough for real-world encoding functions:

$$L\left(\tilde{a}\,\tilde{b}\right) = L\left(\tilde{a}\right) L\left(\tilde{b}\right)$$
$$N\left(a\,b\right) = N\left(a\right) N\left(b\right)$$

Converting into and out of linear space was the subject of Chapter 5, "Dirty Pixels," of *Jim Blinn's Corner: Dirty Pixels*.

# The Good, the Bad, the Ugly

Let's now state the problem in algebraic terms, using the above notation. If we were given linearly encoded input pixel values, the calculation of the linearly encoded result is simple:

$$r = f + (1 - a)\,b$$

This, for example, is the calculation I optimized earlier, in Chapter 7.

On the other hand, if we are given input pixel values that are nonlinearly encoded, and we wish a nonlinearly encoded result, the calculation should first linearize all input quantities, do the calculation, and reencode (nonlinearize) the result:

$$\tilde{r} = N\left(L\left(\tilde{f}\right) + \left(1 - L\left(\tilde{a}\right)\right) L\left(\tilde{b}\right)\right)$$

This is basically the technique I presented in Chapter 17, "'Composting—Practice'" of *Jim Blinn's Corner: Dirty Pixels*. It's slower, but still accurate.

On the third hand, most image manipulation programs don't do this. This might be either because programmers are unaware of the problem or because they are scared of the necessary arithmetic. What they do is simply pretend the problem isn't there and calculate on the nonlinear pixel values as though they were linear. This means that they approximate the correct value with

$$\tilde{r}_{approx} = \tilde{f} + (1 - \tilde{a})\,\tilde{b}$$

So how bad is this? Let's see.

# Scenarios

Before getting into error analysis, I want to generalize a bit. There are actually several varieties of situations that can occur depending on the encoding format of the new foreground image. I will discuss four possibilities:

1. $(\tilde{f}, \tilde{a})$ over $\tilde{b}$. Both foreground color and transparency components are nonlinear. This is the example shown above.
2. $(\tilde{f}, a)$ over $\tilde{b}$. The alpha component is coded linearly. This might seem to make sense; since alpha represents the geometric coverage of a pixel, a display device–dependent alpha might seem wrong. As it turns out, this technique has many problems.
3. $(f, a)$ over $\tilde{b}$. Linear intensity and linear alpha. The foreground pixel might come from some algorithmic calculations such as antialiased lines or a 3D rendering system.
4. $(\tilde{g}, a)$ over $\tilde{b}$. Nonlinear nonpremultiplied foreground image. Both images might come from a scanner or paint program, while the alpha value comes from some algorithmically generated blending matte.

In each case, the correct result comes from linearizing any nonlinear input values, doing the calculation, and then renonlinearizing the result.

# Error Analysis

There will be three things we will want to know about each approximation:

- When is it correct?
- When is it the most incorrect?
- When are these inaccuracies most visible?

## When Correct?

The approximation is correct whenever

$$E \equiv \tilde{r}_{approx} - \tilde{r} = 0$$

You can usually just look at the formulas for $\tilde{r}_{approx}$ and $\tilde{r}$ and guess at some parameter ranges where the error is zero, usually at the extreme values of the parameters. A more general technique, though, is to solve for the surface defined mathematically by $E = 0$. This can be made less messy by approximating the $L$ function with $L(\tilde{x}) \approx \tilde{x}^2$. The resulting equation will be more algebraically tractable, and can give us hints at where the true error function is zero. I'll use this approximation to the $L$ function a lot, so I'll give it the name G2 to imply "Gamma = 2."

## Most Incorrect?

We can usually guess that the maximum error will be on a face or edge of the parameter space. This can reduce the calculation from a three-parameter ordeal to a one- or two-parameter cakewalk. When I solve for these, I will give them the names $E_+$ for the most positive error, and $E_-$ for the most negative error.

## Most Visible?

The worst possible situation for an approximation is when a transparent color is composited over a background of the same color. Ideally, the result should be the original background color. Mathematically, this situation is where

$$f + (1 - a)b = b$$

You can rearrange this to get

$$f/a = b \quad \text{or} \quad f = ab$$

(This makes sense intuitively since $f/a$ is the color of the foreground pixel with the transparency divided out.) Any errors in the approximation on the surface $f = ab$ will be the most visible. I'll denote errors on this surface as $E_v$.

# Scenario 1: $(\tilde{f}, \tilde{a})$ over $\tilde{b}$

The calculations we are comparing are

$$\tilde{r} = N\left(L(\tilde{f}) + (1 - L(\tilde{a}))\, L(\tilde{b})\right)$$
$$\tilde{r}_{approx} = \tilde{f} + (1 - \tilde{a})\tilde{b}$$

The possible values of $\tilde{f}$ and $\tilde{a}$ fill a triangle in the $\tilde{f}$ $\tilde{a}$ plane. The possible values of $\tilde{b}$ extrude this triangle into the third dimension. See Figure 9.2.

Where is the approximation correct? Well, plug $\tilde{a} = 1$ into $\tilde{r}$ and $\tilde{r}_{approx}$ and you see that they simplify down to the value $f$. This is not too surprising; if the foreground pixel is opaque, it completely replaces the background pixel with no error, even with the approximation.

Plug $\tilde{b} = 0$ into the expressions, and they also simplify to $\tilde{f}$. In other words, when compositing over a black background, the approximation always gets the right answer. So far so good.

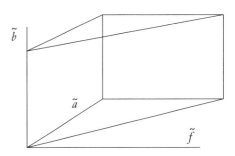

**Figure 9.2** *Parameter space for scenario 1*

To find the general case for zero error, we do the following trick. Equate $L(\tilde{r}) = L(\tilde{r}_{approx})$ to get

$$L(\tilde{f}) + (1 - L(\tilde{a})) L(\tilde{b}) = L(\tilde{f} + (1 - \tilde{a}) \tilde{b})$$

Now use the approximation that $L(\tilde{x}) \approx \tilde{x}^2$ to get

$$\tilde{f}^2 + (1 - \tilde{a}^2) \tilde{b}^2 = (\tilde{f} + (1 - \tilde{a}) \tilde{b})^2$$

A bunch of algebraic canceling and factoring, which I won't bore you with, gives us the equation of the general surface in $(\tilde{f}, \tilde{a}, \tilde{b})$ space where this approximate error is zero:

$$\tilde{b}(1 - \tilde{a})(\tilde{f} - \tilde{a}\tilde{b}) = 0$$

The first two factors are the conditions we knew already. The third, amazingly enough, is just our maximum visibility surface. In fact, plugging it back into the original error formula shows that it is accurate even for general $L$ functions. In other words, $\tilde{r} = \tilde{r}_{approx}$ at just the visual situations where errors would be most apparent, so

$$E_v = E(\tilde{a}\tilde{b}, \tilde{a}, \tilde{b}) = 0$$

Now let's try to find where the error is *worst* over the space of possible values of $(\tilde{f}, \tilde{a}, \tilde{b})$. In Figure 9.3, I've shaded in the three surfaces where the approximation is exact: $\tilde{b} = 0$ (the triangular floor), $\tilde{a} = 1$ (the back wall), and $\tilde{f} = \tilde{a}\tilde{b}$ (the twisting surface that sweeps from the $\tilde{a}$ axis to the $\tilde{f} = \tilde{a}$ edge at $\tilde{b} = 1$). This last surface divides the parameter

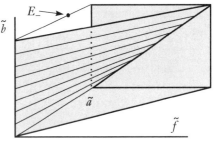

**Figure 9.3** *Zero error surfaces for scenario 1*

volume into two regions, one where the approximation is too high, and one where it's too low. The location of maximum errors will be on the walls farthest from this dividing surface. The largest negative error will be on the $\tilde{f} = 0$ wall; the largest positive error will be on the $\tilde{f} = \tilde{a}$ wall. Let's find these.

The largest negative error will be on the surface:

$$E\left(0, \tilde{a}, \tilde{b}\right) = \left((1 - \tilde{a})\,\tilde{b}\right) - N\left((1 - L(\tilde{a}))L(\tilde{b})\right)$$
$$= (1 - \tilde{a})\,\tilde{b} - N\left(1 - L(\tilde{a})\right)\tilde{b}$$
$$= \tilde{b}\left(((1 - \tilde{a}) - N\left(1 - L(\tilde{a})\right)\right)$$

The error is proportional to $\tilde{b}$, so it is largest where $\tilde{b} = 1$. We can approximate the worst possible value for $\tilde{a}$ along this parameter edge by using G2. This gives us

$$E\left(0, \tilde{a}, 1\right) \approx 1 - \tilde{a} - \left(1 - \tilde{a}^2\right)^{1/2}$$

Setting the derivative of this to zero and solving for $\tilde{a}$ gives us $\tilde{a} = \sqrt{1/2}$, with the error value itself being

$$E_- \approx E\left(0, \sqrt{1/2}, 1\right) \approx 1 - \sqrt{2} \approx -0.414$$

This is a pretty big error out of a total parameter range of 0 to 1! If these values are scaled to an 8-bit byte, the correct $r$ is 180, while the approximate calculation gives 75, for an error of $-105$.

Visually, this means that placing transparent black over white would result in a much darker value than it should. How bad could that be? Just looking at the resulting gray square, you wouldn't have any reference for what the correct value was. What's the worst possible visual effect this can produce?

One place where accurate tonal reproduction is important is in antialiasing. In Figure 9.4, I show an antialiased black line drawn with correct and approximate arithmetic. The approximate line is darker and appears too wide, and the antialiasing has been messed up. I won't vouch for the transfer function of the printing of this figure, but the approximate line looks mighty ropey on my monitor.

**Figure 9.4** *Correct (top), approximate (bottom)*

Next, the largest positive error of our approximation is on the front surface of the parameter space, where $\tilde{f} = \tilde{a}$. This represents various transparencies of white. The location of maximum error is harder to solve for explicitly, but with a little numerical experimentation I found the maximum problem at approximately

$$E_+ \approx E(0.3, 0.3, 0.37) \approx 0.559 - 0.463 = 0.096$$

The visual interpretation of this is that transparent white on a gray background will look too bright. Figure 9.5 shows a white line on a gray background. It's not so ropey as Figure 9.4 since the maximum error is much smaller.

**Figure 9.5**  *Correct (top), approximate (bottom)*

# Scenario 2: $\left(\tilde{f}, a\right)$ over $\tilde{b}$

This is just like scenario 1 but with the alpha component encoded linearly. I originally thought this was a good idea, advocating it in Chapter 17, "'Compositing'—Practice" of *Jim Blinn's Corner: Dirty Pixels*, but the more I've played with it the less I like it. The parameter space appears in Figure 9.6. The $\tilde{f} = \tilde{a}$ surface has become the curved surface $\tilde{f} = N(a)$.

The calculation is

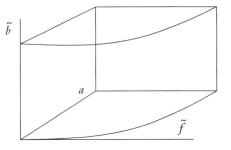

**Figure 9.6**  *Parameter space for scenario 2*

$$\tilde{r} = N\left(L\left(\tilde{f}\right) + (1-a) L(\tilde{b})\right)$$

$$\tilde{r}_{approx} = \tilde{f} + (1-a)\tilde{b}$$

Let's see what effects this coding has on the approximation error.

We again find the zero error surfaces by equating $\tilde{r} = \tilde{r}_{approx}$, applying $L$ to both sides, and using G2. Some algebra and the surfaces of zero error reveal themselves:

$$0 = \tilde{b}(1-a)\left(a\tilde{b} - 2\tilde{f}\right)$$

Once again, we get no error for compositing over a black background, ($\tilde{b} = 0$) or wherever the foreground object is opaque ($\tilde{a} = 1$). The third error-free surface term presents a problem, however. It shows that we no longer have the nice property of zero error where $f/a = b$. This means that it is possible to apply one transparent color over the same colored background and get a visible seam. We can find the worst-case situation by substituting $\tilde{f} = \tilde{a}\tilde{b} = N(a)\tilde{b}$ into the error calculation and get

$$E\left(N\left(a\right)\tilde{b},a,\tilde{b}\right)=\left(N\left(a\right)\tilde{b}+\left(1-a\right)\tilde{b}\right)-N\left(aL\left(\tilde{b}\right)+\left(1-a\right)L\left(\tilde{b}\right)\right)$$
$$=\left(N\left(a\right)\tilde{b}+\tilde{b}-a\tilde{b}\right)-\tilde{b}$$

So

$$E_v=\tilde{b}\left(N\left(a\right)-a\right)$$

The maximum error on this $\tilde{f}=\tilde{a}\tilde{b}$ surface is at $\tilde{b}=1$, $a\approx 1/4$. The visual interpretation of these parameter values is that we are painting a one-quarter transparent white over opaque white. The correct answer is, of course, white: $\tilde{r}=1$. The approximation, however, gives a value of $\tilde{r}_{approx}=5/4$. Wow! Not only is it too big, but it overflows beyond the range

**Figure 9.7** *Linear ghost: correct (top, invisible), approximate (bottom)*

0 to 1. Thus, the "ghost in a snowstorm" (transparent white over white) would be visible using the approximate calculation. Even opaque white over white causes problems if the edges are antialiased. The alphas of the pixels range from 0 outside the edge to 1 inside it. The error in the approximation, as calculated above, is zero for $a = 0$ and for $a = 1$, and maximal in between. The inside of the ghost is invisible, and the outside of the ghost is invisible; just the edges will show up. Figure 9.7 shows a (linear) ghost. I have here drawn light gray over light gray to avoid the overflow problem. I have also made the line thicker and slightly darker than the background so that it shows up for comparison purposes.

What other errors are there? The maximum negative error over the entire parameter space is still along the $\tilde{b}=1$, $\tilde{f}=0$ edge, where

$$E\left(0,a,1\right)=\left(1-a\right)-N\left(1-a\right)$$

Using G2, we can approximate the worst case at

$$E_-\approx E\left(0,1/4,1\right)\approx-0.116$$

Thus, a black antialiased line over a white background will look too dark and ropey, though not as much as with scenario 1. See Figure 9.8.

# Scenario 3: $\left(f,a\right)$ over $\tilde{b}$

**Figure 9.8** *Correct (top), approximate (bottom)*

This common scenario happens when a program generates the foreground image and alpha in linear space by some algorithmic process such as a 3D renderer. This is what happens when we try to overlay computer graphics on top of digital video, for example. The calculations are

$$\tilde{r} = N\left(f + (1-a)L\left(\tilde{b}\right)\right)$$

$$\tilde{r}_{approx} = f + (1-a)\tilde{b}$$

Our technique of finding the general zero-error surface generates a second-order expression that isn't factorable into three simple surfaces. Instead of pursuing this, let's look at a few key locations in parameter space to get an idea of the error shape.

Checking the edges of the parameter space, we find that the error is zero along the five edges:

$$\left(f, a, \tilde{b}\right) = \left(0, 0, \tilde{b}\right); \left(0, 1, \tilde{b}\right); \left(1, 1, \tilde{b}\right); \left(f, f, 1\right); \left(0, a, 0\right)$$

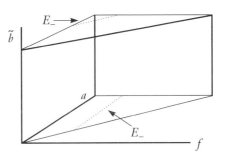

**Figure 9.9** *Zero-error edges and maximal error lines for scenario 3*

I've drawn these edges darkened in Figure 9.9.

Looking at the bottom face, $\tilde{b} = 0$, we discover that

$$E\left(f, a, 0\right) = f - N\left(f\right)$$

Use G2 to find an approximate maximum value of

$$E_- \approx E\left(1/4, a, 0\right) \approx -1/4$$

Note that this maximum error region is a line in parameter space rather than at just one point.

Drawing a white line over a black background will generate parameter values along the $f = a$; $\tilde{b} = 0$ edge that pass across this region and show a maximal problem. The error as a function of $a$ will be

$$E\left(a, a, 0\right) = a - N\left(a\right)$$

See Figure 9.10.

Next, on the top face of the parameter space, $\tilde{b} = 1$, we have

$$E\left(f, a, 1\right) = \left(f - a + 1\right) - N\left(f - a + 1\right)$$

Solving for the maximum error gives

$$E_- \approx E\left(f, f + 3/4, 1\right) \approx -1/4$$

**Figure 9.10** *Correct (top), approximate (bottom)*

Again, this maximum error region is a line in parameter space.

An antialiased black line over a white background generates parameter values that pass across this maximum error region. The error here is

$$E(0, a, 1) = (1 - a) - N(1 - a)$$

This is the same as the line in Figure 9.8.

Finally, let's look at the error on the maximum visibility surface $f = a b = a L(\tilde{b})$. Plug this into the error definition:

$$E_v = E\left(aL(\tilde{b}), a, \tilde{b}\right) = a\left(L(\tilde{b}) - \tilde{b}\right)$$

Thus the error will be maximum at approximately

$$E_{v_-} \approx E\left(1/4, 1, 1/2\right) \approx -1/4$$

Here again we have the "ghost in a snowstorm" effect by compositing dark gray over dark gray. See Figure 9.11. Here, though, the error is worst when $a = 1$, so the ghost appears as a darker body rather than as an outline.

**Figure 9.11** *Gray ghost: correct (top, invisible), approximate (bottom)*

# Scenario 4: $\left(\tilde{g}, a\right)$ over $\tilde{b}$

This scenario occurs when we blend two nonlinearly encoded images, such as painted or scanned images, with a linearly encoded matte. The calculation is

$$\tilde{r} = N\left(aL\left(\tilde{g}\right) + (1 - a)L\left(\tilde{b}\right)\right)$$

$$\tilde{r}_{approx} = a\tilde{g} + (1 - a)\tilde{b}$$

The error is zero at $a = 0$, $a = 1$, and at $\tilde{g} = \tilde{b}$. This last is also the maximum visibility surface for this scenario, so we get no ghost effects:

$$E_v = 0$$

These zero-error surfaces are colored gray in Figure 9.12.

The error is always negative wherever it is not zero. The locations of maximal error are along the edges shown in the figure. They are

$$E(1, a, 0) = a - N(a)$$

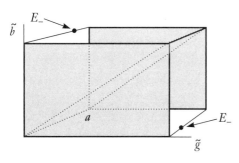

**Figure 9.12** *Parameter space for scenario 4*

and

$$E\left(0,a,1\right)=\left(1-a\right)-N\left(1-a\right)$$

Applying G2, we find that these are approximately at

$$E_{-}\approx E\left(1,1/4,0\right)\approx-1/4$$
$$E_{-}\approx E\left(0,3/4,1\right)\approx-1/4$$

Once again, the worst case is with white over black, or with black over white. The lines look the same as in Figures 9.8 and 9.10.

# What Do We Do about This?

I see three ways to deal with this situation, none of which is ideal:

1. *Live with the error as a real-time approximation to the correct image.*

   The problem with this is that many image-editing programs that do this approximation are not really real-time applications; the image is ultimately destined for a printer somewhere. These programs can very well afford to take the time to generate the correct image. Another problem with this cop-out in real-time systems is that moving images will look optimally bad because the antialiasing is defeated.

2. *Encode all pixels linearly and perform calculations in this space. Then, for display, translate to the appropriate nonlinear display space by using a hardware lookup table.*

   The main problem with this technique is that there is already an extensive library of nonlinearly encoded images (both stills and video). I have another objection to this, at least in the 8-bit arena, which has to do with quantization error. A lookup table that translates "linear" 8-bit pixels into 8-bit DAC inputs through a nonlinear table will, of necessity, map several pixel values at the low end into one output DAC value. As mentioned in *Jim Blinn's Corner: Dirty Pixels*, for a gamma of 2, only 194 distinct values will appear in the table. To preserve the same dark resolution as you have in nonlinear 8-bit encoding, you need at least a 17-bit fixed-point number. A better solution would be to use 16-bit fields for the "linear" representations, but to encode them as a supershort floating-point value.

3. *Linearize pixel values before doing calculation and unlinearize after you are done.*

   This is the slow but correct approach. Actually, depending on when you store the nonlinearized result, this approach merges with the previous one. The search for various ways to speed up the conversions could be a fruitful area for future research. In *Dirty Pixels*, I sped up the calculation as much as I could by using a table lookup for $L$ and a binary search for $N$. Another approach might be to use higher-order approximating functions that are more accurate but that stop short of doing exponential calculations, or by playing with the techniques described in Chapter 8 of this book.

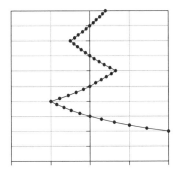

# CHAPTER TEN

# W Pleasure, W Fun

The whole point of doing 3D graphics is the third dimension. But since the screen is only 2D, the third dimension appears only indirectly in terms of perspective and occlusion. Correct occlusion testing is, however, fairly sensitive to precision problems in the depth calculation. In this chapter, I will review the traditional way to represent depth and introduce a new technique that appears in the new generation of 3D graphics boards. This technique has become practical as a side effect of perspective-correct texture-mapping hardware. Both ways have their good and bad points, so I'll finish up by establishing some rules of thumb on which to choose in a given situation.

## Mathematical Niceties

To simplify things a bit in this discussion, I'm not going to include the $y$ coordinates in any calculations. The problem can be adequately understood in terms of only the $x$, $z$, and $w$ coordinates, and the reduction in dimensionality will simplify things considerably.

Next, let's define our coordinate systems. There are three of interest to us:

1. *Eye space*: All objects are translated so that the eye is at the origin and is looking down the positive $z$ axis (this, incidentally, is a left-handed coordinate system).
2. *Perspective space*: This occurs after multiplying points in eye space by a homogeneous perspective transformation.

3. *Screen space*: This occurs after dividing out the $w$ component of the perspective space points.

Finally, there is the question of notation. A mathematical symbol can convey a lot of information if you give it a chance. The mathematical symbols I use here will designate coordinates of various points in various coordinate systems. The three things, then, that we want to explicitly convey are

- The name of the point
- The component ($x$, $z$, or $w$)
- The coordinate system

The symbology available to us consists of letters, subscripts, and other mathematical decorations applied to letters. I will use the following choices:

- The component will be designated by the main letter variable: $x$, $z$, or $w$.
- The coordinate system will be a decoration over the letter as follows:
    $x$ (a bare letter) means eye space
    $\hat{x}$ means perspective space before $w$ division
    $\tilde{x}$ means screen space (perspective space after $w$ division)
    Essentially, the number of wiggles over a letter tell how many transformations it has gone through.
- The name of the point will be a subscript.

For example, the $z$ coordinate of point 0 in perspective space will be denoted as $\hat{z}_0$. Any equations with coordinates that appear without subscripts will indicate generic relations that apply to all points.

# Traditional Perspective

I described the derivation of the homogeneous perspective matrix in Chapters 3 and 18 of *Jim Blinn's Corner: A Trip Down the Graphics Pipeline*. If we only consider the $x$, $z$, and $w$ components, a typical homogeneous perspective matrix looks like

$$\begin{bmatrix} a & 0 & 0 \\ 0 & b & d \\ 0 & c & 0 \end{bmatrix}$$

This gives the following generic relations between components in the various coordinate systems.

Eye to perspective:

$$\begin{bmatrix} x & z & 1 \end{bmatrix} \begin{bmatrix} a & 0 & 0 \\ 0 & b & d \\ 0 & c & 0 \end{bmatrix} = \begin{bmatrix} ax & bz+c & dz \end{bmatrix} = \begin{bmatrix} \hat{x} & \hat{z} & \hat{w} \end{bmatrix}$$

Perspective to screen:

$$\begin{bmatrix} \dfrac{\hat{x}}{\hat{w}} & \dfrac{\hat{z}}{\hat{w}} \end{bmatrix} = \begin{bmatrix} \tilde{x} & \tilde{z} \end{bmatrix}$$

or, composing these two:
   Eye to screen:

$$\begin{bmatrix} \dfrac{ax}{dz} & \dfrac{bz+c}{dz} \end{bmatrix} = \begin{bmatrix} \tilde{x} & \tilde{z} \end{bmatrix}$$

A key property of the homogeneous perspective transform is revealed when we examine what happens to a straight line segment in eye space when it is transformed into screen space. The line segment generated by linear interpolation between eye space endpoints $\begin{bmatrix} x_0 & z_0 \end{bmatrix}$ and $\begin{bmatrix} x_1 & z_1 \end{bmatrix}$ can be represented by the parametric equation

$$\begin{bmatrix} x_L & z_L \end{bmatrix} = \begin{bmatrix} x_0 + \alpha(x_1 - x_0) & z_0 + \alpha(z_1 - z_0) \end{bmatrix}$$

What does this shape transform into in screen space? Plug in the eye-to-screen transform equation and we get

$$\begin{bmatrix} \tilde{x}_L & \tilde{z}_L \end{bmatrix} = \begin{bmatrix} \dfrac{a\left(x_0 + \alpha(x_1 - x_0)\right)}{d\left(z_0 + \alpha(z_1 - z_0)\right)} & \dfrac{b\left(z_0 + \alpha(z_1 - z_0)\right) + c}{d\left(z_0 + \alpha(z_1 - z_0)\right)} \end{bmatrix}$$

At first, this might look fairly mysterious. Our shape is a parametric curve with the x and z coordinates generated by hyperbolic functions of $\alpha$. It never ceases to amaze me that plotting one hyperbola against the other yields . . . a straight line. Over the years, I have collected various ways to show this. The simplest is just to solve $\tilde{x}_L$ for alpha and plug that into the expression for $\tilde{z}_L$ to get a linear equation in $\tilde{x}_L$ and $\tilde{z}_L$. You can never have too many visualizations, however, so here is another one more appropriate for the current discussion. The exposition will be easier to manage if we write the expressions for $\tilde{x}_L$ and $\tilde{z}_L$ as

$$\tilde{x}_L = \frac{A + B\alpha}{E + F\alpha} \qquad\qquad \tilde{z}_L = \frac{C + D\alpha}{E + F\alpha}$$

The key thing to note is that both $\tilde{x}_L$ and $\tilde{z}_L$ have the same denominator. The reason this is significant is that it places the asymptotes of $\tilde{x}_L$ and $\tilde{z}_L$ at the same place: $\alpha = -F/E$. We can therefore move both asymptotes to the origin by changing the parameterization via the replacement:

$$\alpha' = E + F\alpha$$

Putting this into the equation gives

$$\tilde{x}_L = \frac{A + B\left(\dfrac{\alpha' - E}{F}\right)}{\alpha'} = \left(\frac{B}{F}\right) + \frac{1}{\alpha'}\left(\frac{AF - BE}{F}\right)$$

$$\tilde{z}_L = \frac{C + D\left(\dfrac{\alpha' - E}{F}\right)}{\alpha'} = \left(\frac{D}{F}\right) + \frac{1}{\alpha'}\left(\frac{CF - DE}{F}\right)$$

Now this is much more obviously the parametric equation of a straight line segment. And it brings up another important property: equally spaced points in eye space (equal steps in $\alpha$, and therefore in $\alpha'$) transform into nonequally spaced points in screen space (as evinced by the $1/\alpha'$ term). We'll make more of this later.

Anyway, we can now see that straight lines transform into straight lines and, more generally, flat polygons transform into flat polygons. This means that we can calculate values of $\tilde{z}$ at just the triangle vertices and linearly interpolate these values in screen space in order to find the proper value for depth comparisons. A depth buffer implementation of this would properly be called a $\tilde{z}$ buffer in our notation. Figures 10.1(a) and 10.1(b)

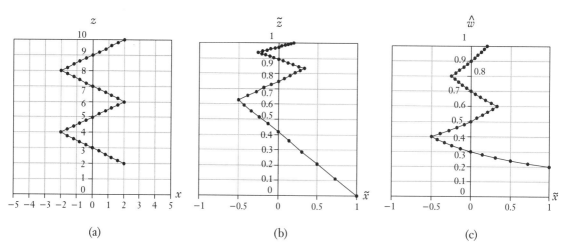

**Figure 10.1** *Transformation of straight lines in eye space: eye space (a), screen space (b), and $\hat{w}$ space (c)*

show the distortion induced on a couple of straight segments due to this perspective transform (ignore Figure 10.1(c) for now).

## $\tilde{z}$ resolution

Now it's time to bow to reality and take a look at some resolution issues. If we use the value of $\tilde{z}$ for depth comparisons, how does resolution in $\tilde{z}$ translate into resolution in eye space $z$? Start with the mapping from eye space $z$ to screen space $\tilde{z}$. We have, generically

$$\tilde{z} = \frac{bz + c}{dz} = \left(\frac{b}{d}\right) + \frac{1}{z}\left(\frac{c}{d}\right)$$

In other words, the $\tilde{z}$ coordinate is a scale and offset applied to one over the eye space $z$ coordinate. The values of the scale and offset will determine the range of values we expect to have to deal with for $\tilde{z}$. It is typical to specify these scales and offsets in terms of two depth values in eye space called $z$-near, $z_n$, and $z$-far, $z_f$, that will map to $\tilde{z}_n = 0$ and $\tilde{z}_f = 1$. A little brain exercise will show that, in order to make this happen, we must have

$$b = d\left(\frac{z_f}{z_f - z_n}\right)$$

$$c = d\left(\frac{-z_n z_f}{z_f - z_n}\right)$$

Putting these together gives the following, which I've written in a whole buncha different ways:

$$\tilde{z} = \frac{bz + c}{dz}$$

$$= \left(\frac{z_f}{z_f - z_n}\right) - \frac{1}{z}\left(\frac{z_n z_f}{z_f - z_n}\right)$$

$$= \left(\frac{z_f}{z_f - z_n}\right)\frac{z - z_n}{z}$$

$$= \frac{\frac{1}{z_n} - \frac{1}{z}}{\frac{1}{z_n} - \frac{1}{z_f}}$$

In a typical application, we would pick $z_n$ and $z_f$ to bracket our data in eye space $z$, set up the matrix appropriately, and throw a bunch of points down it, knowing we will get $\tilde{z}$ values between 0 and 1.

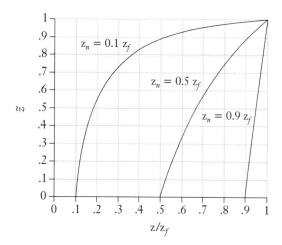

**Figure 10.2** *Distortion of $\tilde{z}$ for various values of $z_n$*

Figure 10.2 shows the mapping from eye space $z$ to screen space $\tilde{z}$ for various values of $z_n$ as a proportion of $z_f$. We note that if $z_n$ is much smaller than $z_f$, the values of $\tilde{z}$ are all smushed together near the value 1, a prospect that is dangerous to the health of our resolution. The recommended practice is to make $z_n$ as far from the eye as possible. This gives the more linear relationship of the curve at the right side of Figure 10.2. Now let's see explicitly how the choice of $z_n$ affects depth resolution.

Suppose we use a fixed-point representation for $\tilde{z}$. The values we can represent are equally spaced along the $\tilde{z}$ axis. That's all very nice, but it's physically more meaningful to see how these quantization bins look in eye space. We can find these by mapping equal steps in $\tilde{z}$ back to the $z$ axis. The different choices for $z_n$ from Figure 10.2 will give the different quantization spacings shown in Figure 10.3(a) using (for clarity) 16 quantization steps. You can see that a low value for $z_n$ gives a rather bad situation. Detail on objects that are far from the eye can all map into the same quantized $\tilde{z}$ value.

If we happen to use floating point for $\tilde{z}$, the situation is even worse. Here, our 16 quantization steps are more or less logarithmically spaced along $\tilde{z}$ in a way that spreads things out even more at large distances. Figure 10.3(b) shows the logarithmic spacing of floating-point values exacerbating the nonlinear spacing of $z$ values.

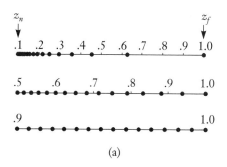

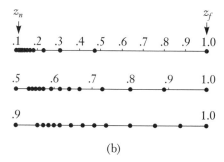

(a)                                              (b)

**Figure 10.3** *Quantization of z space: fixed point $\tilde{z}$ (a) and floating point $\tilde{z}$ (b)*

# Texture Mapping

**N**ow, off on another tangent for a bit.

If you are performing texture mapping on a triangle, it is necessary to calculate, for each pixel, the appropriate $u$, $v$ texture coordinate values. You generally specify the $u$ and $v$ at triangle vertices with the implicit assumption that they will be linearly interpolated across the triangle in eye space. That is, $u$ and $v$ are linear functions of eye space $x$ and $z$. But when rendering, we want to calculate $u$ and $v$ as functions of the screen space $\tilde{x}$. How do we do this? I gave one derivation in Chapter 17, "Hyperbolic Interpolation" of *Jim Blinn's Corner: A Trip Down the Graphics Pipeline*. Here's a different one.

What we have is two categories of parameter. The first category is $x$ and $z$ and any others that are linear functions of $x$ and $z$. These include texture coordinates $u$ and $v$, and perspective space coordinates $\hat{x}$, $\hat{z}$, and $\hat{w}$. If we linearly interpolate $x_L$ and $z_L$ by the parameter $\alpha$ according to

$$x_L = x_0 + \alpha \left( x_1 - x_0 \right)$$
$$z_L = z_0 + \alpha \left( z_1 - z_0 \right)$$

then we can find all these other parameters by interpolating with the same $\alpha$ value:

$$\hat{x}_L = \hat{x}_0 + \alpha \left( \hat{x}_1 - \hat{x}_0 \right)$$
$$\hat{w}_L = \hat{w}_0 + \alpha \left( \hat{w}_1 - \hat{w}_0 \right)$$
$$u_L = u_0 + \alpha \left( u_1 - u_0 \right)$$

The second category of parameters consists of the screen space coordinates $\tilde{x}$ and $\tilde{z}$, which are *not* simple linear combinations of $x$ and $z$. When stepping across a scan line, we interpolate between screen space endpoints by using uniform steps of $\beta$ in the formulas.

$$\tilde{x}_L = \tilde{x}_0 + \beta \left( \tilde{x}_1 - \tilde{x}_0 \right)$$
$$\tilde{z}_L = \tilde{z}_0 + \beta \left( \tilde{z}_1 - \tilde{z}_0 \right) \tag{10.1}$$

We desire a relation between $\alpha$ and $\beta$. Going back to the definition of $\tilde{z}_L$, we can write it in terms of $\alpha$ as

$$\tilde{z}_L = \frac{\hat{z}_L}{\hat{w}_L} = \frac{\hat{z}_0 + \alpha \left( \hat{z}_1 - \hat{z}_0 \right)}{\hat{w}_0 + \alpha \left( \hat{w}_1 - \hat{w}_0 \right)}$$

Now pull in the transformation equations from perspective to screen space, modified slightly:

$$\hat{z}_0 = \tilde{z}_0\, \hat{w}_0$$
$$\hat{z}_1 = \tilde{z}_1\, \hat{w}_1$$

so that

$$\tilde{z}_L = \frac{\tilde{z}_0\, \hat{w}_0 + \alpha \left(\tilde{z}_1\, \hat{w}_1 - \tilde{z}_0\, \hat{w}_0\right)}{\hat{w}_0 + \alpha \left(\hat{w}_1 - \hat{w}_0\right)}$$

Add and subtract $\alpha \tilde{z}_0\, \hat{w}_1$ to the numerator and fiddle around a while, and you can convert this to

$$\tilde{z}_L = \tilde{z}_0 + \left(\frac{\alpha\, \hat{w}_1}{\hat{w}_0 + \alpha \left(\hat{w}_1 - \hat{w}_0\right)}\right)\left(\tilde{z}_1 - \tilde{z}_0\right)$$

Comparing this with Equation (10.1) gives us the following relation connecting interpolation in eye space with interpolation in screen space:

$$\beta = \frac{\alpha\, \hat{w}_1}{\hat{w}_0 + \alpha \left(\hat{w}_1 - \hat{w}_0\right)}$$

Or, solving for $\alpha$:

$$\alpha = \frac{\beta\, \hat{w}_0}{\hat{w}_1 + \beta \left(\hat{w}_0 - \hat{w}_1\right)}$$

Now we can calculate $u_L$ in terms of $\beta$. Plug and shuffle to get

$$u_L = u_0 + \alpha \left(u_1 - u_0\right)$$
$$= u_0 + \frac{\beta \hat{w}_0}{\hat{w}_1 + \beta \left(\hat{w}_0 - \hat{w}_1\right)}\left(u_1 - u_0\right)$$
$$= \frac{u_0 \hat{w}_1 + \beta \left(u_1 \hat{w}_0 - u_0 \hat{w}_1\right)}{\hat{w}_1 + \beta \left(\hat{w}_0 - \hat{w}_1\right)}$$
$$= \frac{\dfrac{u_0}{\hat{w}_0} + \beta \left(\dfrac{u_1}{\hat{w}_1} - \dfrac{u_0}{\hat{w}_0}\right)}{\dfrac{1}{\hat{w}_0} + \beta \left(\dfrac{1}{\hat{w}_1} - \dfrac{1}{\hat{w}_0}\right)}$$

Now it's time to take a deep breath and interpret this result. We calculate the values of $\left(u/\hat{w}\right)$ and $\left(1/\hat{w}\right)$ at each endpoint of a line (or at each vertex of a triangle) and then linearly interpolate *these* values in screen space. Divide them to get $u_L$. This mechanism works for any parameter that is linear in eye space. Since we are going to have to do this for several such values ($u$, $v$, and perhaps even vertex colors), it is best to calculate the value of $\hat{w}$ once and then multiply it by the interpolated values of $\left( u/\hat{w} \right)$. The interpolation equation for $\hat{w}$ is

$$\hat{w}_L = \cfrac{1}{\cfrac{1}{\hat{w}_0} + \beta \left( \cfrac{1}{\hat{w}_1} - \cfrac{1}{\hat{w}_0} \right)}$$

so we linearly interpolate the denominator, that is, $\left( 1/\hat{w}_L \right)$, and do just one division (per pixel) to get $\hat{w}_L$.

# W Buffering

The calculations necessary for texture mapping give us a new way to do depth testing. Since we are going to calculate $\hat{w}$ anyway, doing a divide per pixel, we can simply use $\hat{w}$ (which is really a scaled version of eye space $z$) for depth testing. That is, instead of doing $\tilde{z}$ buffering, we would be doing $\hat{w}$ buffering. Note that this is not the same as the classic error of simply interpolating $\hat{w}$ (or $z$) linearly in screen space. $\hat{w}$ buffering works properly only if we calculate $\hat{w}$ as the correct hyperbolic function of $\beta$ (and hence of screen $x$). This means that flat lines and planes are no longer flat in a $\hat{w}$ buffer scheme. Figure 10.1(c) shows the $\hat{w}$ buffer version of Figures 10.1(a) and 10.1(b).

Note that with $\hat{w}$ buffering, we do not need to specify a value for $z_n$. That's good because this parameter has always been confusing to computer graphics artists. Since it doesn't appear at all in the expressions for $\hat{w}$, we don't need to worry about it anymore.

# Resolution Comparisons

Under what conditions is the resolution of $\hat{w}$ buffering better than $\tilde{z}$ buffering? To properly compare these, we need to scale the anticipated range of $\hat{w}$ to lie between 0 and 1 just as we did for $\tilde{z}$. To do this, just set the value of $d$ in the perspective matrix to $1/z_f$. Since $\hat{w}$ is just a scaled version of eye space $z$, whatever quantization steps we use for $\hat{w}$ will have the same spacing in $z$: equal spacing for fixed point and (approximate) logarithmic spacing for floating point.

To compare the sizes of quantization bins between the two schemes, we can compare the slopes of the depth values as functions of $z$. A large value of derivative is good. It means that a large variation in $\tilde{z}$ or $\hat{w}$ gives a small variation in $z$. To review, we have the two competing depth functions:

$$\hat{w} = dz \qquad \tilde{z} = \frac{bz + c}{dz}$$

The derivatives of these functions are

$$\frac{d}{dz}\hat{w} = d \qquad \frac{d}{dz}\tilde{z} = \frac{-c}{dz^2}$$

So $\tilde{z}$ buffering gives better resolution if

$$\frac{-c}{dz^2} > d$$

that is, if

$$z < \frac{\sqrt{-c}}{d}$$

(Don't panic, $c$ will always be negative.) Applying the definitions of $c$ and $d$, this converts to

$$z/z_f < \sqrt{\frac{z_n/z_f}{1 - z_n/z_f}} \tag{10.2}$$

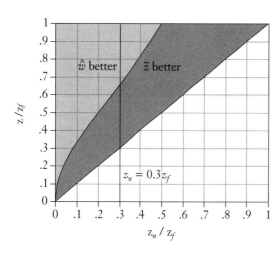

**Figure 10.4** *Tradeoff between $\tilde{z}$ buffering and $\hat{w}$ buffering*

How can we interpret this? Figure 10.4 contains my visualization, showing the proper choice of $\tilde{z}$ or $\hat{w}$ buffering for all possible values of $z_n$. Here's how it works. Each vertical slice of the diagram stands for a choice of $z_n$ as a proportion of $z_f$. We will only need to consider values of $z/z_f$ in the shaded part of that slice, from the diagonal line (representing $z = z_n$) up to the top line (representing $z = z_f$). The curved line is a plot of the right side of Equation (10.2). If $z/z_f$ is below this curve, we would be better off with $\tilde{z}$ buffering; if it's above, we would be better off with $\hat{w}$ buffering. Of course, you have to pick one or the other for the entire scene; this graph just tells you how much of your $z$ range is likely to get into trouble. Finally, note that if $z_n > \frac{1}{2}z_f$, then $\tilde{z}$ buffering always wins.

# Summary

$\widehat{w}$ buffering is best if you must make $z_n$ very small, as for example, in room walk-throughs. $\tilde{z}$ buffering is best if you can get away with making $z_n$ a noticeable fraction of $z_f$, as for example, in CAD, where you are examining a single object held virtually in front of you. This works well in this case mainly because the mapping for $z$ to $\tilde{z}$ becomes pretty close to linear. The breakpoint is at about $z_n = 0.3z_f$. (See the vertical line in Figure 10.4.) If $z_n$ is nearer than that, more of your $z$ range would benefit from $\widehat{w}$ buffering. If $z_n$ is farther than that, more of your $z$ range would benefit from $\tilde{z}$ buffering.

This is not the last word on the subject. We still need to investigate the desirability of using floating point versus fixed point for depth resolution. And how much resolution do you actually need? Maybe you do need more resolution for objects at small $z$ distances because mistakes are more visually apparent when they're close to you.

## Deleted Scene

Test Floating Point $1 - \tilde{z}$: Figure 10.3(b) suggests an alternative that can use the effects of floating-point quantization spacing to cancel out the nonlinearity in $\tilde{z}$: instead of calculating $\tilde{z}$, we calculate $1 - \tilde{z}$. Distant objects map to values near zero, and close objects map to values near 1 with much more evenly spread quantization steps. We, of course, have to reverse the sense of our depth comparison test in this case. Of course, we have to be careful that we aren't fooling ourselves with this. We don't want to calculate $1 - \tilde{z}$ after calculating the quantized (and information-destroyed) $\tilde{z}$. We must build the calculation into the perspective matrix, which then becomes

$$\begin{bmatrix} a & 0 & 0 \\ 0 & d-b & d \\ 0 & c & 0 \end{bmatrix}$$

and the depth value calculation becomes

$$1 - \tilde{z} = \left( \frac{z_n}{z_f - z_n} \right) \frac{z_f - z}{z}$$

I haven't pursued this.

# CHAPTER ELEVEN

# Ten More Unsolved Problems in Computer Graphics

S E P T E M B E R – O C T O B E R   1 9 9 8

At SIGGRAPH 1998, I had the honor of delivering the keynote address in celebration of the 25th annual conference. In my talk, I reminisced about my recollections of all the 25 conferences I had attended. I compared the state of computer graphics then to its state now. I predicted the future of the field. I performed a now-classic routine by listing my choice of ten unsolved problems in computer graphics. I have since realized that a keynote address is like a Ph.D. thesis. After you create it, you can extract it chapter by chapter and publish it as several papers. Here, then, is the first extraction—ten unsolved problems.

## History

Let's start by reviewing some of the past lists of unsolved problems. Judge for yourself how many of these historical problems have been solved by now.

## Sutherland 1966[1]

The tradition of posing unsolved problems in computer graphics goes back, as most CG things do, to Ivan Sutherland. He started it all with a 1966 article in *Datamation* with the following:

1. Cheap machines with basic capability
2. Basic interaction techniques
3. Coupling simulations to their display
4. Describing motion
5. Continuous tone displays
6. Making structure of drawings explicit
7. Hidden line removal
8. Program instrumentation and visualization
9. Automatic placement of elements in network diagrams
10. Working with abstractions (scientific visualization)

## Newell and Blinn 1977[2]

In 1977, Martin Newell and I presented the following thoughts at the ACM national conference. The unsolved problems we focused on were concerned primarily with realistic rendering. We were a bit lazy and could only think of six problems.

1. Increasing scene complexity
2. Fuzzy objects (hair, clouds)
3. Transparency and refraction
4. Extended light sources
5. Antialiasing
6. Systems integration

## Heckbert 1987[3]

Paul Heckbert presented an update to unsolved rendering problems in 1987.

1. Converting implicit models to parametric
2. High-quality texture filtering

---

1  Sutherland, I. E., "Ten Unsolved Problems in Computer Graphics," *Datamation*, Vol. 12, No. 5, May 1966, pp. 22–27.

2  Newell, M., and Blinn, J., "The Progression of Realism in Computer Generated Images," *ACM 77 Proceedings*, October 1977, pp. 444–448.

3  Heckbert, P., "Ten Unsolved Problems in Rendering," *Workshop on Rendering Algorithms and Systems, Graphics Interface 87*, April 1987, Toronto: *www-2.cs.cmu.edu/~ph/unsolved.ps.gz*.

3. Antialiasing
4. Shadows without ray tracing
5. Practical ray tracing
6. Practical radiosity
7. Frame-to-frame coherence
8. Automating model culling
9. Smooth model transitions
10. Affordable real-time rendering hardware

## Siggraph Panel 1991[4]

By 1991, things had become complex enough that it took a whole committee to identify key unsolved problems.

1. Managing scene complexity (Barr)
2. Tools for serious modeling (Brooks)
3. Large-scale user interfaces (Card)
4. Multimedia (Clark)
5. Automatic graphic design (Feiner)
6. Robust geometric algorithms (Forrest)
7. Better rendering (Hanrahan)
8. Graphics standards (van Dam)

# When Is a Problem "Solved"?

So now it's my turn again. But to keep you on pins and needles, before I get into my list of unsolved problems, I want to talk a bit about what the word *solved* means. Is a problem solved when its solution has been shown to be possible even though very expensive? Or does a true solution need to be cheap and easy to implement?

Some of the problems I will describe here have, indeed, been solved in the theoretical sense. The problem remains unsolved in the practical sense, though, because cheap and fast solutions are still elusive. As you will see, many of the problems I present are more sociological and marketing related than technical. Further, many of them have multiple parts, and there is much overlap. I do, after all, have to come up with exactly ten problems.

---

4  "Computer Graphics: More Unsolved Problems," Siggraph Panels 1991.

# Ten More Unsolved Problems

## 1. Novelty

The first problem is simply finding something that hasn't been done yet. Let's face it; all the easy problems have been solved. Sometimes it seems that computer graphics research consists of finding some new subtle lighting effect that hasn't yet been modeled.

## 2. Education

There are two parts to this—learning and teaching.

*Learning* (keeping up with what has been done). Not only do you have to find a problem that hasn't been solved, you have to *know* that it hasn't been solved. It used to be that the yearly SIGGRAPH conference proceedings were about the only place where computer graphics advances were published. Now there are lots of places to show off your work. You can no longer keep up with every new development by reading just the SIGGRAPH proceedings. Nowadays, it's sometimes harder to discover an existing solution to a problem than it is to reinvent the solution yourself. There's lots of reinvention in this field; computer graphics is almost *too* easy in that regard.

*Teaching* (dissemination of new discoveries). Just because somebody solves some problem doesn't mean that others will use that solution. This happens because other graphicists either aren't aware of the solution or don't understand it. You can think of this as a marketing problem. Two examples that come to mind are premultiplied alpha (more about this later) and specular reflection calculation by raising the cosine of some angle to a power. I mean, Phong was a great guy and all, but his use of the cosine power was a simple approximation to a function that we have dramatically improved on many years ago. Despite this, rendering systems still use "cosine power" as a property of surfaces as though it actually had physical meaning.

## 3. Systems Integration

This is the problem of keeping all the balls in the air at once, that is, how to use all the tricks in one production. Just because one researcher can do cloth, one can do faces, and one can do hair, doesn't mean that all animation systems can suddenly put them all together. The new technology of component software and plug-ins to existing software shows promise here.

## 4. Simplicity

I could keep this section simple and just say, "Make things simple." But I won't because life is not so simple.

How can we keep this stuff simple enough to use? Having a separate component for cloth, hair, skin, trees, water, physically based motion, deformations, texture synthesis, weathering, solid textures, multiresolution models, image-based rendering, yadda-yadda . . . could be a bit cumbersome.

But is simplicity even possible? Is it possible to make a simple computer graphics system that can generate complex images? Consider other systems that are complex enough to do interesting things. The telephone system has a conglomeration of old and new technology that still pretty much works. The human brain has several layers of legacy processors inherited from our reptilian and mammalian ancestors. Maybe simplicity is a hopeless goal.

Nonetheless, one should still strive for simplicity. Let's face it, people don't read manuals anymore. If a feature of a program is not obvious from playing with its user interface, then users assume that the feature is broken or nonexistent.

## 5. Better Pixel Arithmetic Theory

Our basic concept of pixels as red, green, blue, and alpha channels is incomplete. I can see at least three main problems. One is largely a matter of definition and education, while the other two involve integration of compositing with other parts of the imaging process.

Problem one concerns premultiplication of the color channels by the alpha channel. We've long known that premultiplication has many advantages. For example, it allows compositing arithmetic on all channels to be identical, linear filtering to commute with compositing, and the set of pixel values to be closed under composition. (This is because the result of any pixel-compositing operation is a premultiplied pixel. Therefore, the first operation in a chain of operations moves us into the premultiplied domain automatically.) Nonetheless, several systems store colors unmultiplied by alpha. This indicates a fundamentally different interpretation of the meaning of the alpha channel: alpha as a cropping stencil. We need to understand this difference and realize that the alpha value has subtly different meanings when used as a fundamental component of a pixel and when it is used as a stencil to shape an existing image. I call this the local/global alpha distinction. Both uses of alpha are important, and systems should support both.

The second problem is that the conventional alpha channel interpretation assumes that edges of a foreground and background object are uncorrelated. Some useful algorithms, on the other hand, divide the screen into nonoverlapping polygonal regions. When two adjacent regions are rasterized, their boundaries, of course, coincide, and are thus completely correlated. These rasterized regions cannot be merged using the standard uncorrelated compositing algebra.

Third, we must consider combining compositing operations with light reflection models. The fundamental operation of light reflection is the simulation of colored light reflecting off a colored surface or transmitting through colored glass. A single alpha channel can only model partial *geometric* occlusion of a pixel. It cannot adequately simulate a colored, partially transparent surface. A separate alpha channel per color is still not the ultimate answer, either. The complete physical simulation of spectral interactions would seem to be necessary, but might be overkill. Some other lighting-related arithmetic operations that must be included are the simulation of after-the-fact shadow application and transparency effects at boundaries of fogged objects.

A complete algebra on pixel values will be embedded in the deep innards of any rendering system. Currently available compositing operations do not address the above concerns. A more complete theory must be devised and installed in the inner polygon tiling loops of future 3D APIs.

## 6. Legacy Compatibility

Time goes on, and we do things differently. Partly this is because we have learned how to do things better than we did before, and partly it is because technological improvements change the tradeoffs to make things practical that weren't before. Unfortunately, our history remains to haunt us in the form of legacy applications and data. This applies to operating systems, 3D APIs, file formats, and on and on. Simply pitching out all legacy items is not a good idea. Instead, progress is a balancing act of how to not abandon the old while allowing the new.

One particularly interesting example of this is the coming convergence (or collision) of television technology with computer imaging. We will have to face the fact that TV pixels (even digital TV pixels) are not the same as computer pixels. For one thing, TV pixels are not square. The standard 4:3 ratio screen has 720:480 pixels, giving an individual pixel the aspect ratio of 8:9. For another thing, TV pixels have a different range than computer pixels. For digital TV, the byte value 16 corresponds to black, and the byte value 235 corresponds to white (220 levels total). And finally, TV pixel values do not linearly represent light intensity; they have a gamma correction value burned into them. Sometimes computer graphics pixels do this, and sometimes they don't. But when it is done, the standard gamma correction for computer graphics is different from the standard for TV pixels (see Chapter 9). Gamma correction has the advantage of giving better resolution to darker regions of an image, but doing correct image compositing with it is slow. The probable eventual solution to this problem is to use 16 bits per color channel. Before this happens, we will need to devise a standard 16-bit encoding (the *meaning* of the 16 bits) that has at least as much dark resolution as 8-bit gamma-corrected pixels, and that allows small negative values and greater-than-one values. Simple fixed-point encoding still doesn't have enough accuracy on the dark end. Extending the current gamma encodings to 16 bits retains all the nonlinear arithmetic problems we currently have. I think the best solution is to use a 16-bit floating-point format.

## 7. Arithmetic Sloppiness

There are a lot of things we are doing wrong in image rendering, and we know it. We do it anyway, though, to appease the great god of speed. Surprisingly, this problem worsens because modern computers are so fast—just fast enough that some algorithms are borderline real time. Programmers are tempted to do a sloppy job of pixel arithmetic to get their speed just over the line into real time. This can often lead to an embarrassing amount of arithmetic sloppiness in pixel calculations. I'll mention a couple of examples of this.

- When processing pixel values, we often ignore the above-mentioned nonlinear gamma encoding. We simply do linear calculations on this nonlinear data. (I discussed this problem in more detail in Chapter 9.)

- Conversions between, say, 5 bits per color channel and 8 bits per color channel are trickier than most people realize. Proper conversion is not a simple 3-bit shift and mask operation. A 5-bit quantity is a number of 1/31 st's; an 8-bit quantity is a number of 1/255 th's. Proper conversion requires multiplying or dividing by the unpleasant value $255/31 \approx 8.22$.

- Texture filtering often takes the form of simple bilinear interpolation between the four nearest texels to the desired pixel. This bad interpolation gives ugly diamond-shaped artifacts to the image.

The problem about all these picky details is that often the proponents of bad arithmetic show images that are visually pretty much the same as correct ones. So what's the big deal? How sloppy can we be and still get an image whose errors are below the threshold of visibility? What we really need are better criteria for how accurate we need to be.

## 8. Antialiasing

At the turn of this century, the director of the U.S. Patent Office stated that all possible inventions had already been invented. Bill Gates is often quoted as having said that 640K of memory is enough for anybody. (He was right.) I think I can become famous, too, by categorically stating what will *not* happen (thus guaranteeing what *will* happen). I will therefore proclaim that

> *Nobody will ever solve the antialiasing problem.*

(This problem, you will note, appears twice on our list of historical unsolved problems.) No one will *ever* figure out how to quickly render legible antialiased text in perspective. Textures in perspective will *always* be either too fuzzy or too jaggy. No one will ever build texture-mapping hardware that uses a 4×4 interpolation kernel or anisotropic filtering. And no one will ever send me tickets to the Digital Domain Siggraph party.

## 9. A Modeling, Rendering, Animation Challenge

OK. So much for the hard sociological problems. How about a simple, straightforward rendering challenge. Here it is:

> *Spaghetti*

No, really. Consider that we can do cloth pretty well now (possibly due to our obsession with rendering the human body). We can model how it drapes and folds without self-intersections. Now cloth is a basically 2D shape. Spaghetti is an essentially 1D shape. It should be even easier to model. Such algorithms could also apply to piles of rope or string and even conceivably to protein folding. And it will give new meaning to the term *Spaghetti code.*

And remember, to respond to this challenge, you must solve all three problems: modeling (shape), rendering (making pictures), and animation (showing evolution over time). Don't forget the sauce.

## 10. Finding a Use for Real-Time 3D

We all know that real-time 3D is cool. And what's incredibly cool, and astonishing to us old-timers, is the fact that you can now get real-time 3D hardware for about a hundred dollars. What's not cool is that the companies making these hardware cards are having a tough time staying solvent.

The main applications for cheap 3D hardware, games, simply don't have enough adherents to support the industry. To keep 3D hardware cheap, we need more large-scale uses for it. And I mean *large* scale, uses that virtually everybody owning a personal computer will lust after. Fruitful areas might include e-commerce and business data visualization.

Here's another idea: a vision of better 3D user interfaces. Currently, operating systems and applications have a lot of persistent settings that indicate preferences and system setup information. In order to examine and change these settings, you have to hunt around through a maze of windows and menus to find the particular one that applies. Suppose we could represent this system state in terms of 3D shapes rather than list settings. The internal state of your program would then look something like an old-fashioned car engine (one simple enough to understand, I mean). You would see interrelations between components as shapes plugged into the "system" shape. Direct manipulation of these shapes via a mouse or data glove would make configuring your system a much more understandable process. (I am reminded of the scene from the movie *Johnny Mnemonic* . . .)

# Get Hopping

I realize that people will mostly pursue the easiest of these: spaghetti. The other problems will likely require group participation but are, probably, rather more important. Whichever challenges you—hop to it! And let me know what you find.

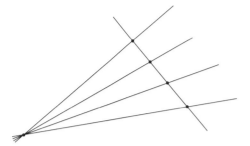

# CHAPTER TWELVE

# The Cross Ratio

**G**eometry is the study of what properties of a figure stay the same as the figure undergoes some transformation. For example, in Euclidean geometry, the allowable transformations are rotations and translations. Properties that stay constant include distances and angles. For projective geometry, such as we use with homogeneous coordinates, the transformations include perspective projections. In this case, one thing that emphatically does *not* stay the same is geometric length. A property that *does*, however, is something called the *cross ratio*. Take a look at Figure 12.1 where lines **p**, **q**, **r**, and **s** all intersect at the same point; the cross ratio is the ratio of the ratios of the following distances:

$$\chi = \frac{|\mathbf{AB}|/|\mathbf{BD}|}{|\mathbf{AC}|/|\mathbf{CD}|}$$

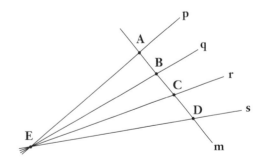

**Figure 12.1** *The cross ratio*

This value is constant no matter where line **m** is placed. It is also constant if the whole diagram undergoes a homogeneous transformation (possibly including perspective).

   This has always puzzled me. If geometric distances aren't preserved, and ratios of geometric distances aren't preserved, then how come the ratio of ratios of geometric distances is preserved? Well, here's a quick demonstration.

# The First Ratio

et's begin by calculating the Euclidean distance between points **A** and **B**. I'll start with the 2D homogeneous coordinates of each point, which I will name as follows:

$$\mathbf{A} = \begin{bmatrix} A_x & A_y & A_w \end{bmatrix}$$
$$\mathbf{B} = \begin{bmatrix} B_x & B_y & B_w \end{bmatrix}$$

To calculate a Euclidean distance, we must turn these into the "real" coordinates by dividing out the homogeneous $w$ coordinate giving the two 2D Euclidean points:

$$\begin{bmatrix} \dfrac{A_x}{A_w} & \dfrac{A_y}{A_w} \end{bmatrix} \text{ and } \begin{bmatrix} \dfrac{B_x}{B_w} & \dfrac{B_y}{B_w} \end{bmatrix}$$

Then subtract giving

$$\begin{bmatrix} \dfrac{A_x}{A_w} - \dfrac{B_x}{B_w} & \dfrac{A_y}{A_w} - \dfrac{B_y}{B_w} \end{bmatrix}$$

The desired distance is the length of this 2D vector. The fact that this quantity doesn't treat all three of the $x$, $y$, and $w$ components symmetrically is a hint that Euclidean distance is not a meaningful concept in projective geometry.

Anyway, if we bash ahead to get the Euclidean length of the above vector, we would need to calculate the square root of the sum of the squares of these two components—wotta pain. Instead, let's pretend for a minute that the line **m** is horizontal and points **A** . . . **D** line up horizontally. In that case, the length of the vector is just the $x$ component of the vector. In other words,

$$\frac{A_x}{A_w} - \frac{B_x}{B_w} = |\mathbf{AB}|$$

In general, though, the line will be at some angle $\theta$. In this case, the $x$ component will equal the length times the cosine of the tilt angle, or

$$\frac{A_x}{A_w} - \frac{B_x}{B_w} = |\mathbf{AB}|\cos\theta$$

For the collinear segment **BD**, tipped by the same angle $\theta$, the $x$ component would be

$$\frac{B_x}{B_w} - \frac{D_x}{D_w} = |\mathbf{BD}|\cos\vartheta$$

Here's where the first ratio will come in to simplify life. The top half of our desired cross ratio is the ratio between these segment **AB** and segment **BD**. And, by similarity, the ratio of the $x$ components is the same as the ratio of the lengths. Taking the ratio of the above two equations, we find

$$\frac{\dfrac{A_x}{A_w} - \dfrac{B_x}{B_w}}{\dfrac{B_x}{B_w} - \dfrac{D_x}{D_w}} = \frac{|\mathbf{AB}|\cos\vartheta}{|\mathbf{BD}|\cos\vartheta} = \frac{|\mathbf{AB}|}{|\mathbf{BD}|}$$

The angle dependency cancels. Yay! We can calculate the ratio of lengths without any squaring and square rooting.

# The Second Ratio

Now let's look at the second ratio in the "ratio of ratios" game. Remember that what we are really interested in is

$$\chi = \frac{|\mathbf{AB}|/|\mathbf{BD}|}{|\mathbf{AC}|/|\mathbf{CD}|}$$

A little algebra on the **AB/BD** ratio turns it into

$$\frac{|\mathbf{AB}|}{|\mathbf{BD}|} = \frac{D_w}{A_w}\left(\frac{A_x B_w - A_w B_x}{B_x D_w - B_w D_x}\right)$$

And by going through the same schtick, but everywhere changing **B** to **C**, we can see that the second of our two ratios is

$$\frac{|\mathbf{AC}|}{|\mathbf{CD}|} = \frac{D_w}{A_w}\left(\frac{A_x C_w - A_w C_x}{C_x D_w - C_w D_x}\right)$$

Now we can see why the ratio of ratios is something interesting homogeneously—it lets us cancel the ugly $w$ component ratios. The whole cross ratio then boils down to

$$\chi = \frac{|\mathbf{AB}|/|\mathbf{BD}|}{|\mathbf{AC}|/|\mathbf{CD}|} = \frac{A_x B_w - A_w B_x}{B_x D_w - B_w D_x}\frac{C_x D_w - C_w D_x}{A_x C_w - A_w C_x}$$

This is much more symmetric in $x$, $y$, and $w$, and closer to the sort of thing we expect we can make homogeneously constant.

# Constancy with Changing m

Now we can ask why this ratio is independent of the position of the line $\mathbf{m}$. The root cause must have something to do with the fact that we generate the points $\mathbf{A}$, $\mathbf{B}$, $\mathbf{C}$, and $\mathbf{D}$ from the lines $\mathbf{p}$, $\mathbf{q}$, $\mathbf{r}$, and $\mathbf{s}$ that have the special relationship of all intersecting at the same point $\mathbf{E}$.

First, then, here's a brief reminder of the relationship between homogeneous points and lines. You can calculate the point at the intersection of two lines by taking the cross product of the line vectors. This means that the point at the intersection of the four lines is any of the six quantities:

$$\mathbf{E} = c_1 \left( \mathbf{p} \times \mathbf{q} \right) = c_2 \left( \mathbf{q} \times \mathbf{r} \right) = c_3 \left( \mathbf{r} \times \mathbf{s} \right)$$
$$= c_4 \left( \mathbf{p} \times \mathbf{r} \right) = c_5 \left( \mathbf{q} \times \mathbf{s} \right) = c_6 \left( \mathbf{p} \times \mathbf{s} \right)$$

The inclusion of the constants $c_i$ recognizes the fact that the cross products can represent the same intersection point even though there might be a homogeneous scale factor applied to all three of the $x$, $y$, and $w$ components.

After some fooling around, I have found that, for our purposes, the neatest algebraic way to use this relationship is to express the lines $\mathbf{q}$ and $\mathbf{r}$ in terms of $\mathbf{p}$ and $\mathbf{s}$. I'll write this as

$$\mathbf{q} = q_\alpha \mathbf{p} + q_\beta \mathbf{s}$$
$$\mathbf{r} = r_\alpha \mathbf{p} + r_\beta \mathbf{s} \tag{12.1}$$

You can think of the pairs $\begin{bmatrix} q_\alpha & q_\beta \end{bmatrix}$ and $\begin{bmatrix} r_\alpha & r_\beta \end{bmatrix}$ as 1D homogeneous coordinates for the collection of lines passing through $\mathbf{E}$, the intersection of $\mathbf{p}$ and $\mathbf{s}$. Any point passing through this intersection has an $\begin{bmatrix} \alpha & \beta \end{bmatrix}$ pair that describes it. Any nonzero multiple of an $\begin{bmatrix} \alpha & \beta \end{bmatrix}$ pair represents the same line though.

Now, let's relate this to our points. Remember, the cross product is how we intersect lines, so we have

$$\mathbf{A} = \mathbf{p} \times \mathbf{m}$$
$$\mathbf{B} = \mathbf{q} \times \mathbf{m}$$
$$\mathbf{C} = \mathbf{r} \times \mathbf{m}$$
$$\mathbf{D} = \mathbf{s} \times \mathbf{m}$$

Write the interior point $\mathbf{B}$ in terms of the outside lines and points:

$$\mathbf{B} = \mathbf{q} \times \mathbf{m} = \left( q_\alpha \mathbf{p} + q_\beta \mathbf{s} \right) \times \mathbf{m}$$
$$= q_\alpha \left( \mathbf{p} \times \mathbf{m} \right) + q_\beta \left( \mathbf{s} \times \mathbf{m} \right)$$
$$= q_\alpha \mathbf{A} + q_\beta \mathbf{D}$$

We can then write the top half of the cross ratio as

$$|\mathbf{AB}|/|\mathbf{BD}| = \frac{A_w}{D_w} \frac{A_x B_w - A_w B_x}{B_x D_w - B_w D_x}$$
$$= \frac{A_w}{D_w} \frac{A_x \left( q_\alpha A_w + q_\beta D_w \right) - A_w \left( q_\alpha A_x + q_\beta D_x \right)}{\left( q_\alpha A_x + q_\beta D_x \right) D_w - \left( q_\alpha A_w + q_\beta D_w \right) D_x}$$
$$= \frac{A_w}{D_w} \frac{q_\beta A_x D_w - q_\beta A_w D_x}{q_\alpha A_x D_w - q_\alpha A_w D_x}$$
$$= \frac{A_w}{D_w} \frac{q_\beta}{q_\alpha}$$

Again, run through this derivation with $\mathbf{C}$ instead of $\mathbf{B}$, and you get

$$|\mathbf{AC}|/|\mathbf{CD}| = \frac{A_w}{D_w} \frac{r_\beta}{r_\alpha}$$

The net cross ratio is now

$$\chi = \frac{|\mathbf{AB}|/|\mathbf{BD}|}{|\mathbf{AC}|/|\mathbf{CD}|} = \frac{q_\beta/q_\alpha}{r_\beta/r_\alpha}$$

The interesting thing about this is that the whole dependence on the location of $\mathbf{m}$ has disappeared, as well as the dependence on which coordinate (here we used $x$) we chose to use as the measure of distance ratios. That is, it is only dependant on the orientations of the lines $\mathbf{q}$ and $\mathbf{r}$ relative to $\mathbf{p}$ and $\mathbf{s}$. Any line $\mathbf{m}'$ intersecting these will generate the same cross ratio. The cross ratio is thus a property of the locations of the four original lines, rather than the extra line $\mathbf{m}$.

As another way of looking at this, start with the equations in (12.1) and cross them with $\mathbf{p}$ and $\mathbf{s}$:

$$\mathbf{q} \times \mathbf{p} = q_\alpha \mathbf{p} \times \mathbf{p} + q_\beta \mathbf{s} \times \mathbf{p} = q_\beta \mathbf{s} \times \mathbf{p}$$
$$\mathbf{q} \times \mathbf{s} = q_\alpha \mathbf{p} \times \mathbf{s} + q_\beta \mathbf{s} \times \mathbf{s} = q_\alpha \mathbf{p} \times \mathbf{s}$$
$$\mathbf{r} \times \mathbf{p} = r_\alpha \mathbf{p} \times \mathbf{p} + r_\beta \mathbf{s} \times \mathbf{p} = r_\beta \mathbf{s} \times \mathbf{p}$$
$$\mathbf{r} \times \mathbf{s} = r_\alpha \mathbf{p} \times \mathbf{s} + r_\beta \mathbf{s} \times \mathbf{s} = r_\alpha \mathbf{p} \times \mathbf{s}$$

These are four vector equations. Turn them into scalars by dotting them with **m**:

$$\mathbf{m} \cdot \mathbf{q} \times \mathbf{p} = q_\beta \mathbf{m} \cdot \mathbf{s} \times \mathbf{p}$$
$$\mathbf{m} \cdot \mathbf{q} \times \mathbf{s} = q_\alpha \mathbf{m} \cdot \mathbf{p} \times \mathbf{s}$$
$$\mathbf{m} \cdot \mathbf{r} \times \mathbf{p} = r_\beta \mathbf{m} \cdot \mathbf{s} \times \mathbf{p}$$
$$\mathbf{m} \cdot \mathbf{r} \times \mathbf{s} = r_\alpha \mathbf{m} \cdot \mathbf{p} \times \mathbf{s}$$

And now you can write the cross product in the following form:

$$\chi = \frac{q_\beta r_\alpha}{q_\alpha r_\beta} = \frac{(\mathbf{m} \cdot \mathbf{q} \times \mathbf{p})(\mathbf{m} \cdot \mathbf{r} \times \mathbf{s})}{(\mathbf{m} \cdot \mathbf{q} \times \mathbf{s})(\mathbf{m} \cdot \mathbf{r} \times \mathbf{p})}$$

Here's another key fact: $\chi$ contains only the ratios of the alpha/beta pairs, so it is also independent of arbitrary homogeneous scalings of the vector for **q** and **r**. For example, if we replaced **q** with $\gamma \mathbf{q}$ (geometrically the same line), it means that we are scaling both $q_\alpha$ and $q_\beta$ by $\gamma$, which will again cancel out in the formula for $\chi$.

# Constancy under Perspective

Now let's see why the cross ratio is unchanged when we transform the four lines via an arbitrary transformation matrix. If we have a transformation **T** that changes our outer two lines as

$$\mathbf{p}' = \mathbf{T}\mathbf{p}$$
$$\mathbf{s}' = \mathbf{T}\mathbf{s}$$

the inner lines will be

$$\mathbf{q}' = \mathbf{T}\mathbf{q} = \mathbf{T}(q_\alpha \mathbf{p} + q_\beta \mathbf{s}) = q_\alpha \mathbf{T}\mathbf{p} + q_\beta \mathbf{T}\mathbf{s}$$
$$= q_\alpha \mathbf{p}' + q_\beta \mathbf{s}'$$

And similarly

$$\mathbf{r}' = r_\alpha \mathbf{p}' + r_\beta \mathbf{s}'$$

Even if we try to disguise line $\mathbf{q}'$ or $\mathbf{r}'$ by multiplying by some homogeneous scale, we get the same value of cross ratio—the ratio of ratios:

$$\chi = \frac{q_\beta / q_\alpha}{r_\beta / r_\alpha}$$

A particularly interesting special case of this occurs when we take the outside lines **p** and **s** as the $x$ and $y$ axes, and transform by a simple nonuniform scale factor. Numerically, this would be

$$\mathbf{p} = \begin{bmatrix} 1 \\ 0 \\ 0 \end{bmatrix}, \ \mathbf{q} = \begin{bmatrix} q_\alpha \\ q_\beta \\ 0 \end{bmatrix}, \ \mathbf{r} = \begin{bmatrix} r_\alpha \\ r_\beta \\ 0 \end{bmatrix}, \ \mathbf{s} = \begin{bmatrix} 0 \\ 1 \\ 0 \end{bmatrix}$$

$$\mathbf{T} = \begin{bmatrix} f_x & 0 & 0 \\ 0 & f_y & 0 \\ 0 & 0 & 1 \end{bmatrix}$$

From this we get

$$\mathbf{p}' = \begin{bmatrix} f_x \\ 0 \\ 0 \end{bmatrix}, \ \mathbf{q}' = \begin{bmatrix} f_x q_\alpha \\ f_y q_\beta \\ 0 \end{bmatrix}, \ \mathbf{r}' = \begin{bmatrix} f_x r_\alpha \\ f_y r_\beta \\ 0 \end{bmatrix}, \ \mathbf{s}' = \begin{bmatrix} 0 \\ f_y \\ 0 \end{bmatrix}$$

The alpha and beta components of **q** and **r** have changed to

$$q'_\alpha = f_x q_\alpha, \quad q'_\beta = f_y q_\beta,$$
$$r'_\alpha = f_x r_\alpha, \quad r'_\beta = f_y r_\beta$$

The lines **p** and **s** haven't moved, but the lines **q** and **r** both have. And the ratios of the $[\alpha, \beta]$ values of the lines **q** and **r** are different:

$$q'_\beta / q'_\alpha = \frac{f_y}{f_x} \left( q_\beta / q_\alpha \right)$$

$$r'_\beta / r'_\alpha = \frac{f_y}{f_x} \left( r_\beta / r_\alpha \right)$$

But sure enough, the ratio of ratios remains the same:

$$\chi = \frac{q'_\beta / q'_\alpha}{r'_\beta / r'_\alpha} = \frac{q_\beta / q_\alpha}{r_\beta / r_\alpha}$$

In other words, even though a transformation might not move the outside lines **p** and **s**, it will move the inside lines **q** and **r** in such a manner that the change in the ratio $\left( q_\beta / q_\alpha \right)$ is matched by the same change in the ratio $\left( r_\beta / r_\alpha \right)$.

# Summary

The cross ratio is as much a property of the four mutually intersecting lines **p**, **q**, **r**, and **s** as it is of the four collinear points **A**, **B**, **C**, and **D**. Any line **m** that you throw across the lines will generate four points with the same cross ratio.

You can, in turn, take any four collinear points **A**, **B**, **C**, and **D**, and throw various collections of four mutually intersecting lines through them. Each of these line collections will have the same cross ratio. Finally, you can project any of these figures perspectively and also get an un-changed cross ratio.

The true homogeneous nature of the cross ratio can best be seen by writing it as

$$\chi = \frac{q_\beta r_\alpha}{q_\alpha r_\beta}$$

and reviewing the effect of an arbitrary homogeneous scaling on each of the four lines. Remember that

$$\mathbf{q} = q_\alpha \mathbf{p} + q_\beta \mathbf{s}$$
$$\mathbf{r} = r_\alpha \mathbf{p} + r_\beta \mathbf{s} \tag{12.21}$$

- Scaling only **q** will scale both $q_\alpha$ and $q_\beta$, but this cancels out.

$$\chi = \frac{\boxed{q_\beta} r_\alpha}{\boxed{q_\alpha} r_\beta}$$

- Scaling only **r** will scale $r_\alpha$ and $r_\beta$, but these will cancel:

$$\chi = \frac{q_\beta \boxed{r_\alpha}}{q_\alpha \boxed{r_\beta}}$$

- Scaling only **p** will require inversely scaling $q_\alpha$ and $r_\alpha$ to keep **q** and **r** the same in Equation (12.1). These again cancel:

$$\chi = \frac{q_\beta \boxed{r_\alpha}}{\boxed{q_\alpha} r_\beta}$$

- Scaling only **s** will require inversely scaling $q_\beta$ and $r_\beta$. Same song, new verse:

$$\chi = \frac{\boxed{q_\beta}\, r_\alpha}{q_\alpha \boxed{r_\beta}}$$

From this, we can see the necessity of this arrangement of ratio of ratios in constructing a quantity that remains homogeneously meaningful.

So, even though perspective transformations do not preserve distances, or ratios of distances, they do preserve these ratios of ratios of distances.

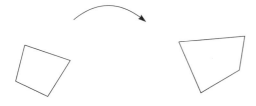

# CHAPTER THIRTEEN

# Inferring Transforms

I n simple 2D texture mapping, you take a 2D image and render it on the screen after some transformation or distortion. To accomplish this, you will need to take each $[X, Y]$ location on the screen and calculate a $[U, V]$ texture coordinate to place there. A particularly common transformation is

$$U = \frac{aX + bY + c}{gX + bY + j}, \quad V = \frac{dX + eY + f}{gX + bY + j}$$

By picking the proper values for the coefficients $a \ldots j$, we can fly the 2D texture around to an arbitrary position, orientation, and perspective projection on the screen. One can, in fact, generate the coefficients by a concatenation of 3D rotation, translation, scale, and perspective matrices, so we, of course, prefer the homogeneous matrix formulation of this transformation:

$$[X \quad Y \quad 1] \begin{bmatrix} a & d & g \\ b & e & h \\ c & f & j \end{bmatrix} = [u \quad v \quad w]$$

$$[U \quad V] = \begin{bmatrix} \dfrac{u}{w} & \dfrac{v}{w} \end{bmatrix}$$

In this chapter, though, I'm going to talk about a more direct approach to finding $a \ldots j$. It turns out that the 2D-to-2D mapping is completely specified if you give four arbitrary points in screen space and the four arbitrary points in texture space they must map to. The only restriction is that no three of the input or output points may be collinear. This method of transformation specification is useful, for example, in taking flat objects digitized in perspective and processing them into orthographic views.

# Our Goal

Let's make the problem explicit by giving names to some quantities. We are given four 2D screen coordinates $\mathbf{s}_i = \begin{bmatrix} X_i & Y_i & 1 \end{bmatrix}$ and four 2D texture coordinates $\mathbf{t}_i = \begin{bmatrix} U_i & V_i & 1 \end{bmatrix}$, and we want to find the $3 \times 3$ homogeneous transformation $\mathbf{M}_{st}$ that maps one to the other so that

$$\mathbf{s}_i \mathbf{M}_{st} = w_i \mathbf{t}_i \qquad (13.1)$$

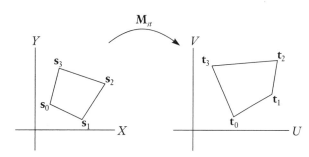

**Figure 13.1** *Desired transform*

See Figure 13.1. Note that we are *not* given the $w_i$ values. Their participation in Equation (13.1) acknowledges the fact that even though the original input and output points are nonhomogeneous (their third component is 1), the output of the matrix multiplication will be homogeneous. We will have to solve for the $w$ values as a side effect of solving for the elements of $\mathbf{M}_{st}$.

# The Conventional Solution

The conventional way to solve this goes as follows. First, using the names $a \ldots j$ for the elements of $\mathbf{M}_{st}$, we can rewrite Equation (13.1) explicitly as

$$\begin{bmatrix} X_i & Y_i & 1 \end{bmatrix} \begin{bmatrix} a & d & g \\ b & e & h \\ c & f & j \end{bmatrix} = w_i \begin{bmatrix} U_i & V_i & 1 \end{bmatrix}$$

Multiplying out and equating each component gives us three equations:

$$aX_i + bY_i + c = w_i U_i$$
$$dX_i + eY_i + f = w_i V_i$$
$$gX_i + hY_i + j = w_i$$

Plug the last equation for $w_i$ into the first two and move everything to the left of the equal sign:

$$aX_i + bY_i + c - gX_iU_i - hY_iU_i - jU_i = 0$$
$$dX_i + eY_i + f - gX_iV_i - hY_iV_i - jV_i = 0$$

Write this as yet another matrix equation in terms of what we are solving for, $a \ldots j$:

$$
\begin{bmatrix}
X_i & Y_i & 1 & 0 & 0 & 0 & -X_iU_i & -Y_iU_i & -U_i \\
0 & 0 & 0 & X_i & Y_i & 1 & -X_iV & -Y_iV_i & -V_i
\end{bmatrix}
\begin{bmatrix}
a \\ b \\ c \\ d \\ e \\ f \\ g \\ h \\ j
\end{bmatrix}
=
\begin{bmatrix}
0 \\ 0
\end{bmatrix}
$$

Each input point gives us two more 9-element rows; four points gives us an 8×9 matrix. Since this is a homogeneous system, that's all we need to solve for the nine values $a \ldots j$ (with an arbitrary global scale factor). One way to calculate each of these nine values is to find the determinant of the 8×8 matrix formed by deleting the matching column of the 8×9 matrix, so . . . nine determinants of 8×8 matrices. This is doable but obnoxious. Looking at all those lovely zeros and ones on the left makes us suspect that there is a better way.

# Heckbert's Improvement

In his 1989 master's thesis, Paul Heckbert[1] made a great leap by splitting the transformation into two separate matrices. He first used one matrix to map the input points to a canonical unit square (with vertices [0, 0], [1, 0], [1, 1], [0, 1]) and then mapped that square into the output points with another matrix. See Figure 13.2.

Each of these matrices will be individually easier to calculate than the complete transformation since the arithmetic is so much simpler. In fact, the arithmetic turns out to be simplest for the second of these transformations, so we will solve that one explicitly. Naming points in the unit-square space $\mathbf{q}$, we want to find $\mathbf{M}_{qt}$ in the equation

$$\mathbf{qM}_{qt} = w_t\mathbf{t}$$

---

1 Heckbert, P., *Fundamentals of Texture Mapping and Image Warping*, master's thesis, University of California, Berkeley, Dept. of Electrical Engineering and Computer Science, 1989 (*www.cs.cmu.edu/~ph/#papers*).

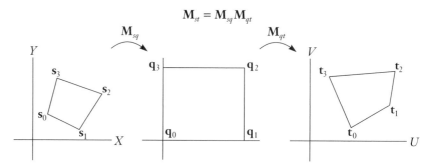

**Figure 13.2** *Two stages of Heckbert decomposition*

Let's explicitly write out all components for all four input/output (**q/t**) point pairs. I'll recycle the names $a \ldots j$ and $w_0 \ldots w_3$ for use in this subcomputation, so be aware that their values are different from those I used in the "conventional" solution:

$$\begin{bmatrix} 0 & 0 & 1 \\ 1 & 0 & 1 \\ 1 & 1 & 1 \\ 0 & 1 & 1 \end{bmatrix} \begin{bmatrix} a & d & g \\ b & e & h \\ c & f & j \end{bmatrix} = \begin{bmatrix} w_0 U_0 & w_0 V_0 & w_0 \\ w_1 U_1 & w_1 V_1 & w_1 \\ w_2 U_2 & w_2 V_2 & w_2 \\ w_3 U_3 & w_3 V_3 & w_3 \end{bmatrix}$$

This generates 12 equations:

$$\begin{array}{ccc}
c = w_0 U_0 & f = w_0 V_0 & j = w_0 \\
a + c = w_1 U_1 & d + f = w_1 V_1 & g + j = w_1 \\
a + b + c = w_2 U_2 & d + e + f = w_2 V_2 & g + h + j = w_2 \\
b + c = w_3 U_3 & e + f = w_3 V_3 & h + j = w_3
\end{array}$$

Substituting the right column of equations into the left two columns gives us

$$\begin{array}{cc}
c = j U_0 & f = j V_0 \\
a + c = (g + j) U_1 & d + f = (g + j) V_1 \\
a + b + c = (g + h + j) U_2 & d + e + f = (g + h + j) V_2 \\
b + c = (h + j) U_3 & e + f = (h + j) V_3
\end{array} \tag{13.2}$$

Then substituting the equations in rows 1, 2, and 4 into the third row gives the two equations

$$(g + j) U_1 + (h + j) U_3 - j U_0 = (g + h + j) U_2$$
$$(g + j) V_1 + (h + j) V_3 - j V_0 = (g + h + j) V_2$$

We juggle this into

$$g\left(U_1-U_2\right)+h\left(U_3-U_2\right)=j\left(U_0-U_1+U_2-U_3\right)$$
$$g\left(V_1-V_2\right)+h\left(V_3-V_2\right)=j\left(V_0-V_1+V_2-V_3\right)$$

(13.3)

Heckbert's original solution did the "without loss of generality" trick and assumed that $j=1$. This works since we can only expect to solve for the matrix elements up to some global scalar multiple, and since $j$ cannot be zero if point 0 is not at infinity. He then solved for $g$ and $h$ and got something that looked like

$$g=\frac{\det\left[stuff_0\right]}{\det\left[stuff_2\right]} \qquad h=\frac{\det\left[stuff_1\right]}{\det\left[stuff_2\right]}$$

I don't really like the $j=1$ assumption though since it leads to these nasty divisions. And we really don't need it if we think homogeneously. We can instead write Equation (13.3) as

$$\begin{bmatrix} g & h & j \end{bmatrix}\begin{bmatrix} U_1-U_2 & V_1-V_2 \\ U_3-U_2 & V_3-V_2 \\ -U_0+U_1-U_2+U_3 & -V_0+V_1-V_2+V_3 \end{bmatrix}=\begin{bmatrix} 0 & 0 \end{bmatrix}$$

And just say that the vector $[g\,h\,j]$ is the cross product of the two columns of the above matrix. This gives us, after a little simplification

$$g=\left(U_3-U_2\right)\left(V_1-V_0\right)-\left(U_1-U_0\right)\left(V_3-V_2\right)$$
$$h=\left(U_3-U_0\right)\left(V_1-V_2\right)-\left(U_1-U_2\right)\left(V_3-V_0\right)$$
$$j=\left(U_1-U_2\right)\left(V_3-V_2\right)-\left(U_3-U_2\right)\left(V_1-V_2\right)$$

Once we have these, it's a simple matter to get $a$ through $f$ using Equation (13.2):

$$c=jU_0 \qquad\qquad f=jV_0$$
$$a=\left(g+j\right)U_1-c \qquad d=\left(g+j\right)V_1-f$$
$$b=\left(h+j\right)U_3-c \qquad e=\left(h+j\right)V_3-f$$

Now that we have $\mathbf{M}_{qt}$, the same simple arithmetic will give us the mapping from the canonical square to the input points. This will be the matrix that satisfies:

$$\mathbf{q}\mathbf{M}_{qs}=w_s\mathbf{s}$$

Invert that (or, better, take its adjoint) and multiply to get our desired net matrix:

$$\mathbf{M}_{st} = \left[\mathbf{M}_{qs}\right]^* \mathbf{M}_{qt}$$

# Olynyk's Improvement

An even better solution recently came from my colleague Kirk Olynyk here at Microsoft Research. His basic idea was to use barycentric coordinates, rather than a unit square, as the intermediate system. Barycentric coordinates represent an arbitrary point in the plane as the weighted sum of three basis points, for example, the first three of our output points. This would represent an arbitrary texture coordinate **t** as

$$\tau_0 \mathbf{t}_0 + \tau_1 \mathbf{t}_1 + \tau_2 \mathbf{t}_2 = \mathbf{t}$$

with the constraint that the barycentric coordinates sum to one: $\tau_0 + \tau_1 + \tau_2 = 1$. Similarly, we can represent an arbitrary input point in barycentric coordinates as

$$\sigma_0 \mathbf{s}_0 + \sigma_1 \mathbf{s}_1 + \sigma_2 \mathbf{s}_2 = \mathbf{s}$$

Kirk then related the two barycentric coordinate systems by coming up with a mapping from $\begin{bmatrix} \sigma_0 & \sigma_1 & \sigma_2 \end{bmatrix}$ to $\begin{bmatrix} \tau_0 & \tau_1 & \tau_2 \end{bmatrix}$ that has the property that the barycentric coordinates of all four input points map to the barycentric coordinates of their respective output points. That is,

$$\begin{bmatrix} 1 & 0 & 0 \end{bmatrix} \mapsto \begin{bmatrix} 1 & 0 & 0 \end{bmatrix}$$
$$\begin{bmatrix} 0 & 1 & 0 \end{bmatrix} \mapsto \begin{bmatrix} 0 & 1 & 0 \end{bmatrix}$$
$$\begin{bmatrix} 0 & 0 & 1 \end{bmatrix} \mapsto \begin{bmatrix} 0 & 0 & 1 \end{bmatrix}$$
$$\begin{bmatrix} \tilde{\sigma}_0 & \tilde{\sigma}_1 & \tilde{\sigma}_2 \end{bmatrix} \mapsto \begin{bmatrix} \tilde{\tau}_0 & \tilde{\tau}_1 & \tilde{\tau}_2 \end{bmatrix}$$

(The two points in the fourth mapping above are the barycentric coordinates of the fourth input/output point pair.) To get the desired mapping, simply multiply each $\sigma_i$ componemt of an arbitrary input point by $\tilde{\tau}_i / \tilde{\sigma}_i$. Then renormalize to a valid barycentric coordinate by dividing by the sum of the components. You can see that this algorithm leaves the coordinates of the first three points intact while properly changing those of the fourth point.

So how do we get the barycentric coordinates of the fourth input/output pair? Start with the matrix formulation of the barycentric coordinates of an arbitrary point. Here's the one for output points:

$$\begin{bmatrix} \tau_0 & \tau_1 & \tau_2 \end{bmatrix} \begin{bmatrix} U_0 & V_0 & 1 \\ U_1 & V_1 & 1 \\ U_2 & V_2 & 1 \end{bmatrix} = \mathbf{t}$$

Note that if $\tau_0 + \tau_1 + \tau_2 = 1$, this guarantees that the $w$ (homogeneous) component of $\mathbf{t}$ will be 1 also. Anyway, plugging in $\mathbf{t} = \mathbf{t}_3$ and moving the matrix over the equal sign gives us

$$\begin{bmatrix} \tilde{\tau}_0 & \tilde{\tau}_1 & \tilde{\tau}_2 \end{bmatrix} = \begin{bmatrix} U_3 & V_3 & 1 \end{bmatrix} \begin{bmatrix} U_0 & V_0 & 1 \\ U_1 & V_1 & 1 \\ U_2 & V_2 & 1 \end{bmatrix}^{-1} \qquad (13.4)$$

This is nice, but it's not ideal. A full-on matrix inversion requires division by the determinant of the matrix. Likewise, the normalization to unit-sum barycentric coordinates requires division by the sum of the coordinates. Kirk dislikes divisions even more than I do, so in his implementation he removed them by homogeneously scaling them out symbolically after the fact. In thinking about this solution, though, I realized that there is a different way of deriving it that better shows its relation to the Heckbert solution.

# Another Interpretation

Heckbert used a unit square as an intermediate coordinate system, and Olynyk used barycentric coordinates. Let's look at this problem anew and try to pick an intermediate coordinate system (call it $b$) that will minimize our arithmetic as much as possible when we solve for $\mathbf{M}_{bt}$ in the equation

$$\mathbf{b}\mathbf{M}_{bt} = w\mathbf{t}$$

We want four points $\mathbf{b}_i$ in our new coordinate system that have as many zeros as possible as components. The four simplest (homogeneous) points I can imagine are [1 0 0], [0 1 0], [0 0 1], and [1 1 1]. It doesn't matter that two of these are points at infinity. All that matters is that no three of these points are collinear. I show this new two-stage transformation in Figure 13.3, although it might be a bit confusing (and unnecessary) to try to make a closed quadrilateral out of the four $\mathbf{b}$ points.

The $\mathbf{b}$ coordinate system is like "homogeneous barycentric coordinates" (with the restriction relaxed that the sum of the components equals one) but is further scaled so that the components of the fourth point are equal.

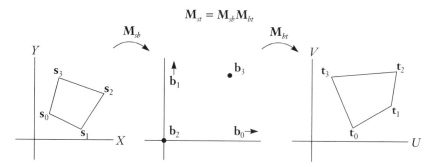

**Figure 13.3**  *Two stages of new decomposition*

So let's solve for $\mathbf{M}_{bt}$. Being extremely ecological, I will again recycle the names $a \ldots j$ for the matrix elements and $w_0 \ldots w_3$ for the (as yet) unknown homogeneous factors. Our four points generate

$$
\begin{bmatrix} 1 & 0 & 0 \\ 0 & 1 & 0 \\ 0 & 0 & 1 \\ 1 & 1 & 1 \end{bmatrix}
\begin{bmatrix} a & d & g \\ b & e & h \\ c & f & j \end{bmatrix}
=
\begin{bmatrix} w_0 U_0 & w_0 V_0 & w_0 \\ w_1 U_1 & w_1 V_1 & w_1 \\ w_2 U_2 & w_2 V_2 & w_2 \\ w_3 U_3 & w_3 V_3 & w_3 \end{bmatrix}
\tag{13.5}
$$

We could solve this by doing the same sort of substitutions that we did in the Heckbert solution, but there's an easier way. Looking at the top three rows on each side, we immediately realize that we have $\mathbf{M}_{bt}$ already staring us in the face; it's just the first three rows of Equation (13.5). Let's write it in factored form:

$$
\mathbf{M}_{bt} =
\begin{bmatrix} a & d & g \\ b & e & h \\ c & f & j \end{bmatrix}
=
\begin{bmatrix} w_0 & 0 & 0 \\ 0 & w_1 & 0 \\ 0 & 0 & w_2 \end{bmatrix}
\begin{bmatrix} U_0 & V_0 & 1 \\ U_1 & V_1 & 1 \\ U_2 & V_2 & 1 \end{bmatrix}
\tag{13.6}
$$

We only need to find $w_0$, $w_1$, and $w_2$, and we are home free. To get these, we take the bottom row of Equation (13.5):

$$
\begin{bmatrix} 1 & 1 & 1 \end{bmatrix} \mathbf{M}_{bt} = \begin{bmatrix} w_3 U_3 & w_3 V_3 & w_3 \end{bmatrix}
$$

and combine it with Equation (13.6) and write

$$
\begin{bmatrix} 1 & 1 & 1 \end{bmatrix}
\begin{bmatrix} w_0 & 0 & 0 \\ 0 & w_1 & 0 \\ 0 & 0 & w_2 \end{bmatrix}
\begin{bmatrix} U_0 & V_0 & 1 \\ U_1 & V_1 & 1 \\ U_2 & V_2 & 1 \end{bmatrix}
= w_3 \begin{bmatrix} U_3 & V_3 & 1 \end{bmatrix}
$$

We can hop the *UV* matrix over the equal sign by inverting it to get

$$\begin{bmatrix} w_0 & w_1 & w_2 \end{bmatrix} = w_3 \begin{bmatrix} U_3 & V_3 & 1 \end{bmatrix} \begin{bmatrix} U_0 & V_0 & 1 \\ U_1 & V_1 & 1 \\ U_2 & V_2 & 1 \end{bmatrix}^{-1} \qquad (13.7)$$

Comparing Equation (13.7) with Equation (13.4), we can see the relationship

$$\begin{bmatrix} w_0 & w_1 & w_2 \end{bmatrix} = w_3 \begin{bmatrix} \tilde{\tau}_0 & \tilde{\tau}_1 & \tilde{\tau}_2 \end{bmatrix}$$

In other words, our $w_0 \ldots w_2$ values are just a homogeneous scaling of the pure barycentric coordinates of the fourth point. Note also that the right-hand column of Equation (13.5) tells us that

$$w_0 + w_1 + w_2 = w_3 \qquad (13.8)$$

Remember that we can determine the $w$'s only up to a homogeneous scale factor, so let's pick something nice for, say, $w_3$. How about using the determinant of the matrix we are inverting? This can never be zero if the three points $\mathbf{t_0}$, $\mathbf{t_1}$, and $\mathbf{t_2}$ aren't collinear. Letting $w_3$ equal this matrix determinant would pleasantly turn the matrix inverse into a matrix adjoint and we have

$$\begin{bmatrix} w_0 & w_1 & w_2 \end{bmatrix} = \begin{bmatrix} U_3 & V_3 & 1 \end{bmatrix} \begin{bmatrix} U_0 & V_0 & 1 \\ U_1 & V_1 & 1 \\ U_2 & V_2 & 1 \end{bmatrix}^{*} \qquad (13.9)$$

So . . . that's half of our final answer. Now for the other half, the matrix $\mathbf{M}_{sb}$. We get the inverse of $\mathbf{M}_{sb}$ by doing the same calculation using the four input coordinate points. First calculate the three homogeneous scale factors, which I'll call $z$, by analogy with Equation (13.9):

$$\begin{bmatrix} z_0 & z_1 & z_2 \end{bmatrix} = \begin{bmatrix} X_3 & Y_3 & 1 \end{bmatrix} \begin{bmatrix} X_0 & Y_0 & 1 \\ X_1 & Y_1 & 1 \\ X_2 & Y_2 & 1 \end{bmatrix}^{*} \qquad (13.10)$$

And then, by analogy with Equation (13.6):

$$\mathbf{M}_{bs} = \begin{bmatrix} z_0 & 0 & 0 \\ 0 & z_1 & 0 \\ 0 & 0 & z_2 \end{bmatrix} \begin{bmatrix} X_0 & Y_0 & 1 \\ X_1 & Y_1 & 1 \\ X_2 & Y_2 & 1 \end{bmatrix}$$

To arrive at our ultimate goal of $\mathbf{M}_{st}$, we need the adjoint of $\mathbf{M}_{bs}$. One very nice feature of the factored form of the matrix that I've written here is that it's arithmetically simpler to adjointify than a general matrix. I'll write it out explicitly:

$$\left[\mathbf{M}_{bs}\right]^* =$$

$$\begin{bmatrix} Y_1 - Y_2 & Y_2 - Y_0 & Y_0 - Y_1 \\ X_2 - X_1 & X_0 - X_2 & X_1 - X_0 \\ X_1 Y_2 - X_2 Y_1 & X_2 Y_0 - X_0 Y_2 & X_0 Y_1 - X_1 Y_0 \end{bmatrix} \begin{bmatrix} z_1 z_2 & 0 & 0 \\ 0 & z_0 z_2 & 0 \\ 0 & 0 & z_0 z_1 \end{bmatrix} \qquad (13.11)$$

Put 'em all together and we get our gigantic punch line:

$$\mathbf{M}_{st} = \left[\mathbf{M}_{bs}\right]^* \mathbf{M}_{bt}$$

Now it's time to name some of the matrices I've been laboriously writing out for so long (actually, I've been cutting and pasting). Up to this point, I've felt that explicitly writing them out has been more informative since it allows comparisons with other parts of the equation. I will name the following matrices:

$$\mathbf{T} \equiv \begin{bmatrix} U_0 & V_0 & 1 \\ U_1 & V_1 & 1 \\ U_2 & V_2 & 1 \end{bmatrix} \qquad \mathbf{S} \equiv \begin{bmatrix} X_0 & Y_0 & 1 \\ X_1 & Y_1 & 1 \\ X_2 & Y_2 & 1 \end{bmatrix}$$

Finally, let's rewrite our final answer slightly to give a nice comparison of this technique with (a homogenized version of) Kirk's original solution:

$$\mathbf{M}_{st} = \mathbf{S}^* \begin{bmatrix} w_0 z_1 z_2 & 0 & 0 \\ 0 & z_0 w_1 z_2 & 0 \\ 0 & 0 & z_0 z_1 w_2 \end{bmatrix} \mathbf{T} \qquad (13.12)$$

The matrix $\mathbf{S}^*$ takes us from screen space to (homogeneous) barycentric coordinates. The $w$ and $z$ diagonal matrices combine to give one diagonal matrix whose elements are just homogeneous scalings of the $\tilde{\tau}_i / \tilde{\sigma}_i$ quantities that Kirk used to go from the screen barycentric system to the texture barycentric system. Matrix $\mathbf{T}$ then takes us to texture coordinates. This form is almost the simplest we can do arithmetically. But let's not give up yet.

# Geometric Interpretations

As Equations (13.9) and (13.10) indicate, we need the adjoints of matrices $\mathbf{T}$ and $\mathbf{S}$ to calculate the $w$ and $z$ values to plug into Equation (13.12). The adjoint $\mathbf{S}^*$ also shows up in Equation (13.12), but we only use $\mathbf{T}^*$ to calculate the $w$'s. Let's look at this $w$ calculation, then, to see if there's some way we can save ourselves some work. While this investigation is initially motivated by performance avarice, it will actually point out some geometric relationships that I think are the most interesting results of this whole problem. In other words, greed is good.

First, let's use the definition in Equation (13.9) to explicitly write out the calculation of $w_0$:

$$w_0 = U_3 \left( V_1 - V_2 \right) + V_3 \left( U_2 - U_1 \right) + \left( U_1 V_2 - U_2 V_1 \right) \qquad (13.13)$$

What does this mean? Well, each row of matrix $\mathbf{T}$ is a point, one of $\mathbf{t}_0$, $\mathbf{t}_1$, or $\mathbf{t}_2$. According to the definition of the adjoint, each column of $\mathbf{T}^*$ is the cross product of two rows (points) of $\mathbf{T}$. This means that each column of $\mathbf{T}^*$ is a homogeneous line. For example, column 0 of $\mathbf{T}^*$ represents the line connecting points $\mathbf{t}_1$ and $\mathbf{t}_2$. The process of multiplying an arbitrary point $\mathbf{t}$ by the matrix $\mathbf{T}^*$ just takes its dot product with the three lines $\mathbf{t}_1\mathbf{t}_2$, $\mathbf{t}_2\mathbf{t}_0$, and $\mathbf{t}_0\mathbf{t}_1$. In other words, it measures the distance from the point to the three lines. That's the essential meaning of barycentric coordinates. In any event, we can now rewrite Equation (13.13) as

$$w_0 = \mathbf{t}_3 \cdot \mathbf{t}_1 \times \mathbf{t}_2$$

This common algebraic expression has a standard geometric interpretation. Thinking of $\mathbf{t}_1$, $\mathbf{t}_2$, and $\mathbf{t}_3$ as 3D vectors, it's the volume of the parallelepiped they define. Thinking, however, of the three points as homogeneous 2D vectors, there's another interpretation: $w_0$ equals twice the area of the triangle $\mathbf{t}_3\mathbf{t}_2\mathbf{t}_1$. We can verify this algebraically by comparing the definition of $w_0$ from Equation (13.13) with twice the integral under the three triangle edges:

$$
\begin{aligned}
w_0 = & \left( U_1 - U_2 \right)\left( V_1 + V_2 \right) \\
& + \left( U_2 - U_3 \right)\left( V_2 + V_3 \right) \\
& + \left( U_3 - U_1 \right)\left( V_3 + V_1 \right)
\end{aligned}
$$

But there's another way to calculate triangle areas: as (half) the length of a cross product. We can rewrite our expression for $w_0$ so that it looks like a cross product of two vectors along the edges of the triangle. For example, taking the third component of the cross product of the vectors $\left( \mathbf{t}_1 - \mathbf{t}_3 \right)$ and $\left( \mathbf{t}_1 - \mathbf{t}_2 \right)$ gives us

$$w_0 = \left( U_1 - U_3 \right)\left( V_2 - V_3 \right) - \left( U_2 - U_3 \right)\left( V_1 - V_3 \right)$$

Now let's calculate $w_1$ (which is half the area of triangle $\mathbf{t}_3\mathbf{t}_0\mathbf{t}_2$) and $w_2$ (half the area of triangle $\mathbf{t}_3\mathbf{t}_1\mathbf{t}_0$). We only need one more vector

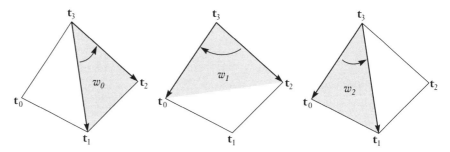

**Figure 13.4** *Geometric interpretation of w's*

difference: $(t_0 - t_3)$. This gives the simplest way I've found to calculate all the $w$'s:

$$w_0 = (U_1 - U_3)(V_2 - V_3) - (U_2 - U_3)(V_1 - V_3)$$
$$w_1 = (U_2 - U_3)(V_0 - V_3) - (U_0 - U_3)(V_2 - V_3) \qquad (13.14)$$
$$w_2 = (U_0 - U_3)(V_1 - V_3) - (U_1 - U_3)(V_0 - V_3)$$

Again, you can verify algebraically that these expressions equal those from Equation (13.9), but the geometric arguments make it seem a bit less magical. Also, you can look at Figure 13.4 for some more geometric inspiration.

# One More Thin Little Mint

There's one last little bit of juice we can squeeze out of this. This, again, came from Kirk, but he found it purely algebraically. I'm going to motivate it by an even more interesting geometric observation. It turns out that there is a magical relationship between the $z_i$ values and the bottom row of **S***. So we have to switch gears and start talking, not about $U, V, w$ but about $X, Y, z$. I'll write the analog to Equation (13.14) and, for good measure, throw in a formula for $z_3$, which is, by analogy with Equation (13.8), the sum of the first three:

$$z_0 = (X_1 - X_3)(Y_2 - Y_3) - (X_2 - X_3)(Y_1 - Y_3)$$
$$z_1 = (X_2 - X_3)(Y_0 - Y_3) - (X_0 - X_3)(Y_2 - Y_3)$$
$$z_2 = (X_0 - X_3)(Y_1 - Y_3) - (X_1 - X_3)(Y_0 - Y_3)$$
$$z_3 = (X_1 - X_0)(Y_2 - Y_0) - (X_2 - X_0)(Y_1 - Y_0)$$

We can now see the missing link: the geometric interpretation of the value $z_3$. It's the area of triangle $s_0 s_1 s_2$. To see this, look at Figure 13.5 and

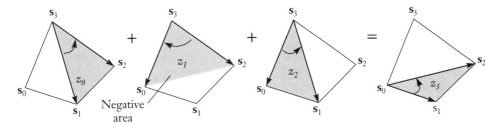

**Figure 13.5**  *Geometric interpretation of z's*

note that $z_0$ plus $z_2$ equals the area of the whole quadrilateral. Now look at $z_1$. Since its edge vectors sweep clockwise, that area is negative and subtracts from the quadrilateral to get triangle $\mathbf{s_0 s_1 s_2}$.

One side note: the area of the whole quadrilateral is

$$z_0 + z_2 = -z_1 + z_3 = (X_1 - X_3)(Y_2 - Y_0) - (X_2 - X_0)(Y_1 - Y_3)$$

This reminds us that the area of the quadrilateral is (twice) the cross product of its diagonals (with appropriate care in algebraic sign).

Now let's take a look at the bottom row of $\mathbf{S}^*$ (inside Equation (13.11)). Again, these look like areas of some sort. In fact, they are the areas of the three triangles connecting the three edges of triangle $\mathbf{t_0 t_1 t_2}$ with the origin. (If this isn't immediately clear, try temporarily imagining point 3 at the origin.) The sum of these areas also equals $z_3$, so we have the following identity, which you can also verify algebraically:

$$\mathbf{S}^*_{20} + \mathbf{S}^*_{21} + \mathbf{S}^*_{22} = z_3$$

This means that

$$\mathbf{S}^*_{20} + \mathbf{S}^*_{21} + \mathbf{S}^*_{22} = z_0 + z_1 + z_2$$

So we can calculate one of the $z$'s in terms of the others. This can, for example, turn the calculation

$$z_0 = X_3 \mathbf{S}^*_{00} + Y_3 \mathbf{S}^*_{10} + \mathbf{S}^*_{20}$$

into

$$z_0 = \mathbf{S}^*_{20} + \mathbf{S}^*_{21} + \mathbf{S}^*_{22} - z_1 - z_2$$

It turns two multiplications into two additions. This may, or may not, be a particularly big deal with current processors.

# Code

```
// Calculate elements of matrix Mst
// From 4 coordinate pairs
// (Ui Vi), (Xi Yi)
U03 = U0-U3;   V03 = V0-V3;
U13 = U1-U3;   V13 = V1-V3;
U23 = U2-U3;   V23 = V2-V3;
w0 = U13*V23 - U23*V13;
w1 = U23*V03 - U03*V23;
w2 = U03*V13 - U13*V03;


Sa00 = Y1-Y2;   Sa10 = X2-X1;
Sa01 = Y2-Y0;   Sa02 = Y0-Y1;
Sa11 = X0-X2;   Sa12 = X1-X0;
Sa20 = X1*Y2 - X2*Y1;
Sa21 = X2*Y0 - X0*Y2;
Sa22 = X0*Y1 - X1*Y0;
z1 = X3*Sa01 + Y3*Sa11 + Sa21;
z2 = X3*Sa02 + Y3*Sa12 + Sa22;
z0 = Sa20+Sa21+Sa22 - z1 - z2;


d0 = w0*z1*z2;
d1 = w1*z2*z0;
d2 = w2*z0*z1;
Sa00*=d0; Sa10*=d0; Sa20*=d0;
Sa01*=d1; Sa11*=d1; Sa21*=d1;
Sa02*=d2; Sa12*=d2; Sa22*=d2;


M00 = Sa00*U0 + Sa01*U1 + Sa02*U2;
M10 = Sa10*U0 + Sa11*U1 + Sa12*U2;
M20 = Sa20*U0 + Sa21*U1 + Sa22*U2;
M01 = Sa01*V0 + Sa01*V1 + Sa02*V2;
M11 = Sa11*V0 + Sa11*V1 + Sa12*V2;
M21 = Sa21*V0 + Sa21*V1 + Sa22*V2;
M02 = Sa00     + Sa01     + Sa02;
M12 = Sa10     + Sa11     + Sa12;
M22 = Sa20     + Sa21     + Sa22;
```

# Down a Dimension

As a mental exercise, let's look at this problem in one dimension. Suppose we want to find a single function relating $X$ and $U$ of the form

$$U = \frac{aX + b}{cX + d}$$

In matrix notation, this would be

$$\begin{bmatrix} X & 1 \end{bmatrix} \begin{bmatrix} a & c \\ b & d \end{bmatrix} = w \begin{bmatrix} U & 1 \end{bmatrix}$$

Here, each input/output pair ($X_i$ and $U_i$) gives us one row in the expression

$$\begin{bmatrix} X_i & 1 & -X_iU_i & -U_i \end{bmatrix} \begin{bmatrix} a \\ b \\ c \\ d \end{bmatrix} = 0$$

Three input/output pairs generate enough rows on the left to make this a fully determined system. Solving for $a \ldots d$ requires the determinants of four $3 \times 3$ matrices. But applying our 2D trick to the 1D problem, we can get the same result by the calculation

$$\begin{bmatrix} w_0 & w_1 \end{bmatrix} = \begin{bmatrix} (U_1 - U_2) & (U_2 - U_0) \end{bmatrix}$$
$$\begin{bmatrix} z_0 & z_1 \end{bmatrix} = \begin{bmatrix} (X_1 - X_2) & (X_2 - X_0) \end{bmatrix}$$
$$\begin{bmatrix} a & c \\ b & d \end{bmatrix} = \begin{bmatrix} 1 & -1 \\ -X_1 & X_0 \end{bmatrix} \begin{bmatrix} z_1w_0 & 0 \\ 0 & z_0w_1 \end{bmatrix} \begin{bmatrix} U_0 & 1 \\ U_1 & 1 \end{bmatrix}$$

Tediously multiplying this out gives the following:

$$a = U_0X_0 (U_2 - U_1) + X_1U_1 (U_0 - U_2) + X_2U_2 (U_1 - U_0)$$
$$b = X_0X_1U_2 (U_1 - U_0) + X_1X_2U_0 (U_2 - U_1) + X_2X_0U_1 (U_0 - U_2)$$
$$c = X_0 (U_2 - U_1) + X_1 (U_0 - U_2) + X_2 (U_1 - U_0)$$
$$d = X_0X_1 (U_1 - U_0) + X_1X_2 (U_2 - U_1) + X_2X_0 (U_0 - U_2)$$

The patterns in these expressions explicitly show something that we expect and implicitly assumed: the transformation will come out the same if we permute the indices of the input/output point pairs.

We will use this 3-point to 3-point transformation to great effect in the next few chapters.

# Up a Dimension

Now, close your eyes and stretch your mind in the other direction. Imagine input/output pairs in homogeneous 3D space. Each pair, connected by a 4×4-element matrix multiplication, gives four equations. The fourth equation gives an expression for $w_i$. Plug it into the other three and rearrange to get three equations that can be written as three rows of stuff times a 16-element column of matrix elements $a \ldots p$. Since this has a zero on the right side, we need one less than 16 equations to solve the homogeneous system. Hmm, 16 minus 1 gives 15, and we get three per input/output pair. That means that we can nail down a 3D homogeneous perspective transform with five input/output pairs. The conventional solution requires a truly excruciating 16 determinants of 15×15 matrices. Opening your eyes in shock, you discover that this exercise in imagination allowed me to get the idea across without making the typesetter hate me.

But now we know better how to solve this. The answer is a fairly straightforward generalization of Equations (13.6) and (13.9) into 4×4 matrices and 4-element vectors like so:

$$\mathbf{M}_{bt} = \begin{bmatrix} w_0 & 0 & 0 & 0 \\ 0 & w_1 & 0 & 0 \\ 0 & 0 & w_2 & 0 \\ 0 & 0 & 0 & w_3 \end{bmatrix} \begin{bmatrix} U_0 & V_0 & T_0 & 1 \\ U_1 & V_1 & T_1 & 1 \\ U_2 & V_2 & T_2 & 1 \\ U_3 & V_3 & T_3 & 1 \end{bmatrix}$$

$$\begin{bmatrix} w_0 & w_1 & w_2 & w_3 \end{bmatrix} = \begin{bmatrix} U_4 & V_4 & T_4 & 1 \end{bmatrix} \begin{bmatrix} U_0 & V_0 & T_0 & 1 \\ U_1 & V_1 & T_1 & 1 \\ U_2 & V_2 & T_2 & 1 \\ U_3 & V_3 & T_3 & 1 \end{bmatrix}^*$$

The details and arithmetic optimization tricks are left as an exercise for you to do (meaning I haven't gotten around to doing it myself).

# CHAPTER FOURTEEN

# How Many Different Rational Parametric Cubic Curves Are There? Part I, Inflection Points

JULY–AUGUST 1999

In my never-ending quest to build intuition about the relationship between algebra and geometry, I have recently turned my attention once again to cubic curves. The basic question is this: what sorts of shapes can a given symbolic expression generate? In Chapter 4, "How Many Different Cubic Curves Are There?" and Chapter 6, "Cubic Curve Update," of *Jim Blinn's Corner: Dirty Pixels* I asked this question about algebraic cubic curves of the form

$$
\begin{aligned}
Ax^3 + \quad 3Bx^2y + \quad 3Cxy^2 + \quad Dy^3 \\
+ 3Ex^2w + 6Fxyw + 3Gy^2w \\
+ 3Hxw^2 + 3\mathcal{J}yw^2 \\
+ Kw^3 = 0
\end{aligned}
$$

I am now going to ask the same question about parametric cubic curves of the form

$$\begin{bmatrix} x(T) & y(T) & w(T) \end{bmatrix} = \begin{bmatrix} T^3 & T^2 & T & 1 \end{bmatrix} \begin{bmatrix} x_3 & y_3 & w_3 \\ x_2 & y_2 & w_2 \\ x_1 & y_1 & w_1 \\ x_0 & y_0 & w_0 \end{bmatrix}$$

As an auxiliary question, I want to see which curve shapes can be generated *both* parametrically and algebraically. Many people have played around with this problem[1,2], what follows is my own personal take on the subject. I found out a lot of things that surprised me at first, but when I thought about them, they became pretty obvious. I hope I can make them obvious to you, too.

The parametric formula includes cubic Bezier curves, cubic B-spline curves, and so on, but those curves usually only consider a segment of the curve between the parameter values 0 and 1. In this chapter, I want to think about the *whole* curve as generated by all possible values of $T$ from minus infinity to plus infinity. This holistic approach is guaranteed to generate points at infinity for some value of $T$ or other. Therefore, in order to *really* understand what's going on with cubic curves, we must be fluent with infinity, both geometric and parametric. This means that we will generalize concepts that use Euclidean coordinates $[X\,Y]$ into those that use projective homogeneous coordinates $[x\,y\,w]$, and we will generalize the parameter $T$ to the homogeneous parameter $[t\,s]$.

Our ultimate goal will be to transform an arbitrary parametric cubic curve both geometrically and parametrically to match one of a set of canonical simple algebraic forms. How many such forms are possible? It turns out that there are exactly three. In order to see this, we will need some basic tools. The most important of these is the ability to find and catalog the inflection points of a curve. That will be the primary focus of this chapter.

# Inflection Points

The main thing that a cubic curve can do, that lower-order curves cannot do, is have inflection points. What is an inflection point? Suppose you

---

1  Patterson, R., "Parametric Cubics as Algebraic Curves," *Computer Aided Geometric Design*, Vol. 5, North Holland Publishers, 1998, pp. 139–159.

2  Stone, M., and DeRose, T., "A Geometric Characterization of Parametric Cubic Curves," *ACM Transactions on Graphics*, Vol. 8, No. 3, July 1989, pp. 147–163.

were driving a car along on the curve. An inflection point would be the place where you switch between "turning right" and "turning left." Circles do not have inflection points. Sine curves have lots of them. We care about inflection points because they're preserved under perspective transformations. So two curves that differ only by a perspective transformation should have the same number of inflection points.

Algebraically, an inflection point occurs when the second derivative of the curve (the acceleration) is not, at time $T$, changing the direction of the first derivative (the tangent). See Figure 14.1. This occurs when the second derivative temporarily points in the same direction as the first derivative. A nonhomogeneous expression of this fact is

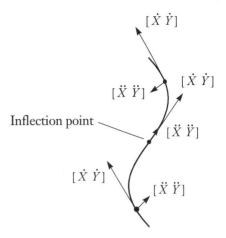

**Figure 14.1** *Relation between inflection point and derivatives*

$$\begin{bmatrix} \dot{X} & \dot{Y} \end{bmatrix} = \alpha \begin{bmatrix} \ddot{X} & \ddot{Y} \end{bmatrix}$$

We don't really care what alpha is, so it's better to express our test as

$$\frac{\dot{X}}{\ddot{X}} = \frac{\dot{Y}}{\ddot{Y}}$$

or

$$\dot{X}\ddot{Y} - \ddot{X}\dot{Y} = \det \begin{bmatrix} \dot{X} & \dot{Y} \\ \ddot{X} & \ddot{Y} \end{bmatrix} = 0$$

This determinant could also be zero, of course, if either the first or second derivative was itself zero. These locations aren't actually inflection points, but they will be useful special points to find, too.

We want to be able to deal fluidly with all possible points, both finite and infinite, so let's recast this in terms of homogeneous coordinates. For the $X$ coordinate, our old friend the chain rule gives us

$$X = \frac{x}{w}$$

$$\dot{X} = \frac{\dot{x}w - x\dot{w}}{w^2}$$

$$\ddot{X} = \frac{(\ddot{x}w - x\ddot{w})w^2 - (\dot{x}w - x\dot{w})2w\dot{w}}{w^4}$$

with similar expressions for $Y$. We can now write the $2 \times 2$ matrix in terms of homogeneous coordinates. Factoring out a few $w$'s, we get

$$\frac{1}{w^2}\begin{bmatrix} \dot{x}w - x\dot{w} & \dot{y}w - y\dot{w} \\ (\ddot{x}w - x\ddot{w}) - 2(\dot{x}w - x\dot{w})\dfrac{\dot{w}}{w} & (\ddot{y}w - y\ddot{w}) - 2(\dot{y}w - y\dot{w})\dfrac{\dot{w}}{w} \end{bmatrix}$$

Look at the mess on the second row and imagine what will happen to it as you take the determinant. You can see that the $-2(\text{stuff})$ terms will cancel out. This leaves us with the much prettier

$$\det\begin{bmatrix} \dot{X} & \dot{Y} \\ \ddot{X} & \ddot{Y} \end{bmatrix} = \frac{1}{w^2}\det\begin{bmatrix} \dot{x}w - x\dot{w} & \dot{y}w - y\dot{w} \\ \ddot{x}w - x\ddot{w} & \ddot{y}w - y\ddot{w} \end{bmatrix}$$

If you multiply out all the terms in this determinant and look at the result, you'll see a pattern. Several terms will cancel out and you will be left with six terms. A little thought and imagination, which I'll leave in your capable hands, will show that the inflection point–sensing determinant is equivalent to

$$\det\begin{bmatrix} \dot{x}w - x\dot{w} & \dot{y}w - y\dot{w} \\ \ddot{x}w - x\ddot{w} & \ddot{y}w - y\ddot{w} \end{bmatrix} = w\det\begin{bmatrix} x & y & w \\ \dot{x} & \dot{y} & \dot{w} \\ \ddot{x} & \ddot{y} & \ddot{w} \end{bmatrix} = 0 \qquad (14.1)$$

## Second-Order Curves Can't Inflect

I claimed that a circle has no inflection points. More generally, no conic sections have inflection points. Let's see why by applying Equation (14.1) to a canonical second-order curve whose matrix representation looks like

$$\begin{bmatrix} x & y & w \end{bmatrix} = \begin{bmatrix} T^2 & T & 1 \end{bmatrix}\begin{bmatrix} x_2 & y_2 & w_2 \\ x_1 & y_1 & w_1 \\ x_0 & y_0 & w_0 \end{bmatrix}$$

To get the first and second derivatives of $x$, $y$, and $w$, you only need to differentiate the $T$ row vector and conclude that

$$\begin{bmatrix} x & y & w \\ \dot{x} & \dot{y} & \dot{w} \\ \ddot{x} & \ddot{y} & \ddot{w} \end{bmatrix} = \begin{bmatrix} T^2 & T & 1 \\ 2T & 1 & 0 \\ 2 & 0 & 0 \end{bmatrix}\begin{bmatrix} x_2 & y_2 & w_2 \\ x_1 & y_1 & w_1 \\ x_0 & y_0 & w_0 \end{bmatrix}$$

Since the determinant of a product equals the product of the determinants, we have

$$\det \begin{bmatrix} x & y & w \\ \dot{x} & \dot{y} & \dot{w} \\ \ddot{x} & \ddot{y} & \ddot{w} \end{bmatrix} = \det \begin{bmatrix} T^2 & T & 1 \\ 2T & 1 & 0 \\ 2 & 0 & 0 \end{bmatrix} \cdot \det \begin{bmatrix} x_2 & y_2 & w_2 \\ x_1 & y_1 & w_1 \\ x_0 & y_0 & w_0 \end{bmatrix}$$

$$= -2 \det \begin{bmatrix} x_2 & y_2 & w_2 \\ x_1 & y_1 & w_1 \\ x_0 & y_0 & w_0 \end{bmatrix}$$

All the $T$'s canceled out. What does this mean? It means that the magic determinant is zero only if the coefficient matrix is singular, independent of $T$. A singular coefficient matrix means that the curve is degenerate; it's something like a circle squashed flat into a line segment. In this case, the tangent and second derivative point in the same direction along the whole curve. A nonsingular matrix, on the other hand, generates a full-fledged conic section. The magic determinant is never zero and therefore conic sections do not have inflection points.

## Third-Order Curves Can

Now let's bump up to third-order curves and see what we can find out. Here we have

$$\begin{bmatrix} x & y & w \\ \dot{x} & \dot{y} & \dot{w} \\ \ddot{x} & \ddot{y} & \ddot{w} \end{bmatrix} = \begin{bmatrix} T^3 & T^2 & T & 1 \\ 3T^2 & 2T & 1 & 0 \\ 6T & 2 & 0 & 0 \end{bmatrix} \begin{bmatrix} x_3 & y_3 & w_3 \\ x_2 & y_2 & w_2 \\ x_1 & y_1 & w_1 \\ x_0 & y_0 & w_0 \end{bmatrix}$$

What can we say about the determinant of this quantity? At first, it looks pretty scary. The final $3 \times 3$ matrix will have $T$-cubed terms on the top row, $T$-squared terms on the second row, and $T$ terms on the bottom row. The determinant of this mess might potentially be sixth order in $T$. Eeeuw.

What was nice in the second-order discussion was that we could separately evaluate the part containing $T$ and the part containing the polynomial coefficients because the determinant of the product of two matrices equals the product of their determinants. We can't take the determinants of the two matrices here since they aren't square. But we can do something similar. To introduce it, I'll start by dropping down a dimension and examine the product of a $2 \times 3$ matrix and a $3 \times 2$ matrix.

# A Useful Identity

Let's look at the determinant of the simpler quantity

$$\det\left(\begin{bmatrix} P_1 & P_2 & P_3 \\ Q_1 & Q_2 & Q_3 \end{bmatrix}\begin{bmatrix} R_1 & S_1 \\ R_2 & S_2 \\ R_3 & S_3 \end{bmatrix}\right)$$

This notation makes it easy to think of the rows of the first matrix as two 3-vectors, **P** and **Q**, and think of the columns of the second matrix as two 3-vectors, **R** and **S**. The matrix product is then

$$\begin{bmatrix} \mathbf{P}\cdot\mathbf{R} & \mathbf{P}\cdot\mathbf{S} \\ \mathbf{Q}\cdot\mathbf{R} & \mathbf{Q}\cdot\mathbf{S} \end{bmatrix}$$

and the determinant in question is

$$\det\begin{bmatrix} \mathbf{P}\cdot\mathbf{R} & \mathbf{P}\cdot\mathbf{S} \\ \mathbf{Q}\cdot\mathbf{R} & \mathbf{Q}\cdot\mathbf{S} \end{bmatrix} = (\mathbf{P}\cdot\mathbf{R})(\mathbf{Q}\cdot\mathbf{S}) - (\mathbf{P}\cdot\mathbf{S})(\mathbf{Q}\cdot\mathbf{R})$$

When I first started playing with this, I multiplied everything out, took the determinant, and stared at the result for a while. A pattern began to emerge. The pattern I saw can be neatly summed up in the vector algebraic identity:

$$(\mathbf{P}\cdot\mathbf{R})(\mathbf{Q}\cdot\mathbf{S}) - (\mathbf{P}\cdot\mathbf{S})(\mathbf{Q}\cdot\mathbf{R}) = (\mathbf{R}\times\mathbf{S})\cdot(\mathbf{P}\times\mathbf{Q})$$

Upon further thought, I realized that this is just an expression of what is called the epsilon-delta rule. I expounded on this at length in Chapters 9 and 10, "Uppers and Downers" (Parts I and II) of *Jim Blinn's Corner: Dirty Pixels*. As desired, it allows us to turn the determinant of a matrix product into the product of two (almost) determinants (if you think of a cross product as a close relative of a determinant).

# Up a Dimension

Now let's step up to the more heady world of $3\times4$ and $4\times3$ matrices. There is a 4D version of the epsilon-delta rule that uses a 4D analog to the cross product. The 4D cross product (which I'll call "$\text{crs}_4$") takes three 4-vectors and generates a 4-vector that is perpendicular to each of them.

You calculate the elements of this result by taking four determinants of three $3 \times 3$ matrices as follows:

$$crs_4 \left( \begin{bmatrix} x_3 \\ x_2 \\ x_1 \\ x_0 \end{bmatrix}, \begin{bmatrix} y_3 \\ y_2 \\ y_1 \\ y_0 \end{bmatrix}, \begin{bmatrix} w_3 \\ w_2 \\ w_1 \\ w_0 \end{bmatrix} \right) = \begin{bmatrix} D_3 & D_2 & D_1 & D_0 \end{bmatrix} \tag{14.2}$$

where

$$D_3 = \det \begin{bmatrix} x_2 & y_2 & w_2 \\ x_1 & y_1 & w_1 \\ x_0 & y_0 & w_0 \end{bmatrix}, \quad D_2 = -\det \begin{bmatrix} x_3 & y_3 & w_3 \\ x_1 & y_1 & w_1 \\ x_0 & y_0 & w_0 \end{bmatrix},$$

$$D_1 = \det \begin{bmatrix} x_3 & y_3 & w_3 \\ x_2 & y_2 & w_2 \\ x_0 & y_0 & w_0 \end{bmatrix}, \quad D_0 = -\det \begin{bmatrix} x_3 & y_3 & w_3 \\ x_2 & y_2 & w_2 \\ x_1 & y_1 & w_1 \end{bmatrix}$$

In 3D, the cross product is perpendicular (has zero dot product) with the two input vectors. Similarly, the 4D cross product satisfies

$$\begin{bmatrix} D_3 & D_2 & D_1 & D_0 \end{bmatrix} \begin{bmatrix} x_3 & y_3 & w_3 \\ x_2 & y_2 & w_2 \\ x_1 & y_1 & w_1 \\ x_0 & y_0 & w_0 \end{bmatrix} = \begin{bmatrix} 0 & 0 & 0 \end{bmatrix}$$

Note that the $crs_4$ of three column vectors is a row vector. Similarly, the $crs_4$ of three row vectors will be a column vector.

Let's give names to each row of the $3 \times 4$ matrix and to each column of the $4 \times 3$ matrix. The 4D epsilon-delta rule can be written in this form as

$$\det \left( \begin{bmatrix} ...\mathbf{A}... \\ ...\mathbf{B}... \\ ...\mathbf{C}... \end{bmatrix} \begin{bmatrix} \vdots & \vdots & \vdots \\ \mathbf{X} & \mathbf{Y} & \mathbf{W} \\ \vdots & \vdots & \vdots \end{bmatrix} \right) = crs_4 (\mathbf{X}, \mathbf{Y}, \mathbf{W}) \cdot crs_4 (\mathbf{A}, \mathbf{B}, \mathbf{C})$$

In other words, the determinant of the matrix product is the dot product of the two 4D cross products. Again, I discussed this identity more fully in "Uppers and Downers."

# Application

Let's see what this tells us about the inflection points on the curve represented by the coefficient matrix. Our inflection point–finding determinant is

$$\det \begin{bmatrix} x & y & w \\ \dot{x} & \dot{y} & \dot{w} \\ \ddot{x} & \ddot{y} & \ddot{w} \end{bmatrix} = \det \left( \begin{bmatrix} T^3 & T^2 & T & 1 \\ 3T^2 & 2T & 1 & 0 \\ 6T & 2 & 0 & 0 \end{bmatrix} \begin{bmatrix} x_3 & y_3 & w_3 \\ x_2 & y_2 & w_2 \\ x_1 & y_1 & w_1 \\ x_0 & y_0 & w_0 \end{bmatrix} \right)$$

We can now separately evaluate the $\mathrm{crs}_4$ of the $\mathbf{T}$ matrix to get

$$\mathrm{crs}_4 \begin{bmatrix} T^3 & T^2 & T & 1 \\ 3T^2 & 2T & 1 & 0 \\ 6T & 2 & 0 & 0 \end{bmatrix} = \begin{bmatrix} -2 \\ 6T \\ -6T^2 \\ 2T^3 \end{bmatrix}$$

(I'll throw out the homogeneous factor of 2 from here on.) Next, the $\mathrm{crs}_4$ of the coefficient matrix will be just the 4-element row of numbers $\begin{bmatrix} D_3 & D_2 & D_1 & D_0 \end{bmatrix}$ from Equation (14.2). We really can't say more about their values than that—they depend on what we were given for the coefficient matrix. The net result, then, is that an inflection point exists for each value of $T$ that satisfies

$$\begin{bmatrix} D_3 & D_2 & D_1 & D_0 \end{bmatrix} \begin{bmatrix} -1 \\ 3T \\ -3T^2 \\ T^3 \end{bmatrix} = D_0 T^3 - 3D_1 T^2 + 3D_2 T - D_3 = 0 \qquad (14.3)$$

This is only third order in $T$ rather than sixth order, as we originally feared. All the higher-order terms have conveniently canceled out.

What does this mean? Since an inflection point lies at the solution of a cubic polynomial, the inflection point count does all the things that roots of cubic equations can do. The five possibilities appear in Table 14.1.

# Collinear Inflection Points

The epsilon-delta trick also gives us a quickie demonstration of the slightly surprising fact that, if three inflection points exist, then they must be collinear, as they are in Figure 14.2.

**Table 14.1** *Five different root structures of cubic equations*

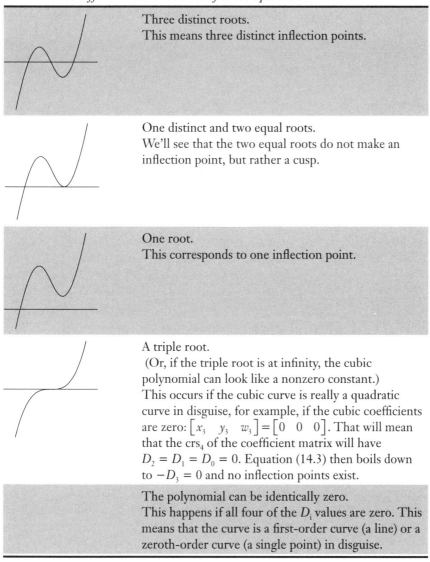

Three distinct roots.
This means three distinct inflection points.

One distinct and two equal roots.
We'll see that the two equal roots do not make an inflection point, but rather a cusp.

One root.
This corresponds to one inflection point.

A triple root.
(Or, if the triple root is at infinity, the cubic polynomial can look like a nonzero constant.)
This occurs if the cubic curve is really a quadratic curve in disguise, for example, if the cubic coefficients are zero: $\begin{bmatrix} x_3 & y_3 & w_3 \end{bmatrix} = \begin{bmatrix} 0 & 0 & 0 \end{bmatrix}$. That will mean that the $crs_4$ of the coefficient matrix will have $D_2 = D_1 = D_0 = 0$. Equation (14.3) then boils down to $-D_3 = 0$ and no inflection points exist.

The polynomial can be identically zero.
This happens if all four of the $D_i$ values are zero. This means that the curve is a first-order curve (a line) or a zeroth-order curve (a single point) in disguise.

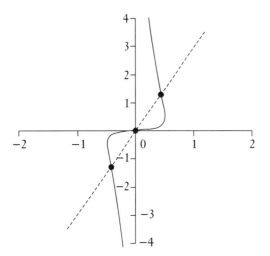

**Figure 14.2** *Cubic with three collinear inflection points*

Suppose we have three solutions to the inflection point equation, $T_0, T_1, T_2$. Then the locations of the three inflection points $\mathbf{I}_0$, $\mathbf{I}_1$, $\mathbf{I}_2$, stacked up into a matrix would be

$$\begin{bmatrix} T_0^3 & T_0^2 & T_0 & 1 \\ T_1^3 & T_1^2 & T_1 & 1 \\ T_2^3 & T_2^2 & T_2 & 1 \end{bmatrix} \begin{bmatrix} x_3 & y_3 & w_3 \\ x_2 & y_2 & w_2 \\ x_1 & y_1 & w_1 \\ x_0 & y_0 & w_0 \end{bmatrix} = \begin{bmatrix} \cdots\mathbf{I}_0\cdots \\ \cdots\mathbf{I}_1\cdots \\ \cdots\mathbf{I}_2\cdots \end{bmatrix}$$

The condition that the three inflection points are collinear is that the determinant of the $\mathbf{I}$ matrix is zero. Look familiar? It's just the same situation as before. The determinant of the $\mathbf{I}$ matrix equals the dot product of the $\mathrm{crs}_4$ of the other two. We already know the $\mathrm{crs}_4$ of the coefficient matrix; it's $\begin{bmatrix} D_3 & D_2 & D_1 & D_0 \end{bmatrix}$. What is the $\mathrm{crs}_4$ of the matrix of $T$'s? We could start taking $3\times3$ determinants and end up with a big mess of $T_0$'s, $T_1$'s, and $T_2$'s to various powers, but it turns out we already know the answer. The $\mathrm{crs}_4$ is just a vector that is perpendicular to each row of the $T$ matrix. Since the $T_i$'s are solutions to Equation (14.3), we know that

$$\begin{bmatrix} T_0^3 & T_0^2 & T_0 & 1 \\ T_1^3 & T_1^2 & T_1 & 1 \\ T_2^3 & T_2^2 & T_2 & 1 \end{bmatrix} \begin{bmatrix} D_0 \\ -3D_1 \\ 3D_2 \\ -D_3 \end{bmatrix} = \begin{bmatrix} 0 \\ 0 \\ 0 \end{bmatrix}$$

So we can evaluate the $\mathbf{I}$ determinant as a 4-vector dot product and find that it is identically zero:

$$\det \begin{bmatrix} \cdots\mathbf{I}_0\cdots \\ \cdots\mathbf{I}_1\cdots \\ \cdots\mathbf{I}_2\cdots \end{bmatrix} = \begin{bmatrix} D_3 & D_2 & D_1 & D_0 \end{bmatrix} \begin{bmatrix} D_0 \\ -3D_1 \\ 3D_2 \\ -D_3 \end{bmatrix} = 0$$

So the three inflection points are indeed collinear.

# The Case of the Missing Inflection Point

There is one more thing we need to do. Consider the following curve equation, which happens to be the one that generated Figure 14.2:

$$\begin{bmatrix} x & y & w \end{bmatrix} = \begin{bmatrix} T^3 & T^2 & T & 1 \end{bmatrix} \begin{bmatrix} 0 & 0 & 1 \\ 1 & 0 & 0 \\ 0 & 0 & 1 \\ 0 & 1 & 0 \end{bmatrix}$$

Now take the $crs_4$ of the coefficient matrix and plug it into Equation (14.3) and you get

$$\begin{bmatrix} 1 & 0 & -1 & 0 \end{bmatrix} \begin{bmatrix} -1 \\ 3T \\ -3T^2 \\ T^3 \end{bmatrix} = -1 + 3T^2 = 0 \qquad (14.4)$$

Fine. Two roots. What happened to the third inflection point? We can see three inflection points staring at us in Figure 14.2. Well . . . one of them is hidden at the parameter value $T = \infty$. This will happen for any curves that have $D_0 = 0$. How can we avoid missing such points? We handle infinite parameter values the same way we handle infinite geometric values, with homogeneous coordinates. Write the parameter $T$ as a 1D homogeneous coordinate $t/s = T$ so that

$$\begin{bmatrix} T^3 & T^2 & T & 1 \end{bmatrix} = \begin{bmatrix} \dfrac{t^3}{s^3} & \dfrac{t^2}{s^2} & \dfrac{t}{s} & 1 \end{bmatrix}$$
$$= \frac{1}{s^3} \begin{bmatrix} t^3 & st^2 & s^2t & s^3 \end{bmatrix}$$

Toss out the common homogeneous factor of $1/s^3$, and our homogeneous parametric curve definition is

$$\begin{bmatrix} x & y & w \end{bmatrix} = \begin{bmatrix} t^3 & st^2 & s^2t & s^3 \end{bmatrix} \begin{bmatrix} x_3 & y_3 & w_3 \\ x_2 & y_2 & w_2 \\ x_1 & y_1 & w_1 \\ x_0 & y_0 & w_0 \end{bmatrix}$$

How does this affect our location of inflection points? It just turns Equation (14.3) into

$$\begin{bmatrix} D_3 & D_2 & D_1 & D_0 \end{bmatrix} \begin{bmatrix} -s^3 \\ 3s^2t \\ -3st^2 \\ t^3 \end{bmatrix} = D_0t^3 - 3D_1st^2 + 3D_2s^2t - D_3s^3 = 0$$

In our problem case, Equation (14.4) becomes

$$\begin{bmatrix} 1 & 0 & -1 & 0 \end{bmatrix} \begin{bmatrix} -s^3 \\ 3s^2t \\ -3st^2 \\ t^3 \end{bmatrix} = -s^3 + 3st^2$$

$$= s\left(\sqrt{3}t + s\right)\left(\sqrt{3}t - s\right) = 0$$

The three inflection points are, then, at the homogeneous parameters

$$[t,s] = [1,0], \left[1, -\sqrt{3}\right], \left[1, \sqrt{3}\right]$$

The solution with $s = 0$ represents the inflection point at $T = t/s = \infty$.

# Next Time

The epsilon-delta rule lets us separate the algebra of the various derivatives of the parameters (which doesn't change from one curve to another) from the algebra on the polynomial coefficients (which does change). In the next chapter, armed with these tools, we'll tackle the problem of transforming an arbitrary parametric cubic to make its coefficient matrix have as many zeros as possible. We'll then look at how many patterns of nonzero elements remain and see what sorts of basic curve shapes are possible.

# How Many Different Rational Parametric Cubic Curves Are There? Part II, The "Same" Game

NOVEMBER–DECEMBER 1999

O K. Here's the deal. I've been playing with the question in the title on and off for over a year now. I'm interested in both the answer to the question and in finding the clearest possible derivation of that answer. My first efforts were very algebra intensive but had an aura of concreteness about them. As I played with the question and went through innumerable drafts of this column, I came up with more and more elegant ways to ward off the brute-force algebra and make the answer more intuitive without reams of calculation. In order for these elegant techniques to work, however, I needed to build up a collection of tools (or lemmas for the mathematically erudite) that themselves took a little time to explain.

The tool that I described in the previous chapter (the use of a particular matrix identity, which I will review here) popped up just before I started to write. I had to scrap my original idea for that chapter and rewrite it to describe this new tool. Using this tool to answer our big question has required major surgery to what you are now seeing in the current chapter.

I have already given you the answer to the big question: three. But deriving that answer in a clear and obvious manner is still a little ways away. But that's OK. The reason we are doing this is really not so much to answer the question as to build our intuition about the algebraic formulas and the geometry that they represent. Let's see, isn't there a phrase that encapsulates this idea? Oh yes: *The journey is the reward.*

# Definition

So, let's reiterate what we are dealing with: parametric cubic curves defined by the formula

$$\begin{bmatrix} x(T) & y(T) & w(T) \end{bmatrix} = \begin{bmatrix} T^3 & T^2 & T & 1 \end{bmatrix} \begin{bmatrix} x_3 & y_3 & w_3 \\ x_2 & y_2 & w_2 \\ x_1 & y_1 & w_1 \\ x_0 & y_0 & w_0 \end{bmatrix} \tag{15.1}$$

We are interested in *all* points generated by this equation, for *all* values of $T$ from $-\infty$ to $+\infty$. Infinite parameter values are easier to manipulate if we use a homogeneous parameterization, something like expressing the parameter in 1D homogeneous coordinates. I will denote the homogeneous parameter coordinates as $[t,s]$, where $T = t/s$. In terms of the homogeneous parameterization, the curve equation is

$$\begin{bmatrix} x(t,s) & y(t,s) & w(t,s) \end{bmatrix} = \begin{bmatrix} t^3 & t^2 s & t s^2 & s^3 \end{bmatrix} \begin{bmatrix} x_3 & y_3 & w_3 \\ x_2 & y_2 & w_2 \\ x_1 & y_1 & w_1 \\ x_0 & y_0 & w_0 \end{bmatrix} \tag{15.2}$$

I'll bounce back and forth between the more familiar nonhomogeneous parameter $T$ and homogeneous parameter representation $[t,s]$ as clarity dictates.

According to the homogeneous convention, any scalar multiple of a $[t,s]$ coordinate represents the same parametric point, and will generate the same geometric point. To generate the whole curve, we must trace out a curve in $[t,s]$ space that looks roughly semicircular around the origin. Why go only halfway around the origin? Well, if the curve starts at $[t_0,s_0]$ and ends at $[-t_0,-s_0]$, it will have returned to its geometric starting point. (If it started at $[x_0\ y_0\ w_0]$, it will now be at $[-x_0\ -y_0\ -w_0]$.) If you went around the parametric origin through a whole circle, you would trace out the curve twice.

The matrix of coefficients contains all the information about the curve, so I will give it a name:

$$\begin{bmatrix} x_3 & y_3 & w_3 \\ x_2 & y_2 & w_2 \\ x_1 & y_1 & w_1 \\ x_0 & y_0 & w_0 \end{bmatrix} \equiv \mathbf{C}$$

# "Different" Means Not the Same

Next, let's concretize what I mean by "different curves" by turning the question around and defining what makes two curves the "same." We will then sort all the parametric cubic curves into groups of the same curves, and see how many groups we have.

### The Same via Transformation

In projective geometry, we are interested in properties of shapes that remain constant even if the shape is subjected to a perspective transformation. The sorts of geometric properties that remain unchanged by such a transformation include intersections, tangency, and inflection points.

Algebraically, we typically express a perspective transformation as a homogeneous matrix multiplication:

$$\begin{bmatrix} x & y & w \end{bmatrix} \mathbf{M} = \begin{bmatrix} \tilde{x} & \tilde{y} & \tilde{w} \end{bmatrix}$$

The coefficient matrix transforms in the same way:

$$\mathbf{CM} = \tilde{\mathbf{C}}$$

Accordingly, if we can find a nonsingular transformation matrix $\mathbf{M}$ that changes one coefficient matrix $\mathbf{C}$ into another one $\tilde{\mathbf{C}}$, we will say that the curves generated by those matrices are the same.

### The Same via Reparametrization

There's another algebraic transformation we can perform on the curve equation that doesn't change the curve shape at all—we can change the parameterization. This change is possible because we're interested in the whole curve generated by the infinite parameter range $-\infty \leq T \leq +\infty$. For example, if we define

$$T = a\hat{T} + c$$

and run $\hat{T}$ from $-\infty$ to $+\infty$, we'll also generate all $T$'s from $-\infty$ to $+\infty$. To see how this affects the algebra of the coefficient matrix, we calculate

$$T^2 = a^2\hat{T}^2 + 2ac\hat{T} + c^2$$
$$T^3 = a^3\hat{T}^3 + 3a^2c\hat{T}^2 + 3ac^2\hat{T} + c^3$$

and write these equations in matrix form:

$$\begin{bmatrix} T^3 & T^2 & T & 1 \end{bmatrix} = \begin{bmatrix} \hat{T}^3 & \hat{T}^2 & \hat{T} & 1 \end{bmatrix} \begin{bmatrix} a^3 & 0 & 0 & 0 \\ 3a^2c & a^2 & 0 & 0 \\ 3ac^2 & 2ac & a & 0 \\ c^3 & c^2 & c & 1 \end{bmatrix}$$

Plugging this into Equation (15.1), we can see that

$$\begin{bmatrix} T^3 & T^2 & T & 1 \end{bmatrix}\mathbf{C} = \begin{bmatrix} \hat{T}^3 & \hat{T}^2 & \hat{T} & 1 \end{bmatrix} \begin{bmatrix} a^3 & 0 & 0 & 0 \\ 3a^2c & a^2 & 0 & 0 \\ 3ac^2 & 2ac & a & 0 \\ c^3 & c^2 & c & 1 \end{bmatrix}\mathbf{C}$$

Evaluating each of these for all values of $T$ and all values of $\hat{T}$ will generate exactly the same set of points. In other words, the coefficient matrices

$$\mathbf{C} \quad \text{and} \quad \begin{bmatrix} a^3 & 0 & 0 & 0 \\ 3a^2c & a^2 & 0 & 0 \\ 3ac^2 & 2ac & a & 0 \\ c^3 & c^2 & c & 1 \end{bmatrix}\mathbf{C}$$

generate exactly the same curve without any geometric distortions.

When we go to the homogeneous parameterization, we can use an even more general transformation, a 1D perspective (rational linear) transform of the form

$$T = \frac{a\hat{T} + c}{b\hat{T} + d} \tag{15.3}$$

A plot of this type of function looks like either a line or a hyperbola. Note that the function is still a one-to-one mapping of $\hat{T}$ to $T$ (including infinite values) and that it's monotonic since the derivative $dT/d\hat{T}$ has a constant sign.

Recasting this function in homogeneous parameter space, we get

$$\frac{t}{s} = \frac{a\dfrac{\hat{t}}{\hat{s}} + c}{b\dfrac{\hat{t}}{\hat{s}} + d} = \frac{a\hat{t} + c\hat{s}}{b\hat{t} + d\hat{s}}$$

Writing this as a matrix gives

$$\begin{bmatrix} t & s \end{bmatrix} = \begin{bmatrix} \hat{t} & \hat{s} \end{bmatrix} \begin{bmatrix} a & b \\ c & d \end{bmatrix}$$

In other words, the reparametrization is a simple linear transformation of [t,s] space. This is OK as long as the transformation is nonsingular, which is as long as $ad - bc \neq 0$.

To see how this reparametrization affects the form of the coefficient matrix, we calculate the following:

$$t^3 = \left(a\hat{t} + c\hat{s}\right)^3$$
$$t^2 s = \left(a\hat{t} + c\hat{s}\right)^2 \left(b\hat{t} + c\hat{s}\right)$$
$$ts^2 = \left(a\hat{t} + c\hat{s}\right)\left(b\hat{t} + c\hat{s}\right)^2$$
$$s^3 = \left(b\hat{t} + c\hat{s}\right)^3$$

Expand this mess all out and write it as a matrix product, and we get

$$\begin{bmatrix} t^3 & t^2 s & ts^2 & s^3 \end{bmatrix} = \begin{bmatrix} \hat{t}^3 & \hat{t}^2\hat{s} & \hat{t}\hat{s}^2 & \hat{s}^3 \end{bmatrix} \mathbf{R} \tag{15.4}$$

where

$$\mathbf{R} \equiv \begin{bmatrix} a^3 & a^2 b & ab^2 & b^3 \\ 3a^2 c & a\,(2bc + ad) & b\,(bc + 2ad) & 3b^2 d \\ 3ac^2 & c\,(bc + 2ad) & d\,(2bc + ad) & -3bd^2 \\ c^3 & c^2 d & cd^2 & d^3 \end{bmatrix}$$

Now we combine Equations (15.2) and (15.4) to get

$$\begin{bmatrix} x & y & w \end{bmatrix} = \begin{bmatrix} \hat{t}^3 & \hat{t}^2\hat{s} & \hat{t}\hat{s}^2 & \hat{s}^3 \end{bmatrix} \mathbf{RC}$$

We say that any coefficient matrix $\mathbf{C}$ generates the same curve as the matrix $\mathbf{RC}$ for any $\mathbf{R}$ constructed with any values $a,b,c,d$ such that $ad - bc \neq 0$.

# The Game

{ o here's what we're going to do. We're going to develop an algorithm that takes an arbitrary coefficient matrix $\mathbf{C}$ and transforms it via a (nonsingular) reparametrization matrix $\mathbf{R}$ and a (nonsingular) geometric transformation matrix $\mathbf{M}$ to turn it into a canonical form:

$$\mathbf{RCM} = \tilde{\mathbf{C}}$$

We'll devise this canonical form to be as simple as possible, with lots of zeros and ones as elements. It will turn out that there are six possible resulting types of $\tilde{\mathbf{C}}$ matrices, three that represent "true" cubics, and three that come from lower-order curves disguised as cubics.

# The Canonical Geometric Transform

A s a warm-up exercise, let's start with an arbitrary second-order curve and simplify it via geometric transformations. We start with

$$\begin{bmatrix} x & y & w \end{bmatrix} = \begin{bmatrix} t^2 & ts & s^2 \end{bmatrix} \begin{bmatrix} x_2 & y_2 & w_2 \\ x_1 & y_1 & w_1 \\ x_0 & y_0 & w_0 \end{bmatrix}$$

Transforming by the matrix $\mathbf{M}$ gives

$$\begin{bmatrix} \hat{x} & \hat{y} & \hat{z} \end{bmatrix} = \begin{bmatrix} t^2 & ts & s^2 \end{bmatrix} \begin{bmatrix} x_2 & y_2 & w_2 \\ x_1 & y_1 & w_1 \\ x_0 & y_0 & w_0 \end{bmatrix} \mathbf{M}$$

We want to find a matrix $\mathbf{M}$ that gives us as simple a product as possible with the coefficient matrix. Gee, what could that be? How about simply picking $\mathbf{M}$ as the inverse of the coefficient matrix. You would get

$$\begin{bmatrix} \hat{x} & \hat{y} & \hat{w} \end{bmatrix} = \begin{bmatrix} t^2 & st & s^2 \end{bmatrix} \begin{bmatrix} 1 & 0 & 0 \\ 0 & 1 & 0 \\ 0 & 0 & 1 \end{bmatrix}$$

Any second-order curve with a nonsingular coefficient matrix is the "same" as this canonical curve, which happens to be a parabola. All conic sections are transformations of this canonical parabola. This means that, according to the rules of our game, there is exactly *one* second-order curve.

There is a bit of a gotcha though. We need to worry about the case where the coefficient matrix is singular. As it happens, this turns out to be linear curve (OK, a line) in disguise, not a true second-order curve. I'll deal with such cases in a separate column.

Now let's see what happens when we try to simplify a cubic in a similar manner. We want to find a transformation $\mathbf{M}$ that will simplify the coefficient matrix

$$\begin{bmatrix} \hat{x} & \hat{y} & \hat{w} \end{bmatrix} = \begin{bmatrix} t^3 & t^2 s & ts^2 & s^3 \end{bmatrix} \begin{bmatrix} x_3 & y_3 & w_3 \\ x_2 & y_2 & w_2 \\ x_1 & y_1 & w_1 \\ x_0 & y_0 & w_0 \end{bmatrix} \mathbf{M}$$

We could shave off the top three rows of the coefficient matrix and transform by the inverse of this $3 \times 3$ matrix. As long as this matrix is nonsingular, we'll get

$$\begin{bmatrix} \hat{x} & \hat{y} & \hat{w} \end{bmatrix} = \begin{bmatrix} t^3 & t^2 s & ts^2 & s^3 \end{bmatrix} \begin{bmatrix} 1 & 0 & 0 \\ 0 & 1 & 0 \\ 0 & 0 & 1 \\ \hat{x}_0 & \hat{y}_0 & \hat{w}_0 \end{bmatrix}$$

So we've boiled our cubic curve down to what, at first, looks like a three-parameter class of curves, depending on what we get for $\hat{x}_0, \hat{y}_0, \hat{w}_0$. To understand what to do next, we must remember our tool from the last chapter.

# Inflection Points Revisited

In the previous chapter, we showed that the inflection points of a cubic curve are at parameter values that are the solutions to a homogeneous cubic polynomial:

$$\begin{bmatrix} D_3 & D_2 & D_1 & D_0 \end{bmatrix} \begin{bmatrix} -s^3 \\ 3ts^2 \\ -3t^2 s \\ t^3 \end{bmatrix} = \qquad (15.5)$$

$$D_0 t^3 - 3D_1 t^2 s + 3D_2 ts^2 - D_3 s^3 = 0$$

where the coefficients $D_i$ are the determinants of the various $3 \times 3$ submatrices of the coefficient matrix:

$$D_3 = \det \begin{bmatrix} x_2 & y_2 & w_2 \\ x_1 & y_1 & w_1 \\ x_0 & y_0 & w_0 \end{bmatrix}, \quad D_2 = -\det \begin{bmatrix} x_3 & y_3 & w_3 \\ x_1 & y_1 & w_1 \\ x_0 & y_0 & w_0 \end{bmatrix},$$

$$D_1 = \det \begin{bmatrix} x_3 & y_3 & w_3 \\ x_2 & y_2 & w_2 \\ x_0 & y_0 & w_0 \end{bmatrix}, \quad D_0 = -\det \begin{bmatrix} x_3 & y_3 & w_3 \\ x_2 & y_2 & w_2 \\ x_1 & y_1 & w_1 \end{bmatrix} \tag{15.6}$$

Notice that the matrix defining $D_0$ is the one we used for the canonical transform above.

# Back to the Game

Now we can relate the values of $\hat{x}_0, \hat{y}_0, \hat{w}_0$ to the values of $D_i$. We start by noting that each row of the coefficient matrix is a homogeneous point in the plane. I'll give names to these row vectors as follows (I include the ellipses to emphasize that the points are row vectors):

$$\begin{bmatrix} x_3 & y_3 & w_3 \\ x_2 & y_2 & w_2 \\ x_1 & y_1 & w_1 \\ x_0 & y_0 & w_0 \end{bmatrix} = \begin{bmatrix} \cdots \mathbf{p}_3 \cdots \\ \cdots \mathbf{p}_2 \cdots \\ \cdots \mathbf{p}_1 \cdots \\ \cdots \mathbf{p}_0 \cdots \end{bmatrix}$$

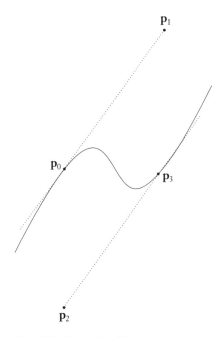

It's interesting to note that the top and bottom rows are points on the curve itself. $\mathbf{p}_0$ is the point at the homogeneous parameter value $[0,1]$ (or at $T = 0$ in the nonhomogeneous formulation), and $\mathbf{p}_3$ is the point at the homogeneous parameter value $[1,0]$ (or at $T = \infty$ in the nonhomogeneous formulation). Furthermore, the line through $\mathbf{p}_0$ and $\mathbf{p}_1$ is tangent to the curve at $\mathbf{p}_0$. And the line through $\mathbf{p}_2$ and $\mathbf{p}_3$ is tangent to the curve at $\mathbf{p}_3$ (see Figure 15.1). Anyway, we can now rewrite the definition of the elements of the $D$ vector from Equation (15.6) as

$$\begin{aligned} D_3 &= \quad \mathbf{p}_2 \cdot \mathbf{p}_1 \times \mathbf{p}_0 \\ D_2 &= -\mathbf{p}_3 \cdot \mathbf{p}_1 \times \mathbf{p}_0 \\ D_1 &= \quad \mathbf{p}_3 \cdot \mathbf{p}_2 \times \mathbf{p}_0 \\ D_0 &= -\mathbf{p}_3 \cdot \mathbf{p}_2 \times \mathbf{p}_1 \end{aligned}$$

**Figure 15.1** *Rows of coefficient matrix interpreted as points*

And the geometric transformation matrix we were using as our canonical transformation is simply

$$\mathbf{M} = \begin{bmatrix} \cdots \mathbf{P}_3 \cdots \\ \cdots \mathbf{P}_2 \cdots \\ \cdots \mathbf{P}_1 \cdots \end{bmatrix}^{-1}$$

We can evaluate the matrix inverse from the cross products of the various row vectors. Each cross product gives a column vector, and the inverse is

$$\begin{bmatrix} \cdots \mathbf{P}_3 \cdots \\ \cdots \mathbf{P}_2 \cdots \\ \cdots \mathbf{P}_1 \cdots \end{bmatrix}^{-1} = \frac{-1}{D_0} \begin{bmatrix} \vdots & \vdots & \vdots \\ \mathbf{P}_2 \times \mathbf{P}_1 & \mathbf{P}_1 \times \mathbf{P}_3 & \mathbf{P}_3 \times \mathbf{P}_2 \\ \vdots & \vdots & \vdots \end{bmatrix}$$

As long as this matrix is nonsingular (that is, the determinant, $D_0$, is nonzero), we can see that our canonical transformation will generate

$$\begin{bmatrix} \cdots \mathbf{P}_3 \cdots \\ \cdots \mathbf{P}_2 \cdots \\ \cdots \mathbf{P}_1 \cdots \\ \cdots \mathbf{P}_0 \cdots \end{bmatrix} \begin{bmatrix} \cdots \mathbf{P}_3 \cdots \\ \cdots \mathbf{P}_2 \cdots \\ \cdots \mathbf{P}_1 \cdots \end{bmatrix}^{-1}$$

$$= \begin{bmatrix} \cdots \mathbf{P}_3 \cdots \\ \cdots \mathbf{P}_2 \cdots \\ \cdots \mathbf{P}_1 \cdots \\ \cdots \mathbf{P}_0 \cdots \end{bmatrix} \frac{-1}{D_0} \begin{bmatrix} \vdots & \vdots & \vdots \\ \mathbf{P}_2 \times \mathbf{P}_1 & \mathbf{P}_1 \times \mathbf{P}_3 & \mathbf{P}_3 \times \mathbf{P}_2 \\ \vdots & \vdots & \vdots \end{bmatrix}$$

$$= \begin{bmatrix} 1 & 0 & 0 \\ 0 & 1 & 0 \\ 0 & 0 & 1 \\ -\dfrac{D_3}{D_0} & -\dfrac{D_2}{D_0} & -\dfrac{D_1}{D_0} \end{bmatrix}$$

This, then, gives the meaning of the bottom row of the candidate canonical matrix. If, however, the original curve gave us a value of $D_0 = 0$, this is not a good choice for a canonical transformation. All is not lost, however. We can pick a transformation matrix as the inverse of any of the other subsets of three of the four rows and get the following possibilities for canonical coefficient matrices:

$$\begin{bmatrix} \cdots \mathbf{p}_3 \cdots \\ \cdots \mathbf{p}_2 \cdots \\ \cdots \mathbf{p}_1 \cdots \\ \cdots \mathbf{p}_0 \cdots \end{bmatrix} \begin{bmatrix} \cdots \mathbf{p}_3 \cdots \\ \cdots \mathbf{p}_2 \cdots \\ \cdots \mathbf{p}_1 \cdots \\ \cdots \mathbf{p}_0 \cdots \end{bmatrix}^{-1} = \begin{bmatrix} 1 & 0 & 0 \\ 0 & 1 & 0 \\ -\dfrac{D_3}{D_1} & -\dfrac{D_2}{D_1} & -\dfrac{D_0}{D_1} \\ 0 & 0 & 1 \end{bmatrix}$$

$$\begin{bmatrix} \cdots \mathbf{p}_3 \cdots \\ \cdots \mathbf{p}_2 \cdots \\ \cdots \mathbf{p}_1 \cdots \\ \cdots \mathbf{p}_0 \cdots \end{bmatrix} \begin{bmatrix} \cdots \mathbf{p}_2 \cdots \\ \cdots \mathbf{p}_1 \cdots \\ \cdots \mathbf{p}_0 \cdots \end{bmatrix}^{-1} = \begin{bmatrix} 1 & 0 & 0 \\ -\dfrac{D_3}{D_2} & -\dfrac{D_1}{D_2} & -\dfrac{D_0}{D_2} \\ 0 & 1 & 0 \\ 0 & 0 & 1 \end{bmatrix}$$

$$\begin{bmatrix} \cdots \mathbf{p}_3 \cdots \\ \cdots \mathbf{p}_2 \cdots \\ \cdots \mathbf{p}_1 \cdots \\ \cdots \mathbf{p}_0 \cdots \end{bmatrix} \begin{bmatrix} \cdots \mathbf{p}_2 \cdots \\ \cdots \mathbf{p}_1 \cdots \\ \cdots \mathbf{p}_0 \cdots \end{bmatrix}^{-1} = \begin{bmatrix} -\dfrac{D_2}{D_3} & -\dfrac{D_1}{D_3} & -\dfrac{D_0}{D_3} \\ 1 & 0 & 0 \\ 0 & 1 & 0 \\ 0 & 0 & 1 \end{bmatrix}$$

Which of these is best to choose will depend on what values we have for the $D_i$'s.

We have therefore been able to recast the question "How many different rational parametric cubic curves are there?" as "How many different homogeneous cubic polynomials are there?" We've gone from needing to understand the 12 numbers in the coefficient matrix to needing to understand the 4 coefficients in a homogeneous cubic polynomial.

# How Does the Game Affect *D*?

The $D$ vector determines where the inflection points are. The reason that inflection points are interesting is that the number of them will not change due to perspective transformations or due to reparametrization. How does this fact show up in the algebra of transformation that we just defined?

### Geometric

When we transform $\mathbf{C}$ by a nonsingular geometric transformation $\mathbf{M}$ to the new matrix $\tilde{\mathbf{C}} = \mathbf{CM}$, what will be the elements of the $D$ vector for this new coefficient matrix? Remember that the determinant of a product is the product of the determinants. So the determinant of any three rows of $\tilde{\mathbf{C}}$ will equal the determinant of the same three rows of $\mathbf{C}$ times the determinant of $\mathbf{M}$. Applying this to each $3 \times 3$ submatrix of $\mathbf{C}$ and $\tilde{\mathbf{C}}$ gives

$$\begin{bmatrix} \tilde{D}_3 & \tilde{D}_2 & \tilde{D}_1 & \tilde{D}_0 \end{bmatrix} = (\det \mathbf{M}) \begin{bmatrix} D_3 & D_2 & D_1 & D_0 \end{bmatrix}$$

In other words, a geometric transformation of the curve will just apply a uniform homogeneous scale of det$\mathbf{M}$ to the $D$ vector. It will not change the location of the roots of the $D$ polynomial, which are the parameter values at the inflection points. This pretty much makes sense.

## Reparametrization

Reparametrization does not change the geometry of the curve at all, so inflection points stay put geometrically, while they may move around parametrically. To see where they move to, let's rewrite Equation (15.5) as

$$D_0 t^3 - 3D_1 t^2 s + 3D_2 ts^2 - D_3 s^3 =$$

$$\begin{bmatrix} t^3 & t^2 s & ts^2 & s^3 \end{bmatrix} \begin{bmatrix} D_0 \\ -3D_1 \\ 3D_2 \\ -D_3 \end{bmatrix} = 0$$

If we reparametrize this using Equation (15.4), we get

$$\begin{bmatrix} \hat{t}^3 & \hat{t}^2 \hat{s} & \hat{t}\hat{s}^2 & \hat{s}^3 \end{bmatrix} \mathbf{R} \begin{bmatrix} D_0 \\ -3D_1 \\ 3D_2 \\ -D_3 \end{bmatrix} = 0$$

In other words, the coefficients of the reparametrized $D$ are

$$\mathbf{R} \begin{bmatrix} D_0 \\ -3D_1 \\ 3D_2 \\ -D_3 \end{bmatrix} = \begin{bmatrix} \hat{D}_0 \\ -3\hat{D}_1 \\ 3\hat{D}_2 \\ -\hat{D}_3 \end{bmatrix}$$

If you plot the function

$$f(t,s) = D_0 t^3 - 3D_1 t^2 s + 3D_2 ts^2 - D_3 s^3$$

and consider what reparametrization does to it, you can see that it is just a rotation and shear of the function in parameter space. It mangles the shape, but one thing it does not do is to change the number and multiplicity of roots of the polynomial.

# Winning the Game

The next order of business is to immerse ourselves in what types of homogeneous cubic polynomials exist under reparametrization. Our goal will be to pick a reparametrization matrix that makes the new values $\hat{D}_i$ as simple as possible. We'll tackle that in the next millennium. (This was written just before New Year's Day 2000. . . . Oh, I really crack myself up.)

# CHAPTER SIXTEEN

# How Many Different Rational Parametric Cubic Curves AreThere? Part III, The Catalog

MARCH – APRIL 2000

Our journey to the answer to the question posed in the title is nearing an end. As I have played around with the ideas in these three chapters, I've begun to feel like I'm experiencing Zeno's paradox—I keep finding subproblems and digressions, each one getting us another halfway to the solution. I'm going to restrain myself a bit this time, though, and power through to a final answer. To do this, I will have to defer some interesting discussions about homogeneous polynomials and their properties. Although this will get us an answer, our purpose here is really insight rather than answers to specific questions. I will therefore reserve the right to go back and revisit these critters in more detail in a later book.

# Our Story So Far

**W**e are interested in rational parametric cubic curves defined by

$$\begin{bmatrix} x(T) & y(T) & w(T) \end{bmatrix} = \begin{bmatrix} T^3 & T^2 & T & 1 \end{bmatrix} \begin{bmatrix} x_3 & y_3 & w_3 \\ x_2 & y_2 & w_2 \\ x_1 & y_1 & w_1 \\ x_0 & y_0 & w_0 \end{bmatrix}$$

I'll name the matrix of polynomial coefficients **C**:

$$\mathbf{C} = \begin{bmatrix} x_3 & y_3 & w_3 \\ x_2 & y_2 & w_2 \\ x_1 & y_1 & w_1 \\ x_0 & y_0 & w_0 \end{bmatrix}$$

We're interested in all points on the curve generated by all values of the parameter, $-\infty \le T \le +\infty$. Dealing with infinity invites homogeneous representations, so I'll express the parameter as the homogeneous coordinates $(t,s)$, where $T = t/s$. The curve equation is then

$$\begin{bmatrix} x(t,s) & y(t,s) & w(t,s) \end{bmatrix} = \begin{bmatrix} t^3 & t^2 s & ts^2 & s^3 \end{bmatrix} \mathbf{C}$$

We can generate all points on the curve by plugging in values of $(t,s)$ along some curve in $(t,s)$ space, for example, the semicircle $(t, s) = (\sin \theta, \cos \theta)$; $-90° \le \theta \le +90°$. We only need half a circle because the parameter values $(-t,-s)$ generate the same homogeneous point as the parameter $(t,s)$.

## Think Different

We are interested in finding out how many essentially different shapes this equation can make. Chapter 15 more precisely defined "different" in terms of what makes two curves the "same." We consider two curves the same if they are merely geometric transformations of each other via some $3 \times 3$ homogeneous transformation matrix **M** (perhaps including perspective). Additionally, we consider two curves the same if one is simply a reparametrization of the other. The particular reparametrization we want to use is a simple linear transformation of the homogeneous parameters:

$$\begin{bmatrix} t & s \end{bmatrix} = \begin{bmatrix} \hat{t} & \hat{s} \end{bmatrix} \begin{bmatrix} a & b \\ c & d \end{bmatrix}$$

Note that I'm actually defining the inverse of the matrix that transforms $(t, s)$ to $(\hat{t}, \hat{s})$. This makes the expression of Equation (16.1) easier. Think of this transformation as a 1D homogeneous (1DH) version of the traditional geometric transformation used in computer graphics. It includes translations and scalings of $T = t/s$ as well as a perspective transformation. As long as the matrix is nonsingular $(ad - bc \neq 0)$, the transformation will be one to one, and all the points generated by all the possible ratios of $(t, s)$ will also be generated by all possible ratios of $(\hat{t}, \hat{s})$. What is the algebraic effect of this on the coefficient matrix? As described in Chapter 15, this reparametrization does not change the algebraic form of the curve since we can write the relation between the various powers of $(t, s)$ and of $(\hat{t}, \hat{s})$ as

$$\begin{bmatrix} t^3 & t^2 s & ts^2 & s^3 \end{bmatrix} = \begin{bmatrix} \hat{t}^3 & \hat{t}^2 \hat{s} & \hat{t}\hat{s}^2 & \hat{s}^3 \end{bmatrix} \mathbf{R} \tag{16.1}$$

where

$$\mathbf{R} \equiv \begin{bmatrix} a^3 & a^2 b & ab^2 & b^3 \\ 3a^2 c & a(2bc + ad) & b(bc + 2ad) & 3b^2 d \\ 3ac^2 & c(bc + 2ad) & d(2bc + ad) & 3bd^2 \\ c^3 & c^2 d & cd^2 & d^3 \end{bmatrix}$$

The coefficient matrix of the reparametrized curve is then $\hat{\mathbf{C}} = \mathbf{RC}$. These two coefficient matrices generate the same curve—they just have their parameter values distributed differently.

So, in sum, two coefficient matrices generate the same curve if it's possible to find a nonsingular reparametrization matrix $\mathbf{R}$ and nonsingular geometric transformation $\mathbf{M}$ such that

$$\tilde{\mathbf{C}} = \mathbf{RCM}$$

Our job now is, given a matrix $\mathbf{C}$, to be able to find $\mathbf{R}$ and $\mathbf{M}$ that will make $\tilde{\mathbf{C}}$ into one of a small set of canonical curves that are as algebraically simple as possible.

## Same-ing Tools

In Chapter 14, we discovered that we can find the inflection points of this curve at parameter values $(t,s)$ that are at the zeros of the homogeneous polynomial:

$$D_0 t^3 - 3D_1 t^2 s + 3D_2 ts^2 - D_3 s^3 = 0$$

where the coefficients $D_i$ are the determinants of the various $3 \times 3$ sub-matrices of $\mathbf{C}$:

$$D_3 = \det \begin{bmatrix} x_2 & y_2 & w_2 \\ x_1 & y_1 & w_1 \\ x_0 & y_0 & w_0 \end{bmatrix}, \quad D_2 = -\det \begin{bmatrix} x_3 & y_3 & w_3 \\ x_1 & y_1 & w_1 \\ x_0 & y_0 & w_0 \end{bmatrix},$$

$$D_1 = \det \begin{bmatrix} x_3 & y_3 & w_3 \\ x_2 & y_2 & w_2 \\ x_0 & y_0 & w_0 \end{bmatrix}, \quad D_0 = -\det \begin{bmatrix} x_3 & y_3 & w_3 \\ x_2 & y_2 & w_2 \\ x_1 & y_1 & w_1 \end{bmatrix},$$

In Chapter 15, we discovered that any two curves that had the same inflection point polynomial—that is, any two whose coefficient matrices generated the same $D_i$ values (up to a scale)—were just geometric transformations of each other (and were therefore the same shape). In particular, we showed that, if the value of $D_1$ for a curve is nonzero, we could transform the curve by the inverse of the matrix that defines $D_1$ and get

$$\begin{bmatrix} x_3 & y_3 & w_3 \\ x_2 & y_2 & w_2 \\ x_1 & y_1 & w_1 \\ x_0 & y_0 & w_0 \end{bmatrix} \begin{bmatrix} x_3 & y_3 & w_3 \\ x_2 & y_2 & w_2 \\ x_0 & y_0 & w_0 \end{bmatrix}^{-1} = \begin{bmatrix} 1 & 0 & 0 \\ 0 & 1 & 0 \\ -\dfrac{D_3}{D_1} & -\dfrac{D_2}{D_1} & -\dfrac{D_0}{D_1} \\ 0 & 0 & 1 \end{bmatrix} \quad (16.2)$$

Or if $D_3 \neq 0$, we could transform via the inverse of the $D_3$ matrix and get

$$\begin{bmatrix} x_3 & y_3 & w_3 \\ x_2 & y_2 & w_2 \\ x_1 & y_1 & w_1 \\ x_0 & y_0 & w_0 \end{bmatrix} \begin{bmatrix} x_2 & y_2 & w_2 \\ x_1 & y_1 & w_1 \\ x_0 & y_0 & w_0 \end{bmatrix}^{-1} = \begin{bmatrix} -\dfrac{D_0}{D_3} & -\dfrac{D_1}{D_3} & -\dfrac{D_2}{D_3} \\ 1 & 0 & 0 \\ 0 & 1 & 0 \\ 0 & 0 & 1 \end{bmatrix} \quad (16.3)$$

Yay. Lots of zeros and ones. Now all we need to do is to figure out how to reparametrize the inflection point polynomial to make its coefficients $D_i$ into zeros and ones. One basic tool will be an equation from Chapter 15 that shows how reparametrization affects the $D_i$ values:

$$\mathbf{R} \begin{bmatrix} D_0 \\ -3D_1 \\ 3D_2 \\ -D_3 \end{bmatrix} = \begin{bmatrix} \hat{D}_0 \\ -3\hat{D}_1 \\ 3\hat{D}_2 \\ -\hat{D}_3 \end{bmatrix}$$

Our other basic tool comes from a somewhat offhand remark in Chapter 13.

# Inferring Transforms

In Chapter 13 I showed how to generate the elements of a homogeneous transformation given a set of desired inputs and outputs. This technique is usually used to determine 2DH transformations from four input/output point pairs. But at the end of the chapter, I mentioned that a 1DH transformation could be derived from any *three* distinct input/output pairs. Translated into our notation, this means that we can find a $2 \times 2$ matrix to transform any three given values $(\hat{t}_i, \hat{s}_i)$ into any three desired values $(t_i, s_i)$ according to the equation

$$\begin{bmatrix} \hat{t}_i & \hat{s}_i \end{bmatrix} \begin{bmatrix} a & c \\ b & d \end{bmatrix} = w_i \begin{bmatrix} t_i & s_i \end{bmatrix}$$

(The three homogeneous scales $w_i$ are also calculated as a side effect of the matrix derivation. We don't have to specify them.) In a nutshell, we calculate the matrix by first finding the intermediate matrices:

$$\mathbf{N} = \begin{bmatrix} t_1 s_2 - t_2 s_1 & 0 \\ 0 & t_2 s_0 - t_0 s_2 \end{bmatrix} \begin{bmatrix} t_0 & s_0 \\ t_1 & s_1 \end{bmatrix}$$

$$\hat{\mathbf{N}} = \begin{bmatrix} \hat{t}_1 \hat{s}_2 - \hat{t}_2 \hat{s}_1 & 0 \\ 0 & \hat{t}_2 \hat{s}_0 - \hat{t}_0 \hat{s}_2 \end{bmatrix} \begin{bmatrix} \hat{t}_0 & \hat{s}_0 \\ \hat{t}_1 & \hat{s}_1 \end{bmatrix}$$

Then the desired matrix will be the adjoint of $\hat{\mathbf{N}}$ times $\mathbf{N}$:

$$\begin{bmatrix} a & c \\ b & d \end{bmatrix} = \hat{\mathbf{N}}^* \mathbf{N}$$

We now use this tool to move the roots of arbitrary polynomials into arithmetically nice canonical positions.

# Types of Homogeneous Cubic Polynomials

A homogeneous cubic polynomial has three roots: $(t_0, s_0)$, $(t_1, s_1)$, and $(t_2, s_2)$. The polynomial is then

$$f(t, s) = (ts_0 - st_0)(ts_1 - st_1)(ts_2 - st_2)$$

Our technique for inferring transformations allows us to reparametrize the polynomial to place these three roots at any three canonical locations we wish. In what follows, I'll pick canonical locations that I've verified lead to nicer arithmetic later on. We're only interested in cases where the final polynomial coefficients are real, so this boils down to five special cases:

1. *Three distinct real roots.* Transform them to the equally radially spaced canonical positions $(\hat{t}, \hat{s}) = (1, 0), (-1, \sqrt{3}), (-1, -\sqrt{3})$. This generates the canonical three-root polynomial $(3\hat{t}^2 - \hat{s}^2)\hat{s}$.

2. *One simple root and one double root.* Transform the simple root to $(-1, 0)$ and the double root to $(0, 1)$. But what do we do for the third input/output pair? It turns out that it doesn't matter. As long as we pick any third input value that is distinct from the original roots and any output value that is distinct from $(-1, 0)$ and $(0, 1)$, we will get some constant factor times the polynomial $-\hat{t}^2\hat{s}$. With some foresight, I will choose to scale this canonical polynomial to be $3\hat{t}^2\hat{s}$.

3. *One real root and two complex conjugate roots.* Transform the real root to $(-1, 0)$, and the complex conjugate roots to $(-i, \sqrt{3}), (-i, -\sqrt{3})$. Feel free to entertain yourself by showing that two complex conjugate input/output pairs will still result in real values for the $2 \times 2$ matrix. The canonical polynomial is $(3\hat{t}^2 + \hat{s}^2)\hat{s}$.

4. *One triple root.* Transform it to $(-1, 0)$. Again, it doesn't matter what choices we make for the other two input/output pairs as long as they are distinct. We'll get the canonical polynomial $\hat{s}^3$.

5. *The zero polynomial.* This may appear trivial, but it does correspond to a valid set of coefficient values. We will, in fact, encounter it later on in some perfectly reasonable situations.

Any homogeneous cubic polynomial (in particular, our inflection point polynomial) can be transformed into exactly one of these five types. So what are the $D_i$ values for each canonical inflection point polynomial? In the final column of Table 16.1, I've lined up the inflection point coefficients with the possible canonical coefficients. We see that $D_0 = D_2 = 0$, and the $D_1$ and $D_3$ values are as listed.

# Generating the Catalog

Now let's put this all together. We will assume we are given a cubic coefficient matrix and want the steps necessary to transform it, both parametrically and geometrically, to a standard form with lots of zeros, and a few ones in the coefficient matrix. We'll then eagerly see what those matrices are.

**Table 16.1** *Catalog of possible homogeneous cubic polynomials*

| Case | Real roots | Canonical polynomial | Canonical coefficient vector $\left[\hat{D}_0 \quad -3\hat{D}_1 \quad 3\hat{D}_2 \quad -\hat{D}_3\right]$ | | | |
|---|---|---|---|---|---|---|
| 1 | $(1,0),\left(-1,\sqrt{3}\right),\left(-1,-\sqrt{3}\right)$ | $\left(3\hat{t}^2 - \hat{s}^2\right)\hat{s}$ | $[0$ | $3$ | $0$ | $-1]$ |
| 2 | Simple: $(-1,0)$, Double: $(0,1)$ | $3\hat{t}^2\hat{s}$ | $[0$ | $3$ | $0$ | $0]$ |
| 3 | $(-1,0)$ | $\left(3\hat{t}^2 + \hat{s}^2\right)\hat{s}$ | $[0$ | $3$ | $0$ | $1]$ |
| 4 | Triple: $(-1,0)$ | $s^3$ | $[0$ | $0$ | $0$ | $1]$ |
| 5 | Infinitely many | $0$ | $[0$ | $0$ | $0$ | $0]$ |

1. Generate the $D$ vector. This just involves taking the four $3\times3$ determinants of the submatrices of the original polynomial coefficients.
2. Figure out the reparametrization of the resulting cubic polynomial that puts it into one of the five canonical forms of Table 16.1. This, of course, involves finding the roots of the cubic. This is a perfectly doable project but I won't get into the mechanics of it here.
3. Apply the same reparametrization to the original polynomial coefficient matrix. We are now guaranteed that the various $3\times3$ subdeterminants of this reparametrized coefficient matrix will have values implied by the fourth column of Table 16.1.
4. We now apply the geometric transformation. For cases 1, 2, and 3, we have $D_1 \neq 0$, so we can use the transformation from Equation (16.2). For case 4, we use Equation (16.3). The final results appear in Table 16.2.

## False Cubics

Let's take a closer look at case 4. The coefficient matrix will generate the following curve points:

$$\begin{bmatrix} x & y & w \end{bmatrix} = \begin{bmatrix} t^3 & t^2s & ts^2 & s^3 \end{bmatrix} \begin{bmatrix} 0 & 0 & 0 \\ 1 & 0 & 0 \\ 0 & 1 & 0 \\ 0 & 0 & 1 \end{bmatrix}$$

$$= s\begin{bmatrix} t^2 & ts & s^2 \end{bmatrix}$$

**Table 16.2** *The catalog of canonical cubic curves*

| Case | $D_1$ | $D_3$ | Transformation equation number | Final coefficient matrix | Description | Picture |
|---|---|---|---|---|---|---|
| 1 | −1 | 1 | (16.2) | $\begin{bmatrix} 1 & 0 & 0 \\ 0 & 1 & 0 \\ 1 & 0 & 0 \\ 0 & 0 & 1 \end{bmatrix}$ | Serpentine | |
| 2 | −1 | 0 | (16.2) | $\begin{bmatrix} 1 & 0 & 0 \\ 0 & 1 & 0 \\ 0 & 0 & 0 \\ 0 & 0 & 1 \end{bmatrix}$ | Cusp | |
| 3 | −1 | −1 | (16.2) | $\begin{bmatrix} 1 & 0 & 0 \\ 0 & 1 & 0 \\ -1 & 0 & 0 \\ 0 & 0 & 1 \end{bmatrix}$ | Loop | |
| 4 | 0 | 1 | (16.3) | $\begin{bmatrix} 0 & 0 & 0 \\ 1 & 0 & 0 \\ 0 & 1 & 0 \\ 0 & 0 & 1 \end{bmatrix}$ | Quadratic | |
| 5 | 0 | 0 | ?? | $\begin{bmatrix} 0 & 0 & 0 \\ 0 & 0 & 0 \\ 0 & 1 & 0 \\ 0 & 0 & 1 \end{bmatrix}$ | Line | |
| | | | | $\begin{bmatrix} 0 & 0 & 0 \\ 0 & 0 & 0 \\ 0 & 0 & 0 \\ 0 & 0 & 1 \end{bmatrix}$ | Point | |

In other words, the curve is not really a cubic curve; it's a quadratic curve masquerading as a cubic by homogeneously scaling itself by a factor of $s$. Not fair. This particular coefficient matrix above will generate a parabola . . . almost. The parabola will be tangent to the point at infinity on the $x$ axis $[1,0,0]$, and that point of tangency happens at the parameter value $s = 0$. Under its cubic disguise, however, that parameter value generates the nonexistent point $[0,0,0]$. So the quadratic pays for its sins by having one of its points lopped off.

Case 5 is even worse. All of the $D_i$'s are zero. This doesn't mean, however, that the curve totally disappears. It's possible to have a perfectly reasonable coefficient matrix that generates $D_i = 0$. The simplest example is

$$\begin{bmatrix} x & y & w \end{bmatrix} = \begin{bmatrix} t^3 & t^2s & ts^2 & s^3 \end{bmatrix} \begin{bmatrix} 0 & 0 & 0 \\ 0 & 0 & 0 \\ 0 & 1 & 0 \\ 0 & 0 & 1 \end{bmatrix}$$

$$= s^2 \begin{bmatrix} 0 & t & s \end{bmatrix}$$

Varying $(t,s)$ will trace out the $y$ axis, so this time we have a linear function masquerading as a cubic curve. This line, too, is missing a point; this time it's the point at infinity on the $y$ axis.

Finally, we can have another situation for case 5:

$$\begin{bmatrix} x & y & w \end{bmatrix} = \begin{bmatrix} t^3 & t^2s & ts^2 & s^3 \end{bmatrix} \begin{bmatrix} 0 & 0 & 0 \\ 0 & 0 & 0 \\ 0 & 0 & 0 \\ 0 & 0 & 1 \end{bmatrix}$$

$$= s^3 \begin{bmatrix} 0 & 0 & 1 \end{bmatrix}$$

This just generates a single point (the origin) for all values of $(t,s)$ except $(t,0)$.

These last three situations—quadratic, linear, and point curves masquerading as cubics—will be the subject of more investigation in a future article. For now, we will not consider them as true cubic curves. This leaves us with the three curves for cases 1, 2, and 3.

## The Number of the Counting Shall Be 3

Our technique for cataloging arbitrary rational cubic curves into equivalence classes took an arbitrary coefficient matrix **C** and found a transformation matrix **M** and a reparametrization matrix **R** that converted it into

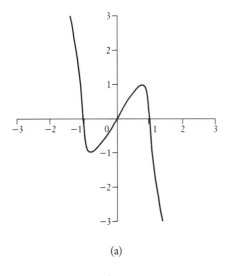

(a)

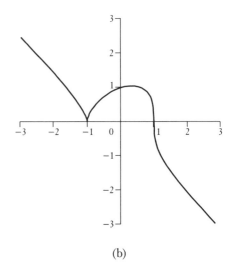

(b)

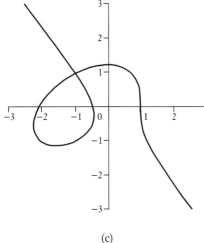

(c)

**Figure 16.1**  *The three canonical parametric cubic curves transformed for best viewing: serpentine (a), cusp (b), and loop (c)*

one of six simple standard forms. Three of these are real cubic curves and three are lower-order curves. Some interesting points follow:

- Each of the canonical forms is a nonrational curve since the $w$ value is constant at 1. In other words, all rational curves are just perspective transformations of some nonrational curve.

- Any rational parametric curve (whether Bezier, B-spline, NURBS, or whatever) is a snippet out of one of these three basic shapes, appropriately reparametrized and perspectively transformed. This reminds me of the story of the guy who copyrighted the note Middle C and then claimed that all compositions were merely transpositions and repetitions of his basic melody.

## Better Pictures

The canonical pictures in Table 16.2 do not really show off the curves to best advantage. The problem is that each of the true cubics has an inflection point at the parameter value (1,0) and with geometric coordinates [1 0 0] (the point at infinity on the $x$ axis). This means that the inflection point is at infinity both geometrically and parametrically. To see all interesting parts of the curve locally, we must do a geometric perspective transform to get the inflection point at [1 0 0] to become a local point.

And when we draw the curve, it will be easier if it is reparametrized so that the (now local) inflection point is not at the parameter value $T = \infty$. Matrices to do this and best show off the shape are different for each of the three cubic types. Figure 16.1 shows the results of hand-tuning nice views of each curve. Note that the three inflection points of the serpentine are on the $x$ axis, and the single inflection point of the cusp and loop is also on the $x$ axis.

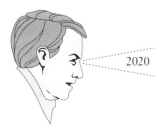

# CHAPTER SEVENTEEN

# A Bright, Shiny Future

*For the January 2000 issue of CG&QA, I was invited, along with other industry notables, to describe my view of the world of 2020. Here's what I want/hope to happen.*

When I was about 15 years old, I performed a calculation. I said to myself, "Let's see, I was born in 1949. That means that in the year 2000, I will be 51 years old. Most people live that long. Therefore I will probably live to see the year 2000." What did I expect to see? Flat-screen color TVs? Yes. Colonies on the moon and Mars? Sure. Personal helicopter backpacks? Why not? Computers? Huh?—I didn't even know what computers *were*. Maybe I expected personal robot slaves, but not computers. But I knew what the future was going to look like. It was going to look like the 1964 New York World's Fair.

Now that I'm 50 years old, I can perform a similar calculation. In the year 2020, I will be 71. Many people live that long. I'll probably live to see the year 2020. What do I expect to see? What do I *want* to see?

## What Will Probably Happen

We know from viewing past predictions that short-term predictions tend to be overly optimistic, and long-term predictions tend to be overly conservative. Here are some short-term predictions that I feel pretty sure of, mainly because most of them are almost here now. They will surely be done deals in 20 years.

## Computers

Computers will be faster. Computers will be cheaper. Computers will have more memory. Computers will still crash.

If present trends continue, computer speeds and main memory sizes will increase by several thousandfold, and nonvolatile storage will increase by several hundred-thousandfold. Small, incredibly cheap, special-purpose computers will abound, all communicating with each other. Ivan Sutherland's "Wheel of Reincarnation" will have gone through another couple of turns, and the main CPU will be doing the graphics again instead of special-purpose processors. Everyone will finally agree that computers are finally fast enough and storage is large enough to satisfy them.

## Display Technologies

CRTs will be gone. We finally really will have cheap flat-panel displays that consume very little power and are lightweight. We'll have small, portable display pads connected to our base CPU or network via wireless LAN technology. Their resolution will be about the same as today's laser printers. We'll watch TV on these devices, do e-mail and voicemail, and read books on them. We will still use large-screen displays for group viewing of movies, but head-mounted displays will be lightweight and common. Direct neural inputs to the brain will be the hot new experimental technology. I can already hear kids saying, "But Dad, all the kids have Neural Internet Receivers."

## Applications

Data rates and storage capacity for large quantities of video and movies will be considered trivial. Bandwidth bottlenecks will diminish but not disappear. Consider the bandwidth hierarchy:

- Bus speed
- Wired LAN speed
- Wireless LAN speed
- Wired WAN speed
- Wireless WAN speed

Each item will advance to the current speeds of the next level or two up. This means that we'll still need to compress file sizes to communicate practically with the next level down in the hierarchy.

The communication between small computers will make the proliferation of remote controls obsolete. We'll be able to control everything from any display or terminal device in the house. These devices will be colorful—no more black-on-black buttons that are impossible to see while watching TV.

Movies will not be distributed as a sequence of images. Instead they will be distributed as the database necessary to construct the images on the fly. What we now think of as computer-rendering techniques will be used as a playback decompression technique. Newly produced movies/videos will be generated directly in this format. Older movies/videos will be stored in this format after some processing to re-extract the layering of the images. (This is basically the intent of MPEG 4; we will probably be up to MPEG 8 or 9 by then.)

The Web will have long since taken over television as the primary communications medium of the world. Much of the world's commerce will be done on the Web. Shipping companies will thrive.

# What Do I Want to Happen?

I want 3D user interfaces and applications to be common. I want this because I think that developing 3D algorithms is fun, and I want there to be enough of a market for them to support their development.

I want to have a sophisticated model of the human visual system that can predict when imaging errors are below the threshold of detectability of the eye. Only then can we properly evaluate tradeoffs in our rendering techniques. We can answer questions like, How much display resolution is really enough? How many bits of precision do you need in pixel-processing arithmetic? And, more abstractly, How realistic do you need to be in your rendering?

I want all legacy idiocies like interlaced video and linear arithmetic on gamma-corrected pixels to go away. In fact, I want pixels to go away as an image archiving and processing method. An image is actually a continuous function. Converting it to pixels requires choosing a resolution and throwing away information beyond that resolution. Choosing a lower resolution generates fewer pixels to store, but throws away more information. When you really think about it, representing an image as pixels is just a bad image compression technique. Better techniques built on discrete cosine transforms or wavelets are attempts to find better sets of image "atoms." Building pictures out of these atoms is more representative of actual images. However, we need still better picture atoms. Converting images to pixels should be a last-minute operation, for display purposes only.

I want special-purpose graphics processors to go away. Programming with these things is just too @#$# hard. I want main CPUs to be fast enough to make the images we want. Special-purpose processors always choke off real algorithmic creativity as they make us try to shoehorn new algorithms into a design model often several years old.

I want computer games (like my favorites Sam and Max Hit the Road, Day of the Tentacle, Monkey Island, and The Fool's Errand) to be archived and downloadable in a format that I will be able to play on future hardware rather than have them disappear from sight because they run on obsolete computers and game consoles. Currently, computer game lifetime is limited by the lifetime of the hardware they run on. And we can't rely on simply keeping a copy of old hardware; these things break.

I want image digitizers to be able to extract all the information from an image. This involves figuring out the maximum spatial resolution and the maximum intensity resolution that a given image actually contains. This would be the limit beyond which the image is just noise. Digitizing devices and software should be able to determine this empirically from any input image.

I want a massive worldwide project to be started to digitize and archive all existing media (books, photographs, TV, and movies) and make them available. I want copyright issues to be addressed so that producers of content get rewarded for their efforts while repurposing of these assets is not a major legal risk. I want all of this because I believe that, in the future, any media not available on the Web will effectively cease to exist.

I want all this stuff to *work*. Not crash a lot, and not destroy data.

And in the future, I want to know everything there is to know about cubic curves.

# Why Do I Want This to Happen?

As a producer of images, mathematical articles, and animations, I want to have better and better tools to use. I want to be able to create mathematics and physics animations as interactive textbooks and distribute them on the future Web. I want to develop new rendering, lighting, and geometric algorithms. And I want an audience for them.

But I am also a consumer of images. And it seems like I am currently accumulating media faster than I am consuming it. So, I want a digitized version of all my books, music, photographs, and videos—both for space considerations and for easy accessibility. I want to be able to download any other books or research reports, old or new, from the Web. I want to have immediate digital access to any old movie or television series that I want to see—all for a reasonable fee.

Since I hate to travel, I want to be able to travel in virtual reality. I want to be able to see interesting places and events at realistic resolution and time delay without the bother of actually going to them. I want to experience the canyons of Mars and the rings of Saturn from my home.

If space travel is inconvenient, time travel is even worse. I want to experience fun past events like, for example, historical world's fairs. One of the things that fascinates me about world's fairs is that they have always had a positive view of the future. I'm tired of the dystopian views currently common in predictions of the future. (How come everything in the future has to be *rusty*?) Architecture in world's fairs was clean and monumental like the grandiose art deco pavilions of the 1939 New York fair. This fair pioneered the concept of the dark ride (an early form of virtual reality), and gave viewers a look at the future world of 1964 containing suburbs, superhighways, automatic dishwashers, fluorescent lights, and voice-actuated robots. You can visit it virtually at

> *websyte.com/alan/nywf.htm*
> *xroads.virginia.edu/g/1930s/DISPLAY/39wf/frame.htm*
> *www.archive.org/movies/index.html*

Then there is my favorite building, the Atomium, a 330-foot-tall building in the shape of a molecule from the 1958 Brussels fair. I have always wondered what it looked like inside this building. Now thanks to the Web, I've discovered that it still exists and have virtually seen inside it via the site

> *www.atomium.be*

In 1962, the fair was in Seattle. I visit that site regularly in real life, since I live nearby. And in 1964, the fair in New York demonstrated touch-tone phones, videophones, fusion power, underwater cities, cultivated deserts, audio animatronics, and multimedia shows (back when multimedia meant lots of slide projectors chunking away simultaneously). It also exhibited a model of an amazing machine that crunches through the jungle laying down a freeway in its wake. (Some of these ideas may appear inadvisable in retrospect.) I actually visited this one in real life, but I can go back virtually at

> *members.aol.com/bbqprod/bbqprod.html*
> *naid.sppsr.ucla.edu/ny64fair/*

I've visited these fairs virtually and through my collection of guidebooks, souvenir books, movie film, and stereo View-Master slides. But it's not enough. I want them digitized and fed to 3D analysis programs to reconstruct 3D digital models. I want the whole experience of seeing a bright, shining future from the point of view of 1939 or 1964 . . . or 2000.

# A Guarantee

There's one prediction I am sure of. In the future, people's predictions of their own future will be no more accurate than ours. In 20 years, things will be vastly different than we expect. But we can do more than just predict the future; we can create it. And that's good because I want the future to be beautiful again.

```
template<class A, class B>
inline const
Sum<P<A>,P<B> >operator+(const A& a,
                          const B& b)
    {return Sum<P<A>,P<B> > (a,b);}
```

# CHAPTER EIGHTEEN

# Optimizing C++ Vector Expressions

R ecently, I've been attempting to delay brain fossilization by studying all the nifty new programming techniques that have been invented since I was in school. I started with C++ and Object-Oriented programming. They say there's no zealot like a convert, and I've become something of a C++ weenie. I am now progressing through generic programming, aspect-oriented programming, partial evaluation, and generative programming. I find all this enormously exciting in theory, but what I'm really interested in is whether all these tricks work in the real world of graphics programming. My answer so far is yes, but. . . . To see "but what?" I'll start by defining one of the problems I want to solve.

## The Goal

f or all my life, I've wanted to have a programming language that defined Vectors and arithmetic between them, so I could say things like

```
Vector A,B,C;
Vector D = A + 3*(B+C);
```

Now C++ weeniness allows me to do this. But perhaps not too surprisingly, it turns out there are various pitfalls in doing this well. This chapter will address one of these pitfalls: the speed of execution of vector arithmetic. The conventional approach turns out to be somewhat slow, but there is a very tricky technique that can make vector arithmetic very fast. It's inspired by the work of Todd Veldhuizen[1] and uses the C++ template mechanism in rather bizarre and unexpected ways. I have to admit that it has taken me quite some time to understand this myself. I will now attempt to pass that understanding on to you.

For clarity of exposition, I will make some simplifications that would not be present in production code.

- I'll use rather terse names for classes, variables, and templates to make the sample code more Spartan.

- I'll just deal with vector addition and scalar products. Vector subtraction, scalar division, and unary minus will be easy for you to add as homework. The vectors will contain simple floats—you can add further templatization yourself to handle other data types.

- In the program fragments, I will make symbolic names boldface when they are first defined. This will make it visually easier for you to wade through the syntactic clutter of type declarations and so on, and see the structure of the code.

# The Basic Vector Class

To start out, here's a basic vector class to construct and access the elements of a 3D vector. I will assume that these definitions are included in all later variants of the Vector class.

```
class Vector {
    float v[3];
public:
    Vector() {;}
    Vector(float d0,float d1,float d2)
        {v[0]=d0; v[1]=d1; v[2]=d2;}
    float operator[](int i) const
        {return v[i];}
    float& operator[](int i)
        {return v[i];}

        ...additional stuff...
};
```

---

1 Veldhuizen, Todd, "Expression Templates," in C++ Gems, Cambridge University Press, 1998. Also available at *http://extreme.indiana.edu/~tveldhui/*.

# Version 1a: The Recommended Arithmetic Operators

W e provide vector addition and scalar multiplication by defining the appropriate operators. Most books (e.g., Scott Meyers, *More Effective C++*, Addison Wesley, 1996, Item22) recommend that you define binary operators like + in terms of their assignment analogues +=. (Doing it the other way around would be less efficient.) Here is how to do this.

```
class Vector {

    basic stuff

Vector& operator+=(const Vector& V2)
    {v[0]+=V2[0];
     v[1]+=V2[1];
     v[2]+=V2[2]; return *this;}

Vector& operator*=(const float S)
    {v[0]*=S; v[1]*=S; v[2]*=S;
     return *this;}
};

inline const
Vector operator+(const Vector& A,
                 const Vector& B)
    {return Vector(A) += B;}

inline const
Vector operator*(const float s,
                 const Vector& V)
    {return Vector(V) *= s;}
```

Notice that we declare the binary operators to return `const Vector` so that the compiler can flag nonsensical statements like A + B = C. Also, the expressions in the return values of the binary operators are carefully crafted to make the optimizer happy (see the Meyers reference above).

This works, but doesn't generate the best possible code. For example, consider the expression

```
D = A+3*(B+C)
```

The problem is that the compiled code evaluates complicated expressions "sideways"—it evaluates all three components for each operation and stores each result in a temporary variable.

```
Vector temp1 = B+C;
Vector temp2 = 3*temp1;
Vector temp3 = A+temp2;
D = temp3
```

We would prefer to calculate the entire expression for each component.

```
D[0] = A[0]+3*(B[0]+C[0]);
D[1] = A[1]+3*(B[1]+C[1]);
D[2] = A[2]+3*(B[2]+C[2]);
```

Theoretically, a really hot optimizer—one that looked at a sufficiently large window of the code—could turn the first version into the second one, but in the real world, it doesn't. Our goal, then, is to help the compiler automatically generate the better implementation.

# Testing

To whet your appetite, let's take a look at some timing comparisons of various implementations that I'm going to progress through (see Figure 18.1). I timed the execution of four different vector expressions:

```
D = A + B;
D = 3*A + 4*B;
D = A + 3*(B+C);
D = 3*A + 4*B + 5*C;
```

All timings are shown relative to the time taken for the simple vector assignment, **D** = **A**, to roughly compare these with simply the memory access time. (All these statements were actually built into a loop that operates on a small buffer of vectors.) Also included in the charts is the relative time to do each calculation "the hard way" by explicitly calculating the elements for a particular operation. One would think that this would be the fastest possible implementation. Happily, some of the techniques shown here are even better, largely because the compiler is able to make better use of registers in these cases. Note that version 2 only works for the expression **A** + **B**, and that version 3 is so slow that it's off the charts and I didn't bother including it.

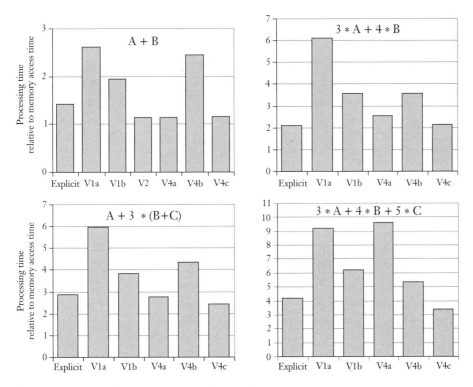

**Figure 18.1** *Timings of various versions of vector classes*

# Version 1b: Explicit Binary Operators

For our first efficiency improvement, let's throw recommended software engineering practice to the wind and define the binary operations directly. In this and all future modifications to the code, the highlighted areas are the only parts that have changed.

```
inline const
Vector operator+(const Vector& A,
                 const Vector& B)
    {return Vector(A[0]+B[0],
                   A[1]+B[1],
                   A[2]+B[2]);}

inline const
Vector operator*(const float s,
                 const Vector& V)
```

```
{return Vector(s*V[0],
               s*V[1],
               s*V[2]);}
```

The plus operation is now defined in two locations (+ and +=), and the code is theoretically less maintainable, but how often do you need to re-define addition? Anyway, in this version, there are fewer temporaries for the optimizer to wade through, and the final code is faster, as shown in Figure 18.1.

# Version 2: Returning a Sum Object

The basic trick of this whole endeavor is to make the binary + operator return, not a Vector object, but a new type of object that represents the sum of two Vectors.

```
class Sum;
```

```
inline const
Sum operator+(const Vector& A,
              const Vector& B)
    {return Sum(A,B);}
```

The actual arithmetic in the vector summation is not performed until that new Sum object is stored into another Vector via a Vector conversion constructor (a Vector constructor that takes a Sum object as a parameter). When you have such a constructor, it's a typical C++ idiom that you also include a conversion assignment operator, but this is purely for efficiency purposes. We will pull out the common functionality from the constructor and the assignment into a routine called Evaluate. Our Vector class now looks like this.

```
class Vector{
        basic stuff

    void Evaluate(const Sum& e);
    Vector(const Sum& e)
        {Evaluate(e);}
    Vector& operator=(const Sum& e)
        {Evaluate(e); return *this;}
};
```

The Sum object only needs to have a constructor and a subscripting operator that evaluates the sum of a particular component.

```
class Sum {
    const Vector &L;
    const Vector &R;
public:
    Sum(const Vector& Linit,
        const Vector& Rinit)
        : L(Linit), R(Rinit) {;}

    float operator[](int i) const
        {return L[i] + R[i];}
};
```

Now we can define the body of Evaluate to simply call Sum::operator[] three times, once for each component, and store the results.

```
inline
void Vector::Evaluate(const Sum& e)
    {v[0]=e[0];
    v[1] =e[1];
    v[2] =e[2];}
```

## How Does This Work?

To see how this works, let's follow what the compiler does for two examples. First, we look at an expression passed as a parameter to a function. We start with

```
void func(const Vector& v){. . .}

Vector A,B;
func(A+B);
```

Let's imagine the steps the compiler goes through in transforming and inlining the function call into code. First we get

```
func (operator+(A,B));
```

This becomes

```
Sum    temp1(operator+(A,B)); //call operator+
Vector temp2(temp1);          //convert to Vector
func   (temp2);               //pass to function
```

And then it becomes

```
Sum    temp1(A,B);    // call Sum constructor
Vector temp2;
```

```
temp2.Evaluate(temp1); //pass to Evaluate routine
func  (temp2);
```

In summary, operator+ creates a temporary Sum object that is passed to the Vector constructor to create a temporary Vector object to pass to func.

Our second example is a vector assignment. This will compile and inline as follows. We start with

```
Vector A,B;
C=A+B;
```

The compiler successively transforms this into

```
C.operator=(operator+(A,B));
```

This becomes

```
Sum temp1(operator+(A,B));
C.operator=(temp1);
```

This becomes

```
Sum temp1(A,B)
C.operator=(temp1);
```

This becomes

```
Sum temp1(A,B);
C.Evaluate(temp1);
```

I've looked at the resulting object code from an optimizing compiler and, without going into machine-dependant details, assure you that it is as optimal as you can get. You can see the effect on the timing by looking at Figure 18.1.

# Version 3: Virtual Functions

Great! Super fast. Now how can we generalize this to the full panoply of vector arithmetic expressions we want to be able to evaluate? We need to handle whole parse trees for arbitrary expressions. In terms of language constructs, we have the following syntactic elements that are *expressions*:

*vector*
*expression* + *expression*
*float* * *expression*
*(expression)*

This is the type of thing that polymorphism was born to do. We first define an abstract base class for *expression* (with the very terse name E) and derive objects from it. The definition of E declares only a pure virtual indexing operator that we will require each of the derived objects to override.

```
class E{
public:
virtual
float operator[](int i) const=0;
};
```

Now let's adjust our definition of Vector. We need to do only two things. Since a raw vector is a valid expression, the Vector class will inherit from E. Next, we use the abstract class E in any spots where we used the explicit Sum class before.

```
class Vector : public E {
        basic stuff
public:
    void Evaluate(const E& e);
        {v[0]=e[0];
         v[1]=e[1];
         v[2]=e[2];}
    Vector(const E& e)
        {Evaluate(e);}
    Vector& operator=(const E& e)
        {Evaluate(e);
         return *this;}
};
```

Now to adjust the Sum object: we inherit from E and change its member data to refer to objects of type E instead of type Vector.

```
class Sum : public E {
    const E& L;
    const E& R;
public:
    Sum(const E& Linit,
        const E& Rinit)
      : L(Linit), R(Rinit) {;}

    virtual
    float operator[](int i) const
      {return L[i] + R[i];}
};
```

We can now proceed to define a similar object that represents scalar multiplication.

```
class Prod : public E {
    float s; const E& V;
public:
    Prod(float Sinit, const E& Vinit)
        : s(Sinit), V(Vinit) {;}

    virtual
    float operator[](int i) const
        {return s*V[i];}
};
```

Finally, we define the binary operators themselves. Again, we just change each operator to accept a general expression of type E.

```
inline const
Sum operator+(const E& A,
              const E& B)
    {return Sum(A,B);}

inline const
Prod operator*(const float s,
               const E& V)
    {return Prod(s,V);}
```

The neat thing about this technique is that it tricks the C++ compile time parser into parsing our expression into the appropriate calls to construct a run-time expression tree. Because of this, we don't need to worry about parenthesized expressions and operator precedence. The C++ parser handles this.

Now I'm going to do something naughty. I know you're not supposed to do this, but I find it most edifying to think of objects in terms of their data layouts. The data layout generated by our test expression A + 3*(B+C) appears in Figure 18.2.

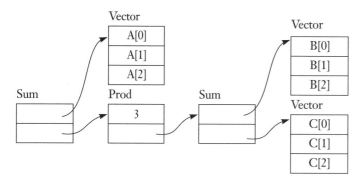

**Figure 18.2** *Data layout for versions 3 and 4a*

The main problem with this code is that it is slow. This is due (indirectly) to the virtual function mechanism. I say "indirectly" because virtual functions are not inherently all that slow, it's just that they interfere with the optimizer and the inlining process, and inlining is the key to getting the best object code. The timing measurements for various expressions gave values of from 15 to 60 in units of memory-access time from Figure 18.1. Plotting this would have required a fold-out page. It didn't seem worth it.

So, we want to get rid of the run-time virtual function calls and make them expand out at compile time. We'll do this by exploiting a somewhat surprising relationship between virtual functions and template functions.

# Similarity between Virtual Functions and Templates

This next trick will involve using templates to express the same sort of functionality that virtual functions provide. How is this possible? First let's take a look at the similarities between the two. Consider the Evaluate routine.

```
void Evaluate(const E& e);
    {v[0]=e[0];
     v[1]=e[1];
     v[2]=e[2];}
}
```

Any such routine that is passed a parameter of type E can expect to be able to call any of the operators listed in the definition of E. The compiler enforces this by making sure any class derived from E defines all the pure virtual functions defined by E. (Here it's just operator[].)

Now consider instead a templatized version of the function.

```
template <class E>
void Evaluate(const E& e)
    {v[0]=e[0];
     v[1]=e[1];
     v[2]=e[2];}
}
```

A program that calls Evaluate can pass it any class of parameter as long as that class defines all of the operations that Evaluate will apply to its parameter. (Here it's again just operator[].) The compiler enforces this indirectly by coughing up an undefined function error if the program attempts to call `Evaluate` on a class that doesn't define `operator[]`.

The difference is that, with the templatized version, all this is done at compile time.

# Version 4a: Expression Templates

To turn this into code within our current scheme, we start with version 3 and mainly convert anything that inherits from a type E into a template function or class parametrized by whatever E used to refer to. The sum object turns into

```
// Sum<L,R>
template <class LexprT,
          class RexprT>
class Sum {
    const LexprT& L;
    const RexprT& R;
public:
    Sum(const LexprT& Linit,
        const RexprT& Rinit)
      : L(Linit), R(Rinit) {;}

    float operator[](int i) const  //no longer virtual
      {return L[i] + R[i];}
};
```

The product object turns into

```
// Prod<V>
template <class VexprT>
class Prod {
    float s;
    const VexprT& V;
public:
    Prod(const float sinit,
         const VexprT& Vinit)
      : s(sinit), V(Vinit) {;}

    float operator[](int i) const  //no longer virtual
      {return s*V[i];}
};
```

The vector object turns into

```
class Vector{             //no longer inherits from E
        basic stuff

template <class T>
    void Evaluate(const T& e)
        {v[0]=e[0];
         v[1]=e[1];
         v[2]=e[2];}

template <class T>
    Vector(const T& e)
        {Evaluate(e);}

template <class T>
    Vector& operator=(const T& e)
        {Evaluate(e);return *this;}
};
```

And the binary operators are

```
template<class A, class B>
inline const
Sum<A,B> operator+(const A& a,
                   const B& b)
    {return Sum<A,B>(a,b);}

template<class A>
inline const
Prod<A> operator*(const float& a,
                  const A& b)
    {return Prod<A>(a,b);}
```

The keeping track of which version of operator[] to call, which used to be controlled by run-time virtual function pointers, is now controlled by the compile-time generation of some rather verbose class names. Let's see how this works by looking at our expression

```
D = A + 3*(B+C)
```

The compiler first expands the expression B + C, which constructs and returns an object of type Sum<Vector,Vector>. Next, it sees the expression 3*(*previous expression*). This generates an object of type

Prod<Sum<Vector,Vector> >. Finally, it compiles the expression A+(*previous stuff*). This generates an object of type Sum<Vector,Prod<Sum<Vector,Vector> > >.

All this happens at compile time and generates calls to constructors to build essentially the same data structure in Figure 18.1. We have no more virtual function calls, and more code can inline. Each of these newly created classes has its own operator[], which calls the correct operator[] for each of its subcomponents.

This machinery is a whole lot faster than virtual functions, as seen in Figure 18.1. But the optimizer still generates some unnecessary temporaries. We can do still better. We ultimately want to give the optimizer a data structure it can completely optimize away.

# Version 4b: Expression Templates with Copying

Let's try to get rid of references by simply changing all the references into actual copies of objects. The only thing that changes is the beginning of the Sum and Prod class definitions.

```
template <class LexprT,
          class RexprT>
class Sum {
    const LexprT L; //no longer a reference but a copy
    const RexprT R; //no longer a reference but a copy

  the rest is same as before
};


template <class VexprT>
class Prod {
    float s;
    const VexprT V; //no longer a reference but a copy

  the rest is same as before
};
```

This means that the parse tree will generate one big, lumpy object instead of a lot of little blocks with pointers. The final expression object that is built looks like Figure 18.3.

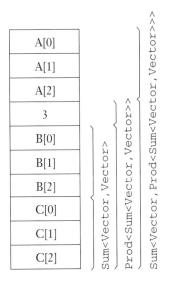

**Figure 18.3** *Data layout for version 4b*

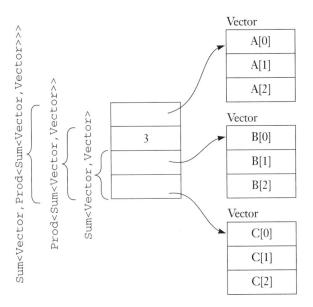

**Figure 18.4** *Data layout for version 4c*

The code to build this object (the calls to all the object constructors) is much simpler since there are no references to initialize. But it does make a copy of each vector. You can see in Table 18.1 that this kills us, speedwise. We want a still simpler expression object. This leads us to our final version.

# Version 4c: Expression Templates with Only Vector References

Figure 18.4 shows what we want our expression object to look like: one object with embedded scalar constants but with references to already existing vectors instead of copies of them. Let's see how we can accomplish this.

Whenever we create a `Sum<. . .,. . .>` or `Prod<. . .>` object using a `Vector` as one of the template parameters, we want to use a `Vector` reference instead of an embedded `Vector` object. Whenever anything else is used as a parameter, we want it to operate as before. This sounds like a job for . . . Template Specialization. We generate another template class for parameters, `P<. . .>`, that is basically a no-op for the default situation. We then specialize this class for vectors to `P<Vector>` to do our needed indirection. The new code to define `P` is

```
template<class anyT>
class P {
    const anyT A; // note this is a copy
public:
    P(const anyT & Ainit) : A(Ainit) {;}
    float operator[](int i) const {return A[i];}
};


class P<Vector> {
    const Vector& V; // note this is a reference
public:
    P(const Vector& Vinit) : V(Vinit) {;}
    float operator[](int i) const {return V[i];}
};
```

All we need now is to wrap any template parameters to
Sum<. . .,. . .> and Prod<. . .> in P<. . .> to get

```
template<class A, class B>
inline const
Sum<P<A>,P<B> >operator+(const A& a,
                                  const B& b)
    {return Sum<P<A>,P<B> > (a,b);}


template<class A>
inline const
Prod<P<A> >operator*(const float& a,
                           const A& b)
    {return Prod<P<A> > (a,b);}
```

The Sum, Prod, and Vector classes are unchanged from the previous
version.

I did have to do one bit of tinkering to make all this inline properly.
We are going to have many nested trivial functions here, and some compilers, by default, won't inline code that is too heavily nested. The compiler I am using (Microsoft VC7) has an override to force inlining at any
depth:

**#pragma inline_depth(255)**

This must be in effect for the compilation of the user's code since that is
what is generating all the template expansions. All this may seem like we're
coddling the compiler. But you have to realize that we are not in conflict
with the compiler; we're in a partnership with it. We want to make it easy
for the compiler to do the right thing.

Version 4c generates optimal code on all the examples I tried. Again, look at the final timings appearing in Figure 18.1. They are actually faster than explicit component-by-component code.

# Summary

All this was pretty complicated, so a fair question to ask is "Is this worth it?" The answer is "Worth it to whom?"

Every programming language has a gimmick. The gimmick of C++ is to put as much intelligence into the class libraries as possible, which makes things as easy as possible for the users of those classes. Even though there is a lot of complexity in the implementation of vector arithmetic, any user of the `Vector` class doesn't see that complexity. They can create `Vectors` and perform arithmetic on them with ease and with confidence that the best possible code will be generated. It makes the class more complicated, but makes life easier for the user of the class. That's the classical tradeoff in C++: the needs of the many outweigh the needs of the few.

$$\det\begin{bmatrix} 2\det\begin{bmatrix} A & B \\ B & C \end{bmatrix} & \det\begin{bmatrix} A & B \\ C & D \end{bmatrix} \\[2ex] \det\begin{bmatrix} A & B \\ C & D \end{bmatrix} & 2\det\begin{bmatrix} B & C \\ C & D \end{bmatrix} \end{bmatrix}$$

# CHAPTER NINETEEN

# Polynomial Discriminants Part I, Matrix Magic

N O V E M B E R – D E C E M B E R    2 0 0 0

I like beautiful equations. But beauty is sometimes subtle or hidden by bad notation. In this chapter and the next, I am going to reveal some of the hidden beauty in the explicit formulation of the discriminants of polynomials. Along the way, I will drag in some clever algebra, promote some notational schemes from mathematical physics, and illustrate some ways of visualizing homogeneous space. This will ultimately lead us to some interesting ways to find roots of these polynomials, a task that will become more and more important as we computer graphicists struggle to break free of the tyranny of the polygon and move into rendering higher-order surfaces.

So first, let's review discriminants.

## Discriminants

I'll soften you up a bit by starting with something already familiar: the quadratic equation.

### Quadratics

A general quadratic equation is

$$ax^2 + bx + c = 0$$

We learn in high school that the solution of this equation is

$$x = \frac{-b \pm \sqrt{b^2 - 4ac}}{2a}$$

The discriminant is the value under the square root sign:

$$\Delta_2 \equiv b^2 - 4ac$$

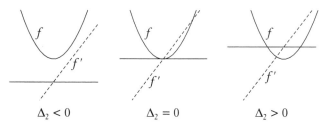

The polynomial will have 0, 1, or 2 real roots depending on the sign of the discriminant. If it is negative, there are no real roots; if it's positive, there are two distinct real roots; and if the discriminant is zero, there is a double root (i.e., two coincident real roots). (See Figure 19.1.) A more generalizable way to derive the discriminant is to note that it is zero if there is some parameter value where both the function and its derivative are zero. In other words, we want to simultaneously solve

$$\Delta_2 < 0 \qquad \Delta_2 = 0 \qquad \Delta_2 > 0$$

**Figure 19.1** *Relation of $\Delta_2$ to roots and derivative of quadratic polynomial f*

$$ax^2 + bx + c = 0$$
$$2ax + b = 0$$

To find if this is possible for a given quadratic, just solve the derivative equation for $x$ and plug it into the quadratic. The result is an expression in *abc* that simplifies to the above discriminant.

## Cubics

Stepping up to cubic equations, we have

$$ax^3 + bx^2 + cx + d = 0$$

As with quadratics, we can find the discriminant by equating the function and its derivative to zero:

$$ax^3 + bx^2 + cx + d = 0$$
$$3ax^2 + 2bx + c = 0 \tag{19.1}$$

We can find the discriminant—the condition on *abcd* that makes this possible—by various methods. We could solve the quadratic for $x$ and substitute that into the cubic equation. A more general technique is to form the, so-called, resultant of the two polynomials. This basically involves taking various linear combinations of them to form new polynomials of lower degree. I won't go into details here, but for cubics this process leads to something called the *Sylvester determinant*[1,2,3]:

$$\Delta_3 = -\frac{1}{a} \det \begin{bmatrix} a & 0 & 3a & 0 & 0 \\ b & a & 2b & 3a & 0 \\ c & b & c & 2b & 3a \\ d & c & 0 & c & 2b \\ 0 & d & 0 & 0 & c \end{bmatrix}$$

A similar technique is Bezout's method.[3] This also takes various linear combinations, and constructs a smaller but more complicated matrix. We ultimately get

$$\Delta_3 = \frac{1}{a} \det \begin{bmatrix} ab & 2ac & 3a \\ 2ac & 3ad + bc & 2b \\ 3ad & 2bd & c \end{bmatrix}$$

Of course, we could take the easy way out and just look it up on the Web. Two sites that have the answer are

*mathworld.wolfram.com/D/DiscriminantPolynomial.html*
*www.britannica.com/seo/d/discriminant*

Converting these to our notation, the result is

$$\Delta_3 = c^2 b^2 - 4db^3 - 4c^3 a + 18abcd - 27d^2 a^2 \tag{19.2}$$

This ungainly mess is rather harder to remember than the quadratic discriminant. But it is useful. As with quadratics, its value (or rather the square root of its value) figures prominently in the solution of the polynomial. If it's negative, the cubic has exactly one real root; if it's positive, there are three distinct real roots. And if it's zero, the cubic has a double root and another single root, or possibly a triple root (see Figure 19.2).

## Quartics

If you think that's bad, take a look at quartic polynomials. The equation is

$$ax^4 + bx^3 + cx^2 + dx + e = 0$$

1  Salmom, George, *Modern Higher Algebra*, Chelsea Publishing Company. Reprinted from the 1885 original.

2  Kurosh, A., *Higher Algebra*, MIR Publishers, Moscow, 1975.

3  Sederberg, T. W., Anderson, D. C., and Goldman, R. N., "Implicit Representation of Parametric Curves and Surfaces," *CVGIP 28*, pp. 72–84, 1984.

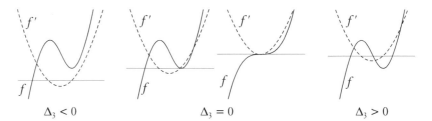

$$\Delta_3 < 0 \qquad\qquad \Delta_3 = 0 \qquad\qquad \Delta_3 > 0$$

**Figure 19.2** *Relation of $\Delta_3$ to roots and derivative of cubic polynomial $f$*

Following the procedure outlined above, we surf over to one of these two sites:

*www.inwap.com/pdp10/hbaker/hakmemgeometry.html*
*mathworld.wolfram.com/DiscriminantPolynomial.html*

We arrive at the truly stunning

$$\begin{aligned}
\Delta_4 = &-27a^2d^4 + 18abcd^3 - 4b^3d^3 - 4ac^3d^2 \\
&+ b^2c^2d^2 + 144a^2cd^2e - 6ab^2d^2e - 80abc^2de \\
&+ 18b^3cde + 16ac^4e - 4b^2c^3e - 192a^2bde^2 \\
&- 128a^2c^2e^2 + 144ab^2ce^2 - 27b^4e^2 + 256a^3e^3
\end{aligned} \tag{19.3}$$

### Aesthetics

These discriminants look really ugly in their explicit form. But there is an interesting pattern embedded in them. Finding that pattern is our mathematical journey for today.

# A Homogeneous Matrix Formulation

My first urge in any algebraic discussion is to write things in homogeneous form, in this case, as homogeneous polynomials. This generalizes the parameter value from the simple quantity $x$ to the homogeneous pair $[x \ w]$.

### Quadratics

The homogeneous quadratic equation is

$$ax^2 + bxw + cw^2 = 0$$

The main thing that homogeneity brings to the party is the addition of a new "parameter at infinity" at the value $\begin{bmatrix} x & w \end{bmatrix} = \begin{bmatrix} 1 & 0 \end{bmatrix}$. This means that if the parameter $a$ is zero, the quadratic does not simply degenerate into a linear equation. Instead, it remains a quadratic, but it simply has one of its roots at infinity ($w = 0$).

Next, I want to indulge an even stronger algebraic urge: to write things in matrix form. To make this a bit neater, I will first modify the notation for the coefficients to build in some constant factors. I'll write the quadratic equation as

$$Ax^2 + 2Bxw + Cw^2 = 0$$

This allows us to write the quadratic equation as a symmetric matrix product:

$$\begin{bmatrix} x & w \end{bmatrix} \begin{bmatrix} A & B \\ B & C \end{bmatrix} \begin{bmatrix} x \\ w \end{bmatrix} = 0 \qquad (19.4)$$

(This way of representing a quadratic is related to a technique known as *blossoming*.) The solutions now become

$$x = \frac{-2B \pm \sqrt{4B^2 - 4AC}}{2A}$$
$$= \frac{-B \pm \sqrt{B^2 - AC}}{A}$$

And the discriminant is

$$\Delta_2 = B^2 - AC$$

We can recognize this as minus the determinant of the coefficient matrix:

$$\Delta_2 = -\det \begin{bmatrix} A & B \\ B & C \end{bmatrix}$$

Neat. We've expressed the formula for the discriminant in terms of a common matrix operation: the determinant.

## Cubics

Bumping up to cubics, I will similarly rename the coefficients

$$Ax^3 + 3Bx^2w + 3Cxw^2 + Dw^3 = 0 \qquad (19.5)$$

Plugging in these renamed coefficients, the discriminant from Equation (19.2) transforms to

$$\Delta_3 = 3C^2B^2 - 4DB^3 - 4C^3A + 6ABCD - D^2A^2 \qquad (19.6)$$

Now, to make a matrix representation of Equation (19.5) analogous to Equation (19.4), we want to arrange these coefficients into a $2 \times 2 \times 2$

symmetric "cube" of numbers. There are various ways to show this, but they are all a bit clunky. About the best you can do with conventional matrix notation is to think of the coefficients as a vector of $2 \times 2$ matrices. Equation (19.5) becomes

$$\begin{bmatrix} x & w \end{bmatrix} \left\{ \begin{bmatrix} \begin{bmatrix} A & B \\ B & C \end{bmatrix} & \begin{bmatrix} B & C \\ C & D \end{bmatrix} \end{bmatrix} \begin{bmatrix} x \\ w \end{bmatrix} \right\} \begin{bmatrix} x \\ w \end{bmatrix} = 0 \qquad (19.7)$$

Once we have this triply indexed cube of numbers, we can hope that the discriminant can be written as some sort of cubical generalization of the determinant. Let's find out what it is.

# A Kinder, Gentler Cubic Discriminant

A defining property of the discriminant is that it is the condition that there is a parameter value where both the function and its derivative are zero. For a homogeneous cubic, we want the condition on $(ABCD)$ that allows simultaneous solution of

$$\begin{aligned} f(x,w) &= Ax^3 + 3Bx^2w + 3Cxw^2 + Dw^3 = 0 \\ f_x(x,w) &= 3Ax^2 + 6Bxw + 3Cw^2 = 0 \\ f_w(x,w) &= 3Bx^2 + 6Cxw + 3Dw^2 = 0 \end{aligned} \qquad (19.8)$$

To visualize what this means, note that having both the partial derivatives of $f$ be zero means that the $f$ function is tangent to the $f = 0$ plane at that point. That is, there is a double root there. See Figure 19.3.

Comparing this with Equation (19.1), it looks at first as if going to homogeneous polynomials gives us an extra equation. But it really doesn't. That's because of the identity

$$3f = xf_x + wf_w$$

So the new derivative is just a linear combination of the function and the original $x$ derivative. This means that we can pick any two equations

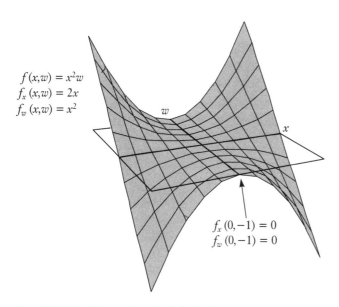

$$f(x,w) = x^2w$$
$$f_x(x,w) = 2x$$
$$f_w(x,w) = x^2$$

$$f_x(0,-1) = 0$$
$$f_w(0,-1) = 0$$

**Figure 19.3** *Double root where both derivatives are zero*

out of Equation (19.8) to work with further. I don't know about you, but the two I'm going to pick are the two lower-order ones. Tossing out a constant factor of 3, we get the following two equations that we want to solve simultaneously:

$$Ax^2 + 2Bxw + Cw^2 = 0$$
$$Bx^2 + 2Cxw + Dw^2 = 0$$

(19.9)

Linear combinations helped us before; let's see what else they can do for us. If the two equations above are both zero, then any linear combination of them also equals zero. We can get an equation without an $x^2$ term by the linear combination

$$B\left(Ax^2 + 2Bxw + Cw^2\right) - A\left(Bx^2 + 2Cxw + Dw^2\right) =$$
$$2\left(B^2 - AC\right)xw + \left(BC - AD\right)w^2 = 0$$

And we can symmetrically get an equation without the $w^2$ term by the combination

$$D\left(Ax^2 + 2Bxw + Cw^2\right) - C\left(Bx^2 + 2Cxw + Dw^2\right) =$$
$$\left(AD - BC\right)x^2 + 2\left(BD - C^2\right)xw = 0$$

Tossing out common factors of $x$ and $w$, we see that we have knocked the simultaneous quadratics in Equation (19.9) down to two simultaneous linear equations.

$$2\left(B^2 - AC\right)x + \left(BC - AD\right)w = 0$$
$$\left(AD - BC\right)x + 2\left(BD - C^2\right)w = 0$$

(19.10)

What we are saying is that if Equation (19.10) can be satisfied, then Equation (19.9) can be also. Each of the equations in (19.10) is easy to solve. The condition that the two solutions be equal leads us to

$$\frac{x}{w} = \frac{AD - BC}{2\left(B^2 - AC\right)} = \frac{-2\left(BD - C^2\right)}{AD - BC}$$

(19.11)

The final expression for the discriminant is then

$$\Delta_3 = 4\left(C^2 - BD\right)\left(B^2 - AC\right) - \left(AD - BC\right)^2$$

(19.12)

If we multiplied this out we would get Equation (19.6), but Equation (19.12) is certainly a lot prettier. But wait, it gets better.

With some imagination, we can recognize that the various parenthesized quantities in Equation (19.12) are (with a few sign flips that cancel each other out) just the determinants of various slices of the cube of coefficients. Let's give them names:

$$\delta_1 = AC - B^2 = \det\begin{bmatrix} A & B \\ B & C \end{bmatrix}$$

$$\delta_2 = AD - BC = \det\begin{bmatrix} A & B \\ C & D \end{bmatrix}$$

$$\delta_3 = BD - C^2 = \det\begin{bmatrix} B & C \\ C & D \end{bmatrix}$$

We can now write the cubic discriminant as

$$\Delta_3 = 4\delta_1\delta_3 - \delta_2^2$$

I love symmetry in algebra. You will note that any time we come up with something that is the difference of two products, I have an irresistible urge to write it as the determinant of a $2\times 2$ matrix. And if it is the difference between the square of something and another product, I want to make it the determinant of a symmetric matrix. Satisfying this urge one more time gives

$$\Delta_3 = \det\begin{bmatrix} 2\delta_1 & \delta_2 \\ \delta_2 & 2\delta_3 \end{bmatrix} \tag{19.13}$$

In other words, the cubic discriminant is a determinant of determinants. If this discriminant is zero, we know that there is a double root. And we know what it is. In fact, we have two formulations of it. Rewriting Equation (19.11) in terms of the $\delta_i$, we have

$$\frac{x}{w} = \frac{\delta_2}{-2\delta_1} = \frac{-2\delta_3}{\delta_2}$$

Or, in more homogeneous terms, the two equivalent formulations become

$$\begin{bmatrix} x & w \end{bmatrix} = \begin{bmatrix} \delta_2 & -2\delta_1 \end{bmatrix}$$

or

$$\begin{bmatrix} x & w \end{bmatrix} = \begin{bmatrix} 2\delta_3 & -\delta_2 \end{bmatrix}$$

It's useful to have a choice here. If two of the $\delta_i$'s are zero, at least one of the two choices still generates a meaningful root.

# Back to Our Roots

There is one more useful piece of information hidden here. To find it, I'll expand the polynomial in terms of its roots. It will also be a little less cluttered if we go back to the nonhomogeneous version:

$$f(x) = (x - r_1)(x - r_2)^2$$
$$= x^3 + (-2r_2 - r_1)x^2 + (r_2^2 + 2r_1r_2)x + (-r_2^2 r_1)$$

The coefficients in our notation scheme are

$$A = 1 \qquad B = \frac{-2r_2 - r_1}{3}$$

$$C = \frac{r_2^2 + 2r_1r_2}{3} \qquad D = -r_2^2 r_1 \qquad (19.14)$$

Plugging these into the definitions of the $\delta_i$ and doing some simplifying, we get

$$\delta_1 = -\frac{(r_2 - r_1)^2}{9}$$

$$\delta_2 = \frac{2r_2(r_2 - r_1)^2}{9} \qquad (19.15)$$

$$\delta_3 = \frac{-r_2^2(r_2 - r_1)^2}{9}$$

This means that if there is a *triple* root, where $r_1 = r_2$, then not only is $\Delta_3 = 0$ but all three components are zero, $\delta_1 = \delta_2 = \delta_3 = 0$. From the definitions of the $\delta_i$ and Equation (19.14), this means that

$$\frac{B}{A} = \frac{C}{B} = \frac{D}{C} = -r_1$$

Or, in homogeneous terms, the triple root has the three equivalent formulations

$$\begin{bmatrix} x & w \end{bmatrix} = \begin{bmatrix} -B & A \end{bmatrix} \text{ or } \begin{bmatrix} -C & B \end{bmatrix} \text{ or } \begin{bmatrix} -D & C \end{bmatrix}$$

Again, the alternative formulations are useful. For example, if $A = 0$ (implying $B = C = 0$) or if $D = 0$ (implying $B = C = 0$), at least one of the choices generates a meaningful root.

So, I'll summarize.

- For a quadratic, write the coefficients as a symmetric $2\times2$ matrix. The discriminant is minus the determinant of the matrix. If this is zero, the quadratic has a double root.

- For a cubic, write the coefficients as a symmetric $2\times2\times2$ cube of numbers. Calculate the three subdeterminants $\delta_1, \delta_2, \delta_3$. If all three are zero, the polynomial has a triple root. Otherwise, the discriminant is the determinant from Equation (19.13). If this is zero, then the cubic polynomial has a double root (and an additional single root).

# Quartics

Emboldened by this success, let's go for broke and see what we can do with quartics. The homogeneous polynomial is

$$q(x, w) = Ax^4 + 4Bx^3w + 6Cx^2w^2 + 4Dxw^3 + Ew^4$$

We can think of this as a $2\times2\times2\times2$ hypercube of coefficients. The best we can do with matrix notation is as a $2\times2$ matrix of $2\times2$ matrices:

$$q(x, w) = \begin{bmatrix} x & w \end{bmatrix} \left\{ \begin{bmatrix} x & w \end{bmatrix} \begin{bmatrix} \begin{bmatrix} A & B \\ B & C \end{bmatrix} & \begin{bmatrix} B & C \\ C & D \end{bmatrix} \\ \begin{bmatrix} B & C \\ C & D \end{bmatrix} & \begin{bmatrix} C & D \\ D & E \end{bmatrix} \end{bmatrix} \begin{bmatrix} x \\ w \end{bmatrix} \right\} \begin{bmatrix} x \\ w \end{bmatrix}$$

Rewriting the big fat Equation (19.3) for the discriminant in terms of our new coefficient names gives

$$
\begin{aligned}
\Delta_4 = {} & A^3E^3 - 12A^2BDE^2 - 18A^2C^2E^2 + 54A^2CD^2E \\
& -27A^2D^4 + 54AB^2CE^2 - 6AB^2D^2E - 180ABC^2DE \\
& +108ABCD^3 - 54AC^3D^2 + 81AC^4E - 27B^4E^2 \\
& +108B^3CDE - 64B^3D^3 - 54B^2C^3E + 36B^2C^2D^2
\end{aligned}
\tag{19.16}
$$

We want to see if there is a prettier way to write this. Let's apply the same technique we used for the cubic; start with the desire to simultaneously solve for the two partial derivatives being zero:

$$
\begin{aligned}
\tfrac{1}{4}q_x &= Ax^3 + 3Bx^2w + 3Cxw^2 + Dw^3 = 0 \\
\tfrac{1}{4}q_w &= Bx^3 + 3Cx^2w + 3Dxw^2 + Ew^3 = 0
\end{aligned}
\tag{19.17}
$$

Now we go through our process of successively knocking down the degree by linear combinations. We form

$$Aq_w - Bq_x = 3(AC - B^2)x^2w + 3(AD - BC)xw^2 + (AE - BD)w^3$$

and

$$Eq_x - Dq_w = (AE - BD)x^3 + 3(BE - CD)x^2w + 3(CE - D^2)xw^2$$

Again, it's beneficial to give names to the parenthesized expressions above. By extension to the terminology for cubics, I will define

$$\begin{aligned}
\delta_1 &= AC - B^2 & \delta_4 &= BE - CD \\
\delta_2 &= AD - BC & \delta_5 &= CE - D^2 \\
\delta_3 &= BD - C^2 & \delta_0 &= AE - BD
\end{aligned} \tag{19.18}$$

So, in these terms, our linear combo trick has resulted in the two simultaneous equations

$$3\delta_1 x^2 + 3\delta_2 xw + \delta_0 w^2 = 0$$
$$\delta_0 x^2 + 3\delta_4 xw + 3\delta_5 w^2 = 0$$

Now we keep turning the crank. We reduce the above quadratics to linears by taking one linear combination to shave the $x^2$ term off one end and another combination to shave the $w^2$ term off the other end. This ultimately results in

$$(9\delta_1\delta_4 - 3\delta_0\delta_2)x + (9\delta_1\delta_5 - \delta_0\delta_0)w = 0$$
$$(9\delta_5\delta_1 - \delta_0\delta_0)x + (9\delta_5\delta_2 - 3\delta_0\delta_4)w = 0$$

Again, mimicking our actions for the cubic, these two linear equations will have a common root if

$$(9\delta_1\delta_4 - 3\delta_0\delta_2)(9\delta_5\delta_2 - 3\delta_0\delta_4) - (9\delta_5\delta_1 - \delta_0\delta_0)^2 = 0 \tag{19.19}$$

The urge to write this as a matrix takes hold and we get

$$\Delta_4 = \det \begin{bmatrix} \det \begin{bmatrix} 3\delta_1 & 3\delta_2 \\ \delta_0 & 3\delta_4 \end{bmatrix} & \det \begin{bmatrix} 3\delta_1 & \delta_0 \\ \delta_0 & 3\delta_5 \end{bmatrix} \\ \det \begin{bmatrix} 3\delta_1 & \delta_0 \\ \delta_0 & 3\delta_5 \end{bmatrix} & \det \begin{bmatrix} 3\delta_2 & \delta_0 \\ 3\delta_4 & 3\delta_5 \end{bmatrix} \end{bmatrix}$$

We might be tempted, then, to say that the quartic discriminant is a determinant of determinants of determinants. But that can't be right. Notice that equation (19.19) is eighth order in *ABCDE* while the correct version in Equation (19.16) is sixth order. What happened?

Watch me pull a rabbit out of my hat. Behold the identity:

$$\delta_1\delta_5 - \delta_2\delta_4 + \delta_0\delta_3 = 0 \tag{19.20}$$

If you like, you can convince yourself of this by plugging in the definitions of the $\delta_i$'s from Equation (19.18), but how did I know to try this? Well, there's an interesting parallel between the arithmetic we did in defining the six $\delta_i$ values and the arithmetic involved in constructing the six components of a 3DH line from two 3DH points. I described this in some detail in "A Homogeneous Formulation for Lines in 3 Space," *SIGGRAPH* 77, pp. 237–241, where I showed that the six values generated by Equation (19.18) must always satisfy Equation (19.20). Now let's use it.

If we multiply out Equation (19.19) and do a little obvious factoring, we get

$$81\delta_1\delta_5\left(\delta_2\delta_4 - \delta_1\delta_5\right) + \delta_0(\text{buncha stuff})$$

Now apply the identity (19.19), and we get

$$81\delta_1\delta_5\left(\delta_0\delta_3\right) + \delta_0(\text{buncha stuff})$$

We now can factor $\delta_0$ out of this to give the correct quartic discriminant:

$$\Delta_4 = 81\delta_1\delta_3\delta_5 - 27\delta_1\delta_4^2 - 27\delta_2^2\delta_5 \\ + 9\delta_0\delta_2\delta_4 + 18\delta_0\delta_1\delta_5 - \delta_0^3$$

Nice but still not nice enough. Watch closely—my fingers never leave the keyboard. By applying the identity again, we can turn this into

$$\Delta_4 = 81\delta_1\delta_3\delta_5 + 9\delta_0\delta_1\delta_5 + 18\delta_0\delta_2\delta_4 \\ - 27\delta_2^2\delta_5 - 27\delta_1\delta_4^2 - 9\delta_0^2\delta_3 - \delta_0^3$$

Which, as anyone can plainly see is

$$\Delta_4 = \det\begin{bmatrix} 3\delta_1 & 3\delta_2 & \delta_0 \\ 3\delta_2 & 9\delta_3 + \delta_0 & 3\delta_4 \\ \delta_0 & 3\delta_4 & 3\delta_5 \end{bmatrix}$$

This is just an application of the formula for the resultant of two cubics given in Kajiya.[4] The two cubics in question are the two derivatives in Equation (19.17).

---

4  Kajiya, J., "Ray Tracing Parametric Patches," *Proc. Siggraph 82*, ACM Press, New York, 1982, p. 248.

This is pretty, but not pretty enough. There is another representation of the discriminant of a quartic that's even better. It's buried in some hundred-year-old lectures by Hilbert, reprinted recently.[5] Hilbert defined two quantities that, translated into our terminology, are

$$I_2 = AE - 4BD + 3C^2$$
$$I_3 = ACE - AD^2 - B^2E + 2BCD - C^3$$

Then the quartic discriminant happens to be

$$\Delta_4 = 27\left(I_3\right)^2 - \left(I_2\right)^3 \tag{19.21}$$

You can verify this for yourself by simple substitution. I won't wait . . .

# Behind the Curtain

The expression for the discriminant in Equation (19.13) is a lot prettier than the one in Equation (19.6). And the expression in Equation (19.21) is a lot prettier than Equation (19.16). But I suspect that you are wondering how I knew to take some of the steps to get there. The answer is that I am using some notational tools that I have not yet told you about. These new tools are motivated by notational clunkiness of Equation (19.7) and are based on the Feynman diagram techniques I wrote about in *Jim Blinn's Corner: Dirty Pixels*, Chapters 9 and 10, "Uppers and Downers" (Parts I and II). Expressing the discriminants using this notation gives us an even more beautiful result. But in order to appreciate it, you must learn this new notational language. We'll do that in the next chapter.

---

5 Hilbert, D., *Theory of Algebraic Invariants*, Cambridge University Press, 1993, pp. 72, 74.

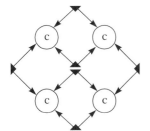

# CHAPTER TWENTY

# Polynomial Discriminants
# Part II, Tensor Diagrams

JANUARY – FEBRUARY 2001

Several years ago, Jim Kajiya lent me a copy of a book called *Diagram Techniques in Group Theory* (G. E. Stedman, Cambridge University Press, Cambridge, England, 1990). This book described a graphical representation of the algebra used to solve various problems in mathematical physics. I was only able to understand the first chapter, but even that was enough to excite me tremendously about adapting the technique to the algebra of homogeneous geometry that we are familiar with in computer graphics. I have written up my initial efforts in Chapters 9 and 10, "Uppers and Downers" (Parts I and II), of *Jim Blinn's Corner: Dirty Pixels*. Recently, I've been playing more and more with these diagrammatic ways of doing algebra and have come up with a lot of interesting results. This chapter presents the first of these—the use of diagrams to compute discriminants of polynomials and to solve a related problem: line-curve tangency. To get into this, I'll briefly review the parts of "Uppers and Downers" that will be useful here.

## 2D Homogeneous Geometry

Two-dimensional homogeneous geometry uses three-element vectors, $3 \times 3$ matrices, $3 \times 3 \times 3$ tensors, and so forth, to represent various objects. I'll denote such quantities in uppercase boldface to distinguish them from polynomials discussed later, for which I'll use lowercase boldface.

**Table 20.1** *Point on a line*

| | |
|---|---|
| (a) | $Ax + By + Cw = 0$ |
| (b) | $\begin{bmatrix} x & y & w \end{bmatrix} \begin{bmatrix} A \\ B \\ C \end{bmatrix} = 0$ |
| (c) | $\mathbf{P} \cdot \mathbf{L} = 0$ |
| (d) | $P^i L_i = 0$ |
| (e) | $\left( P \right) \xrightarrow{i} \left( L \right) = 0$ |

For example, a homogeneous point **P** is a three-element row vector, and a line **L** is a three-element column vector. The point lies on the line if the dot product **P** · **L** is zero. Table 20.1 shows different ways of expressing the dot product. Parts (a), (b), and (c) should be familiar to you. I'll explain parts (d) and (e) shortly.

Moving up to curves, the points on a second-order (quadratic) curve satisfy the equation in Table 20.2(a). We can write this in matrix form by arranging the coefficients into the 3×3 symmetric matrix of Table 20.2(b), and with dot products in 20.2(c).

Next up, the points on a third-order (cubic) curve satisfy Table 20.3(a). We can also write this by arranging the coefficients into a 3×3×3 symmetric generalization of a matrix. Doing this with conventional matrix notation is a bit weird. About the best we can do is to show it as a vector of matrices as in Table 20.3(b).

Now let's talk about transformations. We geometrically transform points by postmultiplying by a 3×3 matrix: **PT** = **P**′, and we transform lines by premultiplying by the adjoint of the matrix: **T\*L** = **L**′. Table 20.4 shows various ways to write these expressions, as well as those for transforming curves.

Finally, the cross product of two point-vectors **P** and **R** gives the line passing through them: **P** × **R** = **L**. See Table 20.5. In a dual fashion, the cross product of two line-vectors **L** and **M** gives their point of intersection: **L** × **M** = **P**.

**Table 20.2** *Point on a quadratic curve*

| | |
|---|---|
| (a) | $Ax^2 + 2Bxy + 2Cxw$ $+Dy^2 + 2Eyw$ $+Fw^2 = 0$ |
| (b) | $\begin{bmatrix} x & y & w \end{bmatrix} \begin{bmatrix} A & B & C \\ B & D & E \\ C & E & F \end{bmatrix} \begin{bmatrix} x \\ y \\ w \end{bmatrix} = 0$ |
| (c) | $\mathbf{P} \cdot \mathbf{Q} \cdot \mathbf{P}^T = 0$ |
| (d) | $P^i Q_{ij} P^j = 0$ |
| (e) | $\left( P \right) \xrightarrow{i} \left( Q \right) \xleftarrow{j} \left( P \right) = 0$ |

# The Problem

In looking over these expressions, we see two hints that our notation has problems. The first is the need to take the transpose of **P** when multiplying by **Q**. This is very fishy; column matrices are supposed to represent lines, not points. In fact, there is something fundamentally different about matrices that represent transformations and matrices that represent quadratic curves. We cannot, however, distinguish between them with standard vector notation. The second hint is inability to conveniently represent entities with more than two indices. Our attempt to arrange the coefficients of a cubic polynomial into a triply indexed "cubical matrix" is an example of the problem.

Fortunately, there are two notational schemes that we can adapt from the world of theoretical physics to alleviate these shortcomings: Einstein

**Table 20.3** *Point on a cubic curve*

(a)
$$Ax^3 + 3Bx^2y + 3Cxy^2 + Dy^3$$
$$+3Ex^2w + 6Fxyw + 3Gy^2w$$
$$+3Hxw^2 + 3\mathcal{J}yw^2$$
$$+Kw^3 = 0$$

(b)
$$\begin{bmatrix} x & y & w \end{bmatrix} \left\{ \left[ \begin{bmatrix} A & B & E \\ B & C & F \\ E & F & H \end{bmatrix} \begin{bmatrix} B & C & F \\ C & D & G \\ F & G & \mathcal{J} \end{bmatrix} \begin{bmatrix} E & F & H \\ F & G & \mathcal{J} \\ H & \mathcal{J} & K \end{bmatrix} \right] \begin{bmatrix} x \\ y \\ w \end{bmatrix} \right\} \begin{bmatrix} x \\ y \\ w \end{bmatrix} = 0$$

(c)
$$???$$

(d)
$$P^i P^j P^k C_{ijk} = 0$$

(e)

$$= 0$$

index notation (EIN) and the diagram notation I referred to in my opening monologue. I originally called these Feynman diagrams, but there are enough differences to give them the more appropriate name *tensor diagrams*. They are more like the diagrams in Kuperberg.[1]

# 2DH Tensor Diagrams

**E**instein index notation differentiates between two types of indices for vector/matrix elements: the point-like ones (which we will call contravariant and write as superscripts) and the line-like ones (which we will call covariant and write as subscripts). Thus an element of a point-vector is $P^i$ and an element of a line-vector is $L_j$. (Note that superscript indices are not the same as exponents. Mathematicians ran out of places to put indices and started overloading their notation. Live with it.) These things are easy to get mixed up and backwards so, for reference, I'll post the following reference diagram:

$$T_{CO(\text{line-like})}^{CONTRA(\text{point-like})}$$

---

1 Kuperberg, Greg, "Involutory Hopf Algebras and 3-Manifold Invariants." *International Journal of Mathematics*, Vol. 2, No. 1, 1991, pp. 41–66.

**Table 20.4** *Transformations*

| | Point | Line | Quadratic | Cubic |
|---|---|---|---|---|
| (b) | $\begin{bmatrix} x & y & w \end{bmatrix} \begin{bmatrix} i & j & k \\ l & m & n \\ o & p & q \end{bmatrix} = \begin{bmatrix} x' & y' & w' \end{bmatrix}$ | $\begin{bmatrix} i^* & j^* & k^* \\ l^* & m^* & n^* \\ o^* & p^* & q^* \end{bmatrix} \begin{bmatrix} A \\ B \\ C \end{bmatrix} = \begin{bmatrix} A' \\ B' \\ C' \end{bmatrix}$ | $\begin{bmatrix} i^* & j^* & k^* \\ l^* & m^* & n^* \\ o^* & p^* & q^* \end{bmatrix} \begin{bmatrix} A & B & C \\ B & D & E \\ C & E & F \end{bmatrix} \begin{bmatrix} i^* & l^* & o^* \\ j^* & m^* & p^* \\ k^* & n^* & q^* \end{bmatrix}$ $= \begin{bmatrix} A' & B' & C' \\ B' & D' & E' \\ C' & E' & F' \end{bmatrix}$ | Messy |
| (c) | $\mathbf{PT} = \mathbf{P'}$ | $(\mathbf{T}^*)\mathbf{L} = \mathbf{L'}$ | $(\mathbf{T}^*)\mathbf{Q}(\mathbf{T}^*)^{\mathrm{T}} = \mathbf{Q}$ | Messy |
| (d) | $P^i T_i^j = (P')^j$ | $(T^*)_j^i L_i = (L')_j$ | $(T^*)_k^i Q_{ij} (T^*)_l^j = (Q')_{kl}$ | $(T^*)_l^i (T^*)_m^j (T^*)_n^k C_{ijk} = (C')_{lmn}$ |
| (e) | | | | |

Dot products happen *only* between matching pairs of covariant and contravariant indices. Thus the dot of a point and a line (using indexes starting at 0) is

$$\mathbf{P} \cdot \mathbf{L} = \begin{bmatrix} P^0 & P^1 & P^2 \end{bmatrix} \cdot \begin{bmatrix} L_0 & L_1 & L_2 \end{bmatrix}$$
$$= \sum_i P^i L_i$$

We simplify further by omitting the sigma and stating that any superscript/subscript pair that has the same letter implicitly implies a summation over that letter. The EIN form of a dot product is then simply

$$P^i L_i$$

A more complicated expression may have many tensors and superscripts and subscripts, and will implicitly be summed over all pairs of identical upper/lower indices. (These summations are also called *tensor contractions*.) We can see this in the EIN for higher-order curves in Tables 20.2(d) and 20.3(d). Note that the expression for EIN is basically a model for the terms that are summed. Each individual factor in the notation is just a number, so the factors can be rearranged in any order, as Table 20.3(d) shows.

## Basic Diagrams

Tensor diagram notation is a translation of EIN into a graph. We represent a point as a node with an outward arrow indicating a contravariant index. A line, with its covariant index, is a node with an inward arrow. The dot product—that is, the summation over the covariant/contravariant pair—is an arc connecting two nodes. See the bottom rows of Tables 20.1 through 20.3 for the diagram notation of the expressions we have seen so far. For many of the diagrams, I will label the arcs with the index they correspond to in EIN. Some later, more complex, diagrams will not need this.

## Transformations

A transformation matrix has one contravariant and one covariant index. Multiplying a point by such a matrix will "annihilate" its covariant index, leaving a result that has a free contravariant index, making the result be a point. Table

**Table 20.5** *The cross product*

(a)
$$\begin{bmatrix} P^1 R^2 - P^2 R^1 \\ P^2 R^0 - P^0 R^2 \\ P^0 R^1 - P^1 R^0 \end{bmatrix} = \begin{bmatrix} L_0 \\ L_1 \\ L_2 \end{bmatrix}$$

(b)
$$\begin{bmatrix} P^0 & P^1 & P^2 \end{bmatrix} \times \begin{bmatrix} R^0 & R^1 & R^2 \end{bmatrix} = \begin{bmatrix} L_0 \\ L_1 \\ L_2 \end{bmatrix}$$

(c)
$$\mathbf{P} \times \mathbf{R} = \mathbf{L}$$

(d)
$$P^i R^j \varepsilon_{ijk} = L_k$$

(e)

20.4(d) shows the EIN form of the transformation of various quantities. Table 20.4(e) shows how this translates into diagram notation. Now we can see the difference between the two types of matrices. A transformation matrix has one of each type of index (denoted with one arrow out and one arrow in); a quadratic matrix has two covariant indices (denoted with both arrows in). In Table 20.2(d), the two contravariant/covariant index pairs annihilate each other to produce a scalar.

## Cross Products and Adjoints

We abbreviate the algebra for cross products and matrix adjoints by defining a three-index $3 \times 3 \times 3$ element antisymmetric tensor called the *Levi-Civita epsilon*. The elements of epsilon are defined to be

$$\varepsilon_{012} = \varepsilon_{120} = \varepsilon_{201} = +1$$
$$\varepsilon_{210} = \varepsilon_{021} = \varepsilon_{102} = -1 \tag{20.1}$$
$$\varepsilon_{ijk} = 0 \quad \text{otherwise}$$

Multiplying two vectors by epsilon forms their cross product. Since epsilon has three subscript indices, multiplying in two points with superscript indices will result in a vector with one remaining subscript index (a line); see Table 20.5(d). The diagram form of epsilon is a node with three inward-pointing arcs. We will show this node as a small dot, as in Table 20.5(e). You can imagine a variant of Table 20.5 for the dual form, the cross product of two lines: $\mathbf{L} \times \mathbf{M} = \mathbf{P}$. Just use a contravariant form of epsilon, $\varepsilon^{ijk}$, so that $L_i M_j \varepsilon^{ijk} = P^k$, and flip the direction of all arrows in the diagram.

We must be careful about how the antisymmetry of epsilon is represented in a tensor diagram. The convention is to label the arcs counterclockwise around the dot. A mirror reflection of an epsilon node will reverse the order of its indices, and therefore flip its algebraic sign.

Epsilon is also useful to form matrix adjoints. Table 20.6 shows various ways to denote the adjoint. Table 20.6(a) explicitly shows that each element of the adjoint is a second-order polynomial of the elements of $\mathbf{Q}$. Table 20.6(b) shows how each column of $\mathbf{Q}^*$ is the cross product of two rows of $\mathbf{Q}$. This gives us a lead-in to the EIN in Table 20.6(d) being constructed of the same epsilons that gave us cross products in Table 20.5. The raw EIN expression $Q_{ij} Q_{kl} \varepsilon^{ikm} \varepsilon^{jln}$ gives twice the adjoint, so I had to insert a factor of $\frac{1}{2}$ to get the correct answer. Table 20.6(e) shows the diagram. Note that the diagram has two $\mathbf{Q}$ nodes, which reflects the fact that the elements of $\mathbf{Q}^*$ are second order in the elements of $\mathbf{Q}$, and also shows another notational convention: I put the scalar factor $-\frac{1}{2}$ into a scalar node, one with

**Table 20.6** *The adjoint of a 3×3 matrix*

(a)
$$DF - E^2 = A^*$$
$$CE - BF = B^*$$
$$\vdots$$

(b)
$$\begin{bmatrix} \det\begin{bmatrix} D & E \\ E & F \end{bmatrix} & -\det\begin{bmatrix} B & E \\ C & F \end{bmatrix} & \det\begin{bmatrix} B & D \\ C & E \end{bmatrix} \\ -\det\begin{bmatrix} B & E \\ C & F \end{bmatrix} & \det\begin{bmatrix} A & C \\ C & F \end{bmatrix} & -\det\begin{bmatrix} A & B \\ C & E \end{bmatrix} \\ \det\begin{bmatrix} B & D \\ C & E \end{bmatrix} & -\det\begin{bmatrix} A & B \\ C & E \end{bmatrix} & \det\begin{bmatrix} A & B \\ B & D \end{bmatrix} \end{bmatrix} =$$

$$\begin{bmatrix} \begin{bmatrix} B & D & E \end{bmatrix} \\ \times \\ \begin{bmatrix} C & E & F \end{bmatrix} \end{bmatrix}, \begin{bmatrix} \begin{bmatrix} C & E & F \end{bmatrix} \\ \times \\ \begin{bmatrix} A & B & C \end{bmatrix} \end{bmatrix}, \begin{bmatrix} \begin{bmatrix} A & B & C \end{bmatrix} \\ \times \\ \begin{bmatrix} B & D & E \end{bmatrix} \end{bmatrix} = \begin{bmatrix} A^* & B^* & C^* \\ B^* & D^* & E^* \\ C^* & E^* & F^* \end{bmatrix}$$

(c)
$$\text{adj}\,\mathbf{Q} = \mathbf{Q}^*$$

(d)
$$\tfrac{1}{2} Q_{ij} Q_{kl} \varepsilon^{ikm} \varepsilon^{jln} = (Q^*)^{mn}$$

(e)

no arrows in or out. Furthermore, I've chosen to mirror the first epsilon in the EIN (and introduce a corresponding minus sign) to make the whole diagram a bit prettier. These factors and signs clutter things up a bit but are necessary.

Now that we have the adjoint, the determinant is not far behind. We use the fact that

$$\mathbf{Q}^*\mathbf{Q} = (\det \mathbf{Q})\,\mathbf{I}$$

We tie up the loose ends, literally, by taking the trace of this getting

$$\text{trace}\,(\mathbf{Q}^*\mathbf{Q}) = 3\det \mathbf{Q}$$

So in diagram terms, connect the adjoint from Table 20.6(e) to another copy of $\mathbf{Q}$ and take the trace by connecting the two dangling arcs. Divide by 3 to get the determinant. The resulting diagram is in Table 20.7(e).

**Table 20.7** *Determinant of 3×3 matrix*

(a)     $ABD + 2BCE - C^2D - E^2A - B^2F = \det \mathbf{Q}$

(b)     $[ABC] \times [BDE] \cdot [CEF]$

(c)     $\det \mathbf{Q}$

(d)     $\frac{1}{6} Q_{ij} Q_{kl} Q_{mn} \varepsilon^{ikm} \varepsilon^{jln}$

(e)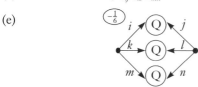

**Table 20.8** *Homogeneous linear equation*

(a)     $Ax + Bw = 0$

(b)     $\begin{bmatrix} x & w \end{bmatrix} \begin{bmatrix} A \\ B \end{bmatrix} = 0$

(c)     $\mathbf{p} \cdot \mathbf{l} = 0$

(d)     $p^i l_i = 0$

(e)     $\boxed{P} \longrightarrow \boxed{l} = 0$

# Homogeneous Polynomials

now let's go down a dimension and take a look at 1D homogeneous geometry. This is effectively the study of homogeneous polynomials. Basically, we have the same thing as before, but everything is now composed of two-element vectors, 2×2 matrices, and 2×2×2 tensors, which I'll write as lowercase boldface. A homogeneous linear equation is written in various notations in Table 20.8.

Table 20.9 shows a homogeneous quadratic equation.

Table 20.10 shows a homogeneous cubic equation. Unfortunately, I find that I have to use the letter C in two contexts, once as a coefficient (italic) and once as a tensor name (bold). Live with it.

**Table 20.9** *Homogeneous quadratic equation*

(a)     $Ax^2 + 2Bxw + Cw^2 = 0$

(b)     $\begin{bmatrix} x & w \end{bmatrix} \begin{bmatrix} A & B \\ B & C \end{bmatrix} \begin{bmatrix} x \\ w \end{bmatrix} = 0$

(c)     $\mathbf{pqp}^T = 0$

(d)     $p^i p^j q_{ij} = 0$

(e)     $\boxed{P} \longrightarrow \boxed{q} \longleftarrow \boxed{P} = 0$

### The 2D Epsilon

The only slightly subtle item is the form of the two-element epsilon. Instead of having three indices, each with three values, the two-element epsilon has two indices (making it a simple matrix), each with two values. By analogy to Equation (20.1) the covariant form of epsilon is

$$\varepsilon_{01} = +1$$
$$\varepsilon_{10} = -1$$
$$\varepsilon_{ij} = 0 \quad \text{otherwise}$$

In other words,

$$\varepsilon = \begin{bmatrix} 0 & 1 \\ -1 & 0 \end{bmatrix}$$

The Einstein notation is simply $\varepsilon_{ij}$ or $\varepsilon^{ij}$, and the diagram notation looks like

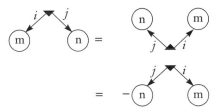

I have purposely constructed this icon to be asymmetrical. The convention is that when the diagram points down (as above), the first index is on the left. A mirror reflection of this diagram will perform a sign flip on the value of the diagram. If the diagram were not asymmetrical, a mirror flip would not be detectable. To drive this home, compare the EIN expressions

$$m_i \varepsilon^{ij} n_j = n_j \varepsilon^{ij} m_i = -n_j \varepsilon^{ji} m_i$$

with their diagram counterparts. The first equality represents a rotation (no sign flip), and the second has a reflection (with a sign flip):

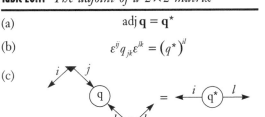

Now let's use the epsilon. The adjoint of a 2×2 matrix, by analogy to Table 20.6, gives us Table 20.11.

We get the determinant by analogy to Table 20.7: multiply **q**\* by **q** and take the trace. This gives twice the determinant. Flip one of the epsilons to make the diagram neater. We get Table 20.12.

**Table 20.10** *Homogeneous cubic equation*

| | |
|---|---|
| (a) | $Ax^3 + 3Bx^2w + 3Cxw^2 + Dw^3 = 0$ |
| (b) | $\begin{bmatrix} x & w \end{bmatrix} \left\{ \begin{bmatrix} x & w \end{bmatrix} \begin{bmatrix} \begin{bmatrix} A & B \\ B & C \end{bmatrix} \\ \begin{bmatrix} B & C \\ C & D \end{bmatrix} \end{bmatrix} \right\} \begin{bmatrix} x \\ w \end{bmatrix} = 0$ |
| (c) | Messy |
| (d) | $p^i p^j p^k c_{ijk} = 0$ |
| (e) | 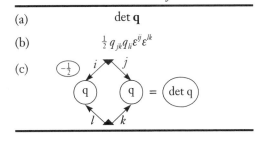 |

**Table 20.11** *The adjoint of a 2×2 matrix*

| | |
|---|---|
| (a) | $\mathrm{adj}\,\mathbf{q} = \mathbf{q}^*$ |
| (b) | $\varepsilon^{ij} q_{jk} \varepsilon^{lk} = (q^*)^{il}$ |
| (c) | (diagram) |

**Table 20.12** *The determinant of a 2×2 matrix*

| | |
|---|---|
| (a) | $\det \mathbf{q}$ |
| (b) | $\frac{1}{2} q_{jk} q_{li} \varepsilon^{ij} \varepsilon^{lk}$ |
| (c) | (diagram) |

# A 1DH Application: Discriminants

The discriminant of a polynomial is a condition on the coefficients that guarantees that the polynomial has a double root. In the previous chapter, we learned how to write this quantity in matrix terms. Now let's see how this looks in diagram form.

## Quadratic

The discriminant of the quadratic polynomial from Table 20.9(a) is

$$\Delta_2 = 4\left(B^2 - AC\right) = -4 \det \begin{bmatrix} A & B \\ B & C \end{bmatrix}$$

In diagram form, this is

$$\Delta_2 = \qquad\qquad\qquad\qquad\qquad\qquad \text{(20.2)}$$

## Cubic

The discriminant of the cubic polynomial of Table 20.10(a) is

$$\Delta_3 = \det \begin{bmatrix} 2\delta_1 & \delta_2 \\ \delta_2 & 2\delta_3 \end{bmatrix} \qquad\qquad \text{(20.3)}$$

where the matrix elements are defined as

$$\delta_1 = AC - B^2 = \det \begin{bmatrix} A & B \\ B & C \end{bmatrix}$$

$$\delta_2 = AD - BC = \det \begin{bmatrix} A & B \\ C & D \end{bmatrix}$$

$$\delta_3 = BD - C^2 = \det \begin{bmatrix} B & C \\ C & D \end{bmatrix}$$

What does this look like in diagram form? Let's look at the individual "slices" of the **c** tensor. We form these by multiplying one index by a "basis vector" like $(1,0)$ or $(0,1)$:

$$(1,0) \longrightarrow \left(\text{c}\right) = \left(\text{c}_1\right) = \begin{bmatrix} A & B \\ B & C \end{bmatrix}$$

$$(0,1) \longrightarrow \left(\text{c}\right) = \left(\text{c}_2\right) = \begin{bmatrix} B & C \\ C & D \end{bmatrix}$$

The determinants of these two matrices are

$$\left(\text{c}_1\right) \quad \left(\text{c}_1\right) = -2\det \begin{bmatrix} A & B \\ B & C \end{bmatrix} = -2\delta_1$$

$$\left(\text{c}_2\right) \quad \left(\text{c}_2\right) = -2\det \begin{bmatrix} B & C \\ C & D \end{bmatrix} = -2\delta_3$$

Now what happens if we mash together $\mathbf{c}_1$ and $\mathbf{c}_2$ as a sort of "cross determinant" with the diagram form

The value of this diagram is, in conventional matrix form,

$$trace \left\{ \begin{bmatrix} A & B \\ B & C \end{bmatrix} \begin{bmatrix} 0 & 1 \\ -1 & 0 \end{bmatrix} \begin{bmatrix} B & C \\ C & D \end{bmatrix} \begin{bmatrix} 0 & 1 \\ -1 & 0 \end{bmatrix} \right\} =$$

$$trace \left\{ \begin{bmatrix} BC - AD & AC - B^2 \\ C^2 - BD & 0 \end{bmatrix} \right\} =$$

$$BC - AD = -\delta_2$$

Now, remembering the definitions of $c_1$ and $c_2$, we have just shown that

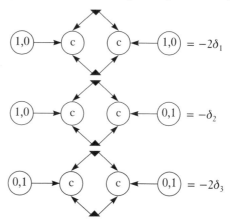

What we have just done is to find expressions for each of the elements of the matrix in Equation (20.3). In other words,

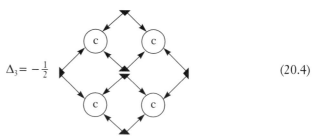

One interesting thing about this demonstration is that it shows why there are factors of 2 for the $\delta_1$ and $\delta_3$ entries, but not for the $\delta_2$. Anyway, the final step is easy. The discriminant of the cubic $c$ equals the determinant of this matrix (with the appropriate minus sign and scale factor):

$$\Delta_3 = -\tfrac{1}{2}$$

(20.4)

You can see this as a nice generalization of the discriminant diagram for the quadratic polynomial. Furthermore, a little scratch work will show that Equation (20.4) is the simplest diagram that can be formed from epsilons and $c$ nodes that is not identically zero.

## Quartic

In the last chapter, I showed a statement by Hilbert that the discriminant of the quartic polynomial

$$f(x, w) = Ax^4 + 4Bx^3w + 6Cx^2w^2 + 4Dxw^3 + Ew^4$$

can be found by first calculating the two quantities

$$I_2 = AE - 4BD + 3C^2$$
$$I_3 = ACE - AD^2 - B^2E + 2BCD - C^3 \tag{20.5}$$

The discriminant is then

$$\Delta_4 = 27\left(I_3\right)^2 - \left(I_2\right)^3$$

Now let's see if we can write this as a tensor diagram. First study Table 20.13, which gives various ways to write the quartic equation. The quartic polynomial is a node with four arcs.

The two simplest diagrams that you can form from four-arc nodes and epsilons are

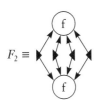

and

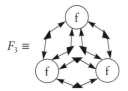

**Table 20.13** *Homogeneous quartic equation*

(a)   $f(x, w) = Ax^4 + 4Bx^3w + 6Cx^2w^2 + 4Dxw^3 + Ew^4$

(b)
$$f(x, w) = \begin{bmatrix} x & w \end{bmatrix} \left\{ \begin{bmatrix} x & w \end{bmatrix} \begin{bmatrix} \begin{bmatrix} A & B \\ B & C \end{bmatrix} & \begin{bmatrix} B & C \\ C & D \end{bmatrix} \\ \begin{bmatrix} B & C \\ C & D \end{bmatrix} & \begin{bmatrix} C & D \\ D & E \end{bmatrix} \end{bmatrix} \begin{bmatrix} x \\ w \end{bmatrix} \right\} \begin{bmatrix} x \\ w \end{bmatrix}$$

(c)   Messy, messy

(d)   $f(p) = p^i p^j p^k p^l f_{ijkl}$

(e)
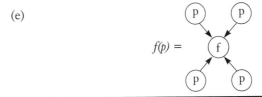

Using techniques similar to those in the next chapter, I've been able to evaluate these diagrams and verify that

$$F_2 = 2AE - 8BD + 6C^2$$
$$= 2I_2$$
$$F_3 = -6ACE + 6AD^2 + 6B^2E - 12BCD + 6C^3$$
$$= -6I_3$$

Hot damn . . . Hilbert's invariants match up with the two simplest possible diagrams. Some fiddling with constants gives us

$$\Delta_4 = 27\left(\frac{F_3}{-6}\right)^2 - \left(\frac{F_2}{2}\right)^3$$
$$= \tfrac{1}{8}\left(6(F_3)^2 - F_2^3\right)$$

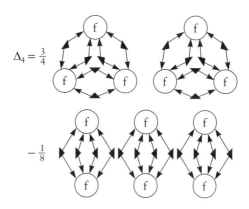

## The Invariance of Invariants

The discriminant of a polynomial is an example of an "invariant" quantity. Invariant, in this case, means invariant under parameter transformations. When you calculate such a quantity for a polynomial, its sign will remain unchanged if the polynomial is transformed parametrically. This makes sense since the number and multiplicity of roots of a polynomial do not change under parameter transformation.

### iDH

Tensor diagrams are particularly useful to express invariant quantities because of the following identity:

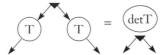

We can easily verify this by explicit calculation

$$\mathbf{T}\varepsilon\mathbf{T}^T = \begin{bmatrix} a & b \\ c & d \end{bmatrix}\begin{bmatrix} 0 & 1 \\ -1 & 0 \end{bmatrix}\begin{bmatrix} a & c \\ b & d \end{bmatrix}$$

$$= \begin{bmatrix} 0 & ad-bc \\ bc-ad & 0 \end{bmatrix}$$

$$= (ad-bc)\begin{bmatrix} 0 & 1 \\ -1 & 0 \end{bmatrix}$$

Now, let's apply this to the simplest of our discriminants, the quadratic. We start with

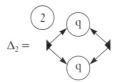

We now do a parameter transformation on **q.** The 1DH analog to the equations in Table 20.4 is

Putting this into our discriminant equation and applying our identity gives

In other words,

$$\operatorname{discr} \mathbf{q} = (\det \mathbf{T})^2 \operatorname{discr} \mathbf{q}'$$

As long as we don't do anything silly, like transform by a singular matrix, the sign of the discriminant of a quadratic is invariant under coordinate transformation.

This seems pretty obvious, but there's a bigger idea lurking in it. It should be pretty simple to see that

*Any diagram made up of a collection of nodes glued together with the appropriate number of epsilon nodes will represent a transformationally invariant quantity.*

If there are an even number of epsilons, the sign is invariant; if there are an odd number of epsilons, just the zeroness of the quantity is invariant.

You can imagine any number of diagrams formed in this way; each of them represents some invariant quantity under parameter transformation. Many of these, however, will be uninteresting. For example, you can show that the following diagram is identically zero:

$$\text{C} \diamondsuit \text{C} = 0$$

Hilbert's book (referenced in the previous chapter) is all about algebraic rules for generating invariant quantities. We can do this much more simply with tensor diagrams. For example, we know that the two expressions in Equation (20.5) are invariant simply because they can be generated by tensor diagrams.

## 2DH

The 2DH epsilon has a similar identity involving transformation matrices that we had in 1DH:

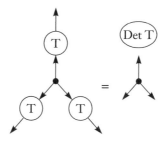

This means that any 2DH tensor diagram made up of polynomial nodes and epsilons represents a transformational invariant.

# A 2DH Application: Tangency

Now let's use these 1DH results to solve a 2DH geometry problem: tangency.

## Quadratic with Line

Table 20.2 gave us the condition of a point **P** being on a quadratic curve **Q**. How can we generate an expression that determines if a line **L** is tangent to curve **Q**? (I've stated the answer to this before; now I'm going to prove it.) Let's start by assuming that we have two points on **L**, call them **R** and **S**. (We don't need to know how we found these two points. In fact, they will disappear shortly.) A general point on the line is then

$$\mathbf{P}(\alpha, \beta) = \alpha\mathbf{R} + \beta\mathbf{s}$$

In matrix notation,

$$\mathbf{P} = \begin{bmatrix} \alpha & \beta \end{bmatrix} \begin{bmatrix} R^0 & R^1 & R^2 \\ S^0 & S^1 & S^2 \end{bmatrix}$$

$$\mathbf{P} = \mathbf{aV}$$

The $2 \times 3$ matrix **V** is a sort of conversion from the world of 2D (1DH) vectors (homogeneous polynomials) to the world of 3D (2DH) vectors (homogeneous curves). Let's write this in diagram form. (For these mixed-mode diagrams, I'll make thicker arrows for the three-element summations and thinner arrows for the two-element summations.)

$$\boxed{P} \longrightarrow \; = \; \boxed{a} \longrightarrow \boxed{V} \longrightarrow$$

If we plug this into the quadratic curve equation, we get a homogeneous polynomial in $(\alpha, \beta)$ that evaluates the quadratic function at each point on the line:

$$\boxed{P} \longrightarrow \boxed{Q} \longleftarrow \boxed{P} \; =$$

$$\longrightarrow \boxed{a} \longrightarrow \boxed{V} \longrightarrow \boxed{Q} \longleftarrow \boxed{V} \longleftarrow \boxed{a} \; =$$

$$\boxed{a} \longrightarrow \boxed{q} \longleftarrow \boxed{a}$$

We've turned the $3 \times 3$ symmetric quadratic curve matrix **Q** into a $2 \times 2$ symmetric quadratic polynomial matrix that we'll call **q**. Writing just **q** by itself we get

$$\longrightarrow \boxed{V} \longrightarrow \boxed{Q} \longleftarrow \boxed{V} \longleftarrow \; = \; \longrightarrow \boxed{q} \longleftarrow$$

The condition of the line being tangent to the curve is the same as the condition that there is a double root to this polynomial. The polynomial has a double root if the determinant of its matrix formulation is zero.

Plugging the above into the diagram form of the determinant and setting it to zero gives us the condition that the polynomial has a double root, and thus that the line hits the curve at exactly one point:

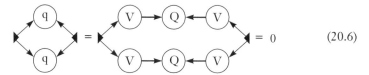

$$\tag{20.6}$$

Now let's look more closely at the following diagram fragment:

Write this as a matrix product:

$$
\begin{bmatrix} R^0 & S^0 \\ R^1 & S^1 \\ R^2 & S^2 \end{bmatrix}
\begin{bmatrix} 0 & 1 \\ -1 & 0 \end{bmatrix}
\begin{bmatrix} R^0 & R^1 & R^2 \\ S^0 & S^1 & S^2 \end{bmatrix} =
$$

$$
\begin{bmatrix}
0 & R^0S^1 - R^1S^0 & R^0S^2 - R^2S^0 \\
R^1S^0 - R^0S^1 & 0 & R^1S^2 - R^2S^1 \\
R^2S^0 - R^0S^2 & R^2S^1 - R^1S^2 & 0
\end{bmatrix}
$$

You can recognize the elements of this matrix as the components of the cross product of the two points **R** and **S**. But these are just the elements of the line-vector **L** arranged into an antisymmetric matrix. In diagram form, we can show this as

$$
L \!\!-\!\!\!< \quad = \quad
\begin{bmatrix}
0 & L_2 & -L_1 \\
-L_2 & 0 & L_0 \\
L_1 & -L_0 & 0
\end{bmatrix}
$$

We can therefore say that

$$\tag{20.7}$$

Note that the right-hand side of this doesn't contain any explicit points on **L**. So if all you have are the **L** components, you do not need to explicitly find points on **L**. Putting Diagrams (20.6) and (20.7) together, we get the condition that the line **L** is tangent to curve **Q**:

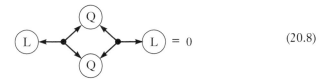

$$\text{(20.8)}$$

This diagram, without the **L** nodes, is just the expression of the adjoint of the matrix **Q** from Table 20.9(c) (times minus two). In other words, while we use **Q** to test for point incidence, we use **Q\*** to test for line incidence (tangency):

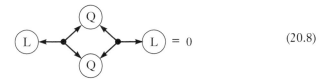

$$\mathbf{L}^T \left( \mathbf{Q}^{\cdot} \right) \mathbf{L} = 0$$

## Cubic with Line

So, going up an order, what is the condition of line **L** being tangent to a cubic curve **C**? That is, we want an expression involving the vector **L** and the cubic coefficient tensor **C** that is zero if **L** is tangent to **C**. With the groundwork we've laid, this is easy. First, compare Diagrams (20.6) and (20.8) to see how we converted the 1DH quadratic polynomial discriminant into a 2DH quadratic curve tangency equation. We just replaced each 2D epsilon with a 3D epsilon attached to a copy of **L**, and replaced **q** with **Q**. Now do the same thing with the discriminant of a cubic polynomial (20.4). We get

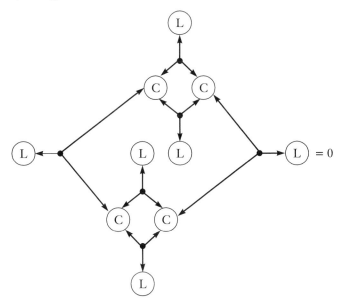

This diagram represents a polynomial expression that is fourth order in **C** and sixth order in **L**. Since it has 18 arcs, the EIN version of this would require 18 index letters. All in all, it is something that would be rather difficult to arrive at in any other, nondiagram, way.

Since the tangency expression is sixth order in **L**, it is reasonable to expect that it is possible to find a situation where there are six tangents to a cubic from a given point. This seems excessive, but it is possible as Figure 20.1 shows.

# A 2DH Application: Discriminants

The concept of the discriminant also bumps up from 1DH-land to 2DH-land. Again, the discriminant being zero tells us that there are places where both the function and its derivatives are zero. Geometrically, this means that there are places on the curve (function = 0) where the tangent is not defined (derivative vector = 0). This can happen if the curve is factorable into lower-order curves; the points in question are the points of intersection of the lower-order curves. Or it can mean that there are cusps or self-intersections in the curve. We'll see examples of all these below.

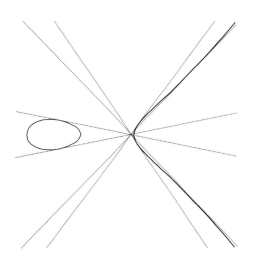

**Figure 20.1** *Six tangents from a point to a cubic curve*

## Quadratic

The discriminant of a quadratic curve is just the determinant of the matrix **Q**. We saw this in Chapter 1. In diagram notation, this looks like

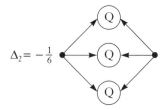

If this discriminant is zero, it means that the quadratic is factorable into two linear terms. Geometrically, it means that the curve is not a simple conic section, but a degenerate one consisting of two intersecting straight lines. See Figure 20.2.

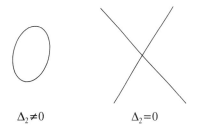

$\Delta_2 \neq 0$         $\Delta_2 = 0$

**Figure 20.2** *Relation between quadratic discriminant and geometry*

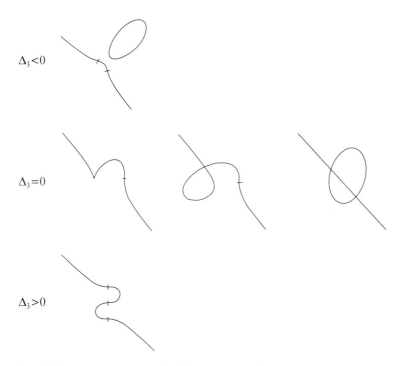

$\Delta_3 < 0$

$\Delta_3 = 0$

$\Delta_3 > 0$

**Figure 20.3**  *Relation between cubic discriminant and geometry*

## Cubic

An equivalent expression for the cubic curve case is considerably more complicated. Paluszny and Patterson describe the cubic discriminant as a polynomial that is degree 12 in the coefficients $A$. . .$F$ and that has over 10,000 terms.[2] Manipulating this thing explicitly is . . . inconvenient. Actually, it's not that complicated. George Salmon showed that the discriminant is a function of two simpler quantities:

$$\Delta_3 = T^2 + 64S^3$$

where $S$ is degree 4 in $A$. . .$K$ and has 25 terms, and $T$ is degree 6 in $A$. . .$K$ and has 103 terms.[3] Salmon worked out all these terms by hand (it's amazing what people had time to do before the invention of television). The cubic discriminant relates to the geometry of the cubic curve as shown in Figure 20.3. Notice the varieties of cusp, self-intersection, and lower-order-curve intersection that can happen when $\Delta_3 = 0$.

---

2  Paluszny, M., and Patterson, R. "A Family of Tangent Continuous Cubic Algebraic Splines," *ACM Transactions on Graphics*, Vol. 12, No. 3, July 1993, p. 212.

3  Salmon, G. *A Treatise on the Higher Plane Curves*, G. E. Stechert & Co., New York, 1934. A photographic reprint of the third edition of 1879, pp. 191, 192, and 199.

How can we express this as a tensor diagram? Let's work backwards and see what sorts of simple diagrams we can make out of **C** nodes and epsilons. After some fooling around, I came up with the following two:

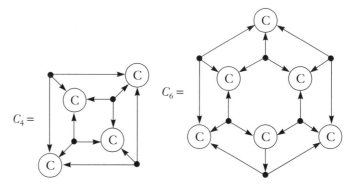

Using the program described in the next chapter, I have been able to verify that

$$C_4 = -24S$$
$$C_6 = -6T$$

Pastafazola! Salmon's invariants correspond to the two simplest tensor diagrams we can make for cubic curves! Some more fiddling with constants gives us

$$\Delta_3 = \left(\frac{C_6}{-6}\right)^2 + 64\left(\frac{C_4}{-24}\right)^3$$
$$= \frac{1}{6^3}\left(6\left(C_6\right)^2 - \left(C_4\right)^3\right)$$

# Relationships

There's something even more interesting going on here. Notice the similarity between the formula for the discriminants of a 1DH quartic polynomial and a 2DH cubic curve:

$$\text{1DH:}\ \ \Delta_4 = \tfrac{1}{2^3}\left(6\left(F_3\right)^2 - \left(F_2\right)^3\right)$$
$$\text{2DH:}\ \ \Delta_3 = \tfrac{1}{6^3}\left(6\left(C_6\right)^2 - \left(C_4\right)^3\right)$$

This means that there is a relationship between the possible root structures of a fourth-order polynomial and the possible degeneracies of a third-order curve. That's one of the things I'm currently trying to understand.

# Notation, Notation, Notation

A lot of the notational language of mathematics consists of the art of creative abbreviation. For example, a vector-matrix product $\mathbf{pT}$ is an abbreviation for a lot of similar-looking algebraic expressions. However, clunky expressions like Table 20.3(b) showed that this notation is not powerful enough to allow us to easily manipulate the sort of expressions that we are encountering here. Einstein index notation has this power, but often gets buried under an avalanche of index letters. The tensor diagram method of drawing EIN is a better way to handle the index bookkeeping. What I've shown here is only the tip of the iceberg. There are a lot of other things that diagram notation can do well that I will cover in future columns.

Our languages help form how we think. I believe that this notation can help us think about these and similar problems and allow us to come up with solutions that we wouldn't find any other way.

```
class Polynomial
{
   TermList Terms;
public:
   Polynomial& operator+=(const Term& T)
   {
      Terms[T.Monomial] += T.Coefficient;
      return *this;
   }
};
```

# CHAPTER TWENTY-ONE

# Tensor Contraction in C++

MARCH – APRIL 2001

In the previous chapter, I talked about a notational device for matrix alge-bra called *tensor diagrams*. This time I'm going to get real and write some C++ code to evaluate these quantities symbolically. This gives me a chance to play with some as yet untried (by me) features in the C++ Standard Library, like strings and STL container classes. For more on STL, check out my favorite book on the subject: *The C++ Standard Library* by Nicolai M. Josuttis (Addison Wesley, 1999). I am trying to figure out if I like these new-fangled programming tools by seeing how much code I can get away with not writing these days. My initial impression is positive. So this article is partially a demo/advertisement of the benefits of the STL. If you spend some time learning these tools, you too can write less code that does more.

## The Basic Objects

Since this chapter is mostly about C++, I will review just enough of the algebra to motivate the code. We are interested in algebraic curves de-fined by $F(x, y, w) = 0$. The simplest of these is a straight line, represented by the equation

$$Ax + By + Cw = 0$$

A quadratic curve is represented by the equation

$$Ax^2 + 2Bxy + 2Cxw$$
$$+ Dy^2 + 2Eyw$$
$$+ Fw^2 = 0$$

A cubic curve is represented by the equation

$$Ax^3 + 3Bx^2y + 3Cxy^2 + Dy^3$$
$$+ 3Ex^2w + 6Fxyw + 3Gy^2w$$
$$+ 3Hxw^2 + 3Jyw^2$$
$$+ Kw^3 = 0$$

We want to relate various geometric properties of these curves with algebraic combinations of the coefficients $A$. . .$K$. The first step is to arrange the coefficients in arrays that, in mathematical lingo, are called *tensors*. For a line, we arrange the coefficients into a column vector:

$$\mathbf{L} = \begin{bmatrix} A \\ B \\ C \end{bmatrix}$$

For the quadratic, we define the symmetric matrix

$$\mathbf{Q} = \begin{bmatrix} A & B & C \\ B & D & E \\ C & E & F \end{bmatrix}$$

For the cubic curve equation, we arrange the coefficients into a $3 \times 3 \times 3$ tensor that we can write (clumsily) as a vector of matrices:

$$\mathbf{C} = \begin{bmatrix} \begin{bmatrix} A & B & E \\ B & C & F \\ E & F & H \end{bmatrix} & \begin{bmatrix} B & C & F \\ C & D & G \\ F & G & J \end{bmatrix} & \begin{bmatrix} E & F & H \\ F & G & J \\ H & J & K \end{bmatrix} \end{bmatrix}$$

When we write an element of one of these tensors, the convention is to label its location in the array with indices written as subscripts. These are called *covariant indices* and look like

$$L_i, Q_{ij}, C_{ijk}$$

A point, on the other hand, is written as a row vector:

$$\mathbf{P} = \begin{bmatrix} x & y & w \end{bmatrix}$$

When we write an element of the point, we label it with an index written as a superscript. (This does not mean exponentiation. It's just a place to put the index.) These indices are called *contravariant* and look like

$$P^i$$

Finally, we will have use for a constant $3 \times 3 \times 3$ contravariant tensor called *epsilon* whose elements are defined to be

$$\varepsilon^{012} = \varepsilon^{120} = \varepsilon^{201} = +1$$
$$\varepsilon^{210} = \varepsilon^{021} = \varepsilon^{102} = -1$$
$$\varepsilon^{ijk} = 0 \quad \text{otherwise}$$

# The Basic Operation

The basic quantity we want to calculate is a "contraction" of two or more tensors. Vector dot products and vector/matrix products are special cases of tensor contractions. More generally, we want to evaluate expressions such as

$$\sum_{ijklmn} \varepsilon^{ijk} \varepsilon^{lmn} \mathbf{Q}_{il} \mathbf{Q}_{jm} \mathbf{Q}_{kn} \tag{21.1}$$

And, being lazy, we will abbreviate expressions like Equation (21.1) by leaving out the summation sign. Any index that appears exactly twice in an expression, once as covariant and once as contravariant, will be assumed summed over.

So, I want to come up with a simple symbolic algebra manipulation program that is good at these sorts of expressions and doesn't really need to handle anything more general. We saw in Chapter 20 that Equation (21.1) should evaluate to six times the determinant of $\mathbf{Q}$. So if we translate Equation (21.1) into C++ code, we want the program to print out something like this:

$$6ADF + 12BCE - 6C^2D - 6AE^2 - 6B^2F \tag{21.2}$$

Incidentally, if this polynomial is zero, it tells us that the quadratic is really the product of two linear factors—that is, the equation stands for two straight lines.

# The Epsilon Routine

The most obvious first step is to define a routine to calculate epsilon as follows:

```
int epsilon(int i, int j, int k)
{
    if(i==0 && j==1 && k==2) return  1;
    if(i==1 && j==2 && k==0) return  1;
    if(i==2 && j==0 && k==1) return  1;
    if(i==2 && j==1 && k==0) return -1;
    if(i==0 && j==2 && k==1) return -1;
    if(i==1 && j==0 && k==2) return -1;
    return 0;

}
```

We are ultimately going to define a class `Polynomial` to hold the final answer and a subroutine `Q(i,j)` that returns the symbolic value in element *i,j*. If we design these properly, we can write code to evaluate Equation (21.1) that simply loops through all values of *i, j, k, l, m, n* and adds up the terms, like so (note that I am using the STL-like convention for loop bounds).

```
#define forIndex(I) for(int I=0;I!=3;++I)

Polynomial E;
forIndex(i)
forIndex(j)
forIndex(k)
forIndex(l)
forIndex(m)
forIndex(n)
E += epsilon(i,j,k)*epsilon(l,m,n)*
                      Q(i,l)*Q(j,m)*Q(k,n);
cout << E << endl;
```

This, however, gets out of hand pretty quickly. The epsilon tensor is mostly zeros; in fact, only 6 out of the 27 entries are nonzero (or $\frac{2}{9}$ of them). If you have two epsilons in your expression, then only 6*6 out of the 27*27 possible combinations are nonzero (about 1 in 20). Some of the diagrams we will be ultimately interested in can have eight or more epsilons. This means that only $6^8$ out of the $27^8$ iterations (about 1 in 168,151) actually adds anything to `E`. And for each epsilon, you have three nested loops. There must be a better way.

There is. We'll turn the loops inside out. Instead of generating all combinations of indices, we will have each loop go through the six non-zero epsilon values and return to us their indices and signs. The new epsilon function looks like

```
int epsilon (int which, int* pI, int* pJ, int* pK)
{
static int Ix1[6]={0,1,2, 2, 0, 1};
static int Ix2[6]={1,2,0, 1, 2, 0};
static int Ix3[6]={2,0,1, 0, 1, 2};
static int Sgn[6]={1,1,1,-1,-1,-1};
    *pI=Ix1[which];
    *pJ=Ix2[which];
    *pK=Ix3[which];
    return Sgn[which];
}
```

And the loop to evaluate Equation (21.1) will look like

```
#define forEpsilon(e) for (int e=0; e!=6; ++e)

Polynomial P;
forEpsilon(e1)
forEpsilon(e2)
{
    int i,j,k, l,m,n;
    int sign=epsilon(e1,&i,&j,&k)
            *epsilon(e2,&l,&m,&n);
    P +=sign*Q(i,l)*Q(j,m)*Q(k,n);
}
cout << P<<endl;
```

Note that I broke the summation statement into two. This is because the calls to `epsilon` return the index values and must be executed before the calls to `Q`. Putting these into the same statement *might* work, but it's a bit dicey. The above paranoia guarantees correct operation.

# The Polynomial Object

▐ ow let's look at what we must do, in C++ terms, to make the following statement make sense:

```
P += sign*Q(i,l)*Q(j,m)*Q(k,n);
```

The result we expect from this, Equation (21.2), is a sum of five terms, each of which is some integer coefficient times a monomial consisting of the product of three elements of the **Q** matrix. So, programwise, a `Polynomial` is some sort of list of `Terms`. And each `Term` consists of an integer, `Coefficient`, and some sort of list of variable names called

`Monomial`. There are many ways to manage lists in C++, but to see which one is best we must look at how the lists will be used.

What must happen when the above statement executes? The code for the `operator+=` must search through the existing elements of `P` to see if there is already one there that has the same `Monomial` as the `Term` being added. If there is, it adds `sign` to the `Coefficient` field of the `Term`. If such a `Term` doesn't exist, we must insert one and initialize the `Coefficient` field to `sign`. So, what are the basic operations we will be doing a lot of? We will be searching the `Polynomial` list for an entry containing a desired `Monomial`, which implies doing a lot of comparisons between various `Monomial` lists. My first design decision, then, is to only allow single characters for symbolic variables and to make the `Monomial` list be a C++ standard `string`. A simple, built-in, string comparison can then compare two `Monomial` lists.

Now, what kind of list should we use for the `Polynomial` object? My first try (as all first tries should be) was to use an STL `vector` and use all the standard `vector` operations for searching and inserting into it. Then, after reading a bit further in the STL manual, I found another collection object that is more ideally suited for the `Polynomial` class—it's called a `map`. A `map` is a collection of key/value pairs that are kept sorted on the key value for easy lookup. What we will do is make the key the `Monomial` string and the value field the `Coefficient` integer. That is, instead of making `Polynomial` be an explicit list of `Term`'s, we'll make it a map from `Monomial` values to `Coefficient` values. And what's really nice about the STL implementation of the `map` is that it can be accessed syntactically as though it were an associative array; the subscription operator is overloaded to do a lookup (and insertion if necessary) and return a reference to the appropriate value field. The whole `Polynomial` class becomes almost trivial.

```
class Term
{
    int     Coefficient;
    string  Monomial;
    friend class Polynomial;
// definition shown below
};


typedef map<const string,int> TermList;


class Polynomial
{
    TermList Terms;
```

```
public:
    Polynomial& operator+=(const Term& T)
    {
        Terms[T.Monomial] += T.Coefficient;
        return *this;
    }
};
```

That's really all there is to it; anything else you need is provided by default by the C++ compiler. For printing purposes, we need an insertion operator that uses the standard STL mechanism for iterating through the map. To do this, just add the following to the definition of `Polynomial`:

```
friend ostream&
operator<< (ostream& out, const Polynomial& P)
{
    TermList::const_iterator i;
    for(i =P.Terms.begin();
        i!=P.Terms.end();
        ++i)
        out <<showpos<< i->second << i->first;
    return out;
}
```

# The Term Object

Now we need to gen up some arithmetic operators that will allow the C++ expression

```
sign*Q(i,l)*Q(j,m)*Q(k,n)
```

to construct the appropriate `Term` object to pass to `Polynomial::operator+=`. Recall that the variable `sign` is the integer result of multiplying several calls to `epsilon`. Simply having `Q` return a single `char` won't work since C++ is perfectly happy to add `int`s and `char`s as numeric quantities. No, we must have a user-defined class `Symbol` that wraps the return from `Q` and allows us to define some multiplication operators within `Term` that accept `int`s and `Symbol`s.

```
class Symbol
{

    char c;
```

```
public:
    Symbol(const char ci):c(ci) {}
    char asChar() const {return c;}
};
```

The conversion constructor from char to Symbol allows us to write the Q routine simply:

```
Symbol Q(int i, int j)
{
    static char V[]="ABC"
                    "BDE"
                    "CEF";
    return V[i*3+j];
}
```

Next, we make a Term constructor that will convert the integer sign into a Term with a null Monomial string. Then we make a multiplication operator for Term*Symbol that simply takes the character from Symbol and appends it to the Monomial string. Finally, to make these strings mathematically comparable by doing a string comparison, we will keep Monomial sorted. Fortunately, there is a handy algorithm in STL that makes this easy. The final Term class looks like

```
class Term
{
    int     Coefficient;
    string  Monomial;
public:
    Term(int s): Coefficient(s), Monomial() {;}

    Term& operator*=(const Symbol& s)
    {
        Monomial += s.asChar();
        sort(Monomial.begin(),Monomial.end());
        return *this;
    }
};

const Term
operator*(const Term& lhs, const Symbol& S)
    {return Term(lhs) *= S;}
```

# It Works

That's all there is to it. We just mash this together with the header files.

```
#include <string>
#include <iostream>
#include <algorithm>
#include <map>

using namespace std;
```

And the code prints out the desired result:

```
+6ADF-6AEE-6BBF+12BCE-6CCD
```

# Examples

Now let's play with this. First, I want to define some more general tensor objects. These should be callable in the same manner as Q above. Each of them will, upon creation, store a single char for each element and will provide a parenthesis operator to return an element of the tensor as a Symbol. Keeping things as simple as possible, the definitions are

```
class Vector
{
    char V[3];
public:
    Vector(const char v[3])
        {copy(&v[0],&v[3],V);}    //STL copy algorithm
    Symbol operator()(int i) const
        {return V[i];}
};

class Matrix
{
    char V[9];
public:
    Matrix(const char v[9])
        {copy(&v[0],&v[9],V);}
    Symbol operator()(int i, int j) const
        {return V[i*3+j];}
};
```

```
class Tensor3
{
    char V[27];
public:
    Tensor3(const char v[27])
        {copy(&v[0],&v[27],V);}
    Symbol operator()(int i, int j, int k) const
        {return V[(i*3+j)*3+k];}
};
```

## Cross Product

The original motivation for defining epsilon was as an abbreviation for the cross product. Here we verify that it works by evaluating

$$P^k = \varepsilon^{ijk} L_i M_j$$

In the diagram notation of the previous chapter, this looks like

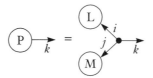

The cross product has one free index (*k* here), so it necessitates the use of an array of Polynomial objects.

```
Vector      L("abc");
Vector      M("def");
Polynomial  P[3];
forEpsilon(e)
{
    int i,j,k;
    int sign = epsilon(e,&i,&j,&k);
    P[k] += sign*L(i)*M(j);
}
forIndex(k)
    cout <<"P("<<k<<")="<<C[k]<<endl;
```

This prints

```
P(+0)=+1bf-1ce
P(+1)=-1af+1cd
P(+2)=+1ae-1bd
```

## Line/Quadratic Tangency

The condition that a line **L** is tangent to a quadratic curve **Q** is

$$\varepsilon^{ijk}\varepsilon^{lmn}Q_{il}Q_{km}L_jL_n = 0$$

Or in diagram notation,

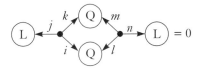

Evaluate this by the following code:

```
Matrix      Q("ABC"
              "BDE"
              "CEF");
Vector      L("abc");
Polynomial P;
forEpsilon(e1)
forEpsilon(e2)
{
    int i,j,k, l,m,n;
    int s = epsilon(e1,&i,&j,&k)
            * epsilon(e2,&l,&m,&n);
    P += s*Q(i,l)*Q(k,m)*L(j)*L(n);
}
cout << P << endl;
```

This prints

```
-2ADcc+4AEbc-2AFbb+2BBcc-4BCbc-4BEac
+4BFab+2CCbb+4CDac-4CEab-2DFaa+2EEaa
```

In particular, if **Q** is a unit circle at the origin, we would have

$$\mathbf{Q} = \begin{bmatrix} 1 & 0 & 0 \\ 0 & 1 & 0 \\ 0 & 0 & -1 \end{bmatrix}$$

Manually plugging this into our printed expression, we get

```
-2cc+2bb+2aa
```

In other words, line **L** is tangent to the unit circle if its elements satisfy

$$a^2 + b^2 - c^2 = 0$$

### An Epsilon Identity

Here is a confirmation of an identity I showed in the previous chapter. We apply three copies of a $3\times 3$ transformation matrix to the three indices of epsilon and get a bare epsilon times the scalar det**T**:

$$\varepsilon^{ijk}T_i^l T_j^m T_k^n = \varepsilon^{lmn}\left(\det T\right)$$

or in diagram notation

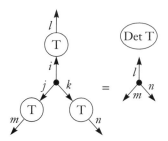

This expression has three free indices, $l,m,n$, but we can do this one without an array of `Polynomials`.

```
Matrix T("abc"
         "def"
         "ghj");
forIndex(l)
forIndex(m)
forIndex(n)
{
    Polynomial P;
    forEpsilon(e1)
    {
        int i,j,k;
        int s = epsilon(e1,&i,&j,&k);
        P += s*T(i,l)*T(j,m)*T(k,n);
    }
cout <<l<<m<<n<<" "<<P<<endl;
}
```

This prints the following imposing stuff:

```
+0+0+0  +0adg
+0+0+1  +0adh+0aeg+0bdg
+0+0+2  +0adj+0afg+0cdg
+0+1+0  +0adh+0aeg+0bdg
+0+1+1  +0aeh+0bdh+0beg
```

```
+0+1+2  +1aej-1afh-1bdj+1bfg+1cdh-1ceg
+0+2+0  +0adj+0afg+0cdg
+0+2+1  -1aej+1afh+1bdj-1bfg-1cdh+1ceg
+0+2+2  +0afj+0cdj+0cfg
+1+0+0  +0adh+0aeg+0bdg
+1+0+1  +0aeh+0bdh+0beg
+1+0+2  -1aej+1afh+1bdj-1bfg-1cdh+1ceg
+1+1+0  +0aeh+0bdh+0beg
+1+1+1  +0beh
+1+1+2  +0bej+0bfh+0ceh
+1+2+0  +1aej-1afh-1bdj+1bfg+1cdh-1ceg
+1+2+1  +0bej+0bfh+0ceh
+1+2+2  +0bfj+0cej+0cfh
+2+0+0  +0adj+0afg+0cdg
+2+0+1  +1aej-1afh-1bdj+1bfg+1cdh-1ceg
+2+0+2  +0afj+0cdj+0cfg
+2+1+0  -1aej+1afh+1bdj-1bfg-1cdh+1ceg
+2+1+1  +0bej+0bfh+0ceh
+2+1+2  +0bfj+0cej+0cfh
+2+2+0  +0afj+0cdj+0cfg
+2+2+1  +0bfj+0cej+0cfh
+2+2+2  +0cfj
```

You can, if you like, make this neater by jiggering the operator<< routine to avoid printing monomials with a coefficient of zero. It's sometimes interesting, though, to see what monomials were added and subtracted (with net coefficient of zero) to an expression.

## Some Cubic Identities

The following quantity is identically zero for all values of **C**:

$$Z_l^k = \varepsilon^{ijk} C_{ijl}$$

In diagram notation,

We verify this by

```
Tensor3 C("ABE" "BCF" "EFH"
          "BCF" "CDG" "FGJ"
          "EFH" "FGJ" "HJK");
forIndex(l)
{
    Polynomial Zl[3];
    forEpsilon(e1)
    {
        int i,j,k;
        int s = epsilon(e1,&i,&j,&k);
        Zl[k] += s * C(i,j,l);
    }
    forIndex(k)
    cout <<"Z("<<l<<k<<")="<<Zl[k]<<endl;
}
```

The printout is

```
Z(+0+0)=+0F
Z(+0+1)=+0E
Z(+0+2)=+0B
Z(+1+0)=+0G
Z(+1+1)=+0F
Z(+1+2)=+0C
Z(+2+0)=+0J
Z(+2+1)=+0H
Z(+2+2)=+0F
```

This means that if we see such a diagram fragment embedded in a larger diagram, we can immediately say that the whole thing is zero.

Likewise, the following expression containing a cubic is also identically zero for any tensor **C**:

$$\varepsilon^{ijk}\varepsilon^{lmn}\varepsilon^{pqr}C_{ilp}C_{jmq}C_{knr}$$

In diagram form,

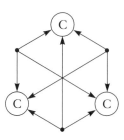

As code,

```
Polynomial P;
forEpsilon(e1)
forEpsilon(e2)
forEpsilon(e3)
{
    int i,j,k, l,m,n, p,q,r;
    int s = epsilon(e1,&i,&j,&k)
          * epsilon(e2,&l,&m,&n)
          * epsilon(e3,&p,&q,&r);
    P +=s*C(i,l,p)*C(j,m,q)*C(k,n,r);
}
cout <<P<<endl;
```

This prints out

```
+0ADK+0AGJ+0BCK+0BFJ+0BGH
+0CEJ+0CFH+0DEH+0EFG+0FFF
```

The final example is a bit more complex. We will evaluate the $C_4$ invariant of a 2DH cubic curve as described in Chapter 20.

$$\varepsilon^{ijk}\varepsilon^{lmn}\varepsilon^{pqr}\varepsilon^{tuv}C_{nqv}C_{jru}C_{kmt}C_{ilp}$$

For fairly obvious reasons, I call it the "cube invariant" because of the diagram

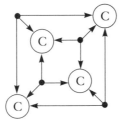

I'm going to do something slightly different this time for the C++ code. All our examples so far have made the code mimic the algebraic expression. This is easy to use, but can be a bit slow. That's because there is a lot of creation, sorting, and destruction of temporary `Term` variables during execution of the binary multiply operator. I'll write the code for the following example to show an alternative way to generate the `Term` that uses our existing machinery, but avoids unnecessary creation and deletion.

```
Polynomial P;
forEpsilon(e1)
forEpsilon(e2)
```

```
forEpsilon(e3)
forEpsilon(e4)
{
    int i,j,k, l,m,n, p,q,r, t,u,v;
    Term T(epsilon(e1,&i,&j,&k)
         * epsilon(e2,&l,&m,&n)
         * epsilon(e3,&p,&q,&r)
         * epsilon(e4,&t,&u,&v)); // create once
    T *= C( n,q,v);        // modify existing one
    T *= C(j ,r,u);
    T *= C(k,m, t);
    T *= C(i,l,p );
    P += T;
}
cout << P << endl;
```

This generates the following:

```
+24ACGK-24ACJJ-24ADFK+24ADHJ+24AFGJ
-24AGGH-24BBGK+24BBJJ+24BCFK-24BCHJ
+24BDEK-24BDHH-24BEGJ-48BFFJ+72BFGH
-24CCEK+24CCHH+72CEFJ-24CEGH-48CFFH
-24DEEJ+24DEFH+24EEGG-48EFFG+24FFFF
```

# How Do I Like This?

C++ giveth and C++ taketh away. The internal machinery of the map object keeps its key/value pairs stored in some sort of binary tree thingy so that searching is very fast. This is something I would not have felt like getting into myself. That's good. But the simple mimicking of an algebraic expression by a C++ expression implies a lot of strange jiggery-pokery going on during the creation of a Term. That's not so good. But who cares really. The execution time of the examples shown here is negligible. It's only when you get upwards of eight epsilons that the program takes a noticeable amount of time. Rewriting the expressions as in the final example helps here. For even more complex situations, it would be easy to add an explicit Term constructor that is passed a sign and some fixed number of Symbols. This constructor could resize Monomial once, assign the Symbols to it explicitly, and only need to sort it once. I'll leave that as an exercise for you to do yourselves.

# What's Next

One can imagine any number of extensions to this code to handle more general expressions. But what we have here is good enough to serve as a check on our theoretical investigations to make sure we don't miss any constant factors or stray minus signs. Now that we can verify some of our computations, we can look for the geometric meaning of transformationally invariant algebraic quantities (invariant because they can be written as tensor diagrams). That will be the topic of future columns.

# Appendix

This appendix contains definitions for the vector and matrix classes necessary to compile the code fragments in Chapters 1 and 2. I have included only those functions actually used in the examples. A complete implementation would require quite a few more operations.

## Vector3

```cpp
class Vector3
{
    float v[3];
public:
//Constructor
    Vector3();

//Element access
    float& operator[](int i);
    float operator[](int i) const;

//Assignment operators
    Vector3& operator+=(const Vector3&);
    Vector3& operator*=(const float&);
};

//Vector sum and scalar product
const Vector3 operator+(const Vector3&, const Vector3&);
const Vector3 operator*(const float& , const Vector3&);
```

## Matrix33

```cpp
class Matrix33
{
Vector3 rows[3]; // vector of rows
public:
//Constructor
```

```
    Matrix33();
    Matrix33(float m00, float m01, float m02,
             float m10, float m11, float m12,
             float m20, float m21, float m22);

//Element Access
    float& operator() (int iRow, int jCol);
    float operator() (int iRow, int jCol) const;

//Standard matrix functions
    const Matrix33 Adjoint() const;
};
```

# Vector4

```
class Vector4
{
    float v[4];
public:
//Constructor
    Vector4();
    Vector4(float v0, float v1, float v2, float v3);

//Element access
    float& operator[](int i);
    float operator[](int i) const;

//Assignment and unary operators
    Vector4& operator/=(const float&);
    Vector4 operator-() const;
};

//Vector sum and scalar product
const Vector4 operator+(const Vector4&, const Vector4&);
const Vector4 operator*(const float& , const Vector4&);
const Vector4 operator/(const Vector4&, const float& );

//4D cross product
const Vector4 Cross(const Vector4&,const Vector4&,const
Vector4&);
```

# Matrix44

```
class Matrix44
{
```

```
    Vector4 rows[4];
public:
//Identity matrix
    static Matrix44 Identity;

//Constructor
    Matrix44();

//Element Access
    float& operator() (int iRow, int jCol);
    float operator() (int iRow, int jCol) const;

//Column Access
    void setCol(int iCol,const Vector4&);
    Vector4 Col(int iCol) const;

//Matrix * Matrix^t (fast if matrix is stored as rows)
    Matrix44 TimesTranspose(const Matrix44&) const;

//Standard matrix functions
    const Matrix44 Adjoint() const;
    const Matrix44 Inverse() const;
};

// scalar and matrix products
const Matrix44 operator*(const float&    , const
Matrix44&);
const Vector4 operator*(const Matrix44&, const Vector4&
);
const Matrix44 operator*(const Matrix44&, const
Matrix44&);
```

# Index

# About the Author

For almost three decades, eminent computer graphicist Jim Blinn has coupled his scientific knowledge and artistic abilities to foster the growth of the computer graphics field. His many contributions include the *Voyager* Flyby animations of space missions to Jupiter, Saturn, and Uranus; The Mechanical Universe, a 52-part telecourse of animated physics; and the computer animation of Carl Sagan's PBS series *Cosmos*. In addition, Blinn, the recipient of the first SIGGRAPH Computer Graphics Achievement Award, has developed many widely used graphics techniques, including bump mapping, environment mapping, and blobby modeling.

Jim Blinn is widely known in the computer graphics community as an artist of picture, word, and science. He is considered one of the founding fathers of the field. While working on his Ph.D. at the University of Utah, Blinn developed bump mapping and, along with Martin Newell, reflection mapping (techniques that are still widely used today).

Jim has been recognized numerous times for his contributions, most recently with the Steven Anson Coons Award at SIGGRAPH '99. In 1983, Blinn was the first recipient of the SIGGRAPH Computer Graphics Achievement Award for his work in lighting and surface modeling. He was awarded a MacArthur Fellowship in 1991 to support his work in educational animation. NASA gave him the Exceptional Service medal for the *Voyager* Flyby animations, and the IEEE recognized Blinn with the Outstanding Contribution Award for his column. In 1995, the Parsons School of Design presented him with an Honorary Doctor of Fine Arts degree for his contributions to computer graphics. In 2000, he was elected to the National Academy of Engineering. And in 2001, he appeared in Richard Saul Wurman's book *1000: Who's Really Who, Richard Saul Wurman's 1000 Most Creative Individuals in the USA* (TOP Publications).